KOREAN POP CULTURE BEYOND ASIA

Edited by David C. Oh and Benjamin M. Han

·······

KOREAN POP CULTURE BEYOND ASIA

·······

Race and Reception

·······

University of Washington Seattle

Korean Pop Culture beyond Asia was supported by a grant from the
Donald R. Ellegood International Publications Endowment.

Copyright © 2024 by the University of Washington Press

All rights reserved. No part of this publication may be reproduced or transmitted in any
form or by any means, electronic or mechanical, including photocopy, recording, or any
information storage or retrieval system, without permission in writing from the publisher.

UNIVERSITY OF WASHINGTON PRESS *uwapress.uw.edu*

LIBRARY OF CONGRESS CATALOGING-IN-PUBLICATION DATA

Names: Oh, David C., editor. | Han, Benjamin M., editor.

Title: Korean pop culture beyond Asia : race and reception /
Edited by David C. Oh and Benjamin M. Han.

Description: Seattle : University of Washington Press, 2024. |
Includes bibliographical references and index.

Identifiers: LCCN 2024003680 | ISBN 9780295752952 (hardcover) |
ISBN 9780295752969 (paperback) | ISBN 9780295752976 (ebook)

Subjects: LCSH: Popular culture—Korea. | Mass media and culture—Korea.

Classification: LCC HM621 .K69155 2024 | DDC 306.095195—dc23/eng/20240515

LC record available at https://lccn.loc.gov/2024003680

♾ This paper meets the requirements of ANSI/NISO Z39.48-1992 (Permanence of Paper).

To our children,
Noah, Aaron, and Aaron,
who use the symbolic
resources of transnational
Korean popular media
to empower their
own identifications.

Contents

Acknowledgments • ix

Introduction • DAVID C. OH AND BENJAMIN M. HAN • 1

• • • • • • •

PART I • Transcultural Affinity, Excess, and Contradiction

1 • The Road to Fandom: Joy and Black "Fans" in K-pop
CRYSTAL S. ANDERSON • 33

2 • Between Appreciation and Appropriation: Race-Transitioning among Hallyu Fans • MIN JOO LEE • 52

3 • Korean Romance for Wholesomeness and Racism?
The Transcultural Reception of the Reality Dating Show
Single's Inferno • WOORI HAN • 74

4 • K-pop and the Racialization of Asian American Popular Musicians • DONNA LEE KWON • 98

5 • "Soft" Koreans and "Sensual" Cubans:
Race, Gender, and the Reception of South Korean Popular Culture in Cuba • LAURA-ZOË HUMPHREYS • 122

PART II • Intersectional Connection and Imaginaries

6 • Latin Orientalism and Anglo Hegemony in Korean Rock:
Seo Taiji's "Moai" (2009) • MOISÉS PARK • 149

7 • "I Was Probably Korean in a Previous Life": Transracial Jokes
and Fantasies of Hallyu Fans • IRINA LYAN • 171

8 • Hallyu Dreaming: Making Sense of Race
and Gender in K-dramas in the US Midwest and Ireland
REBECCA CHIYOKO KING-O'RIAIN • 194

9 • When K-pop Meets Islam: Cultural Appropriation
and Fan Engagement • YOUNG JUNG • 216

10 • "I Can Do Both": Queering K-pop Idols
through the White Discursive Standpoint of TikTok Users
JULIA TRZCIŃSKA AND DAVID C. OH • 238

• • • • • • • •

List of Contributors • 261

Index • 267

Acknowledgments

Korean Pop Culture beyond Asia: Race and Reception would not have been possible without the contributions of our authors, a mix of dynamic early-career scholars and established researchers in Korean popular culture studies. We fully recognize that our book is only as good as our contributors' work, and we are grateful for their faith in this project, the contributions of their intellectual labor, their willingness to meet our requests for revisions, and their patience dealing with us, their editors. Far too often editors act as if they are providing a benefit to their authors, but the reverse is true. Our contributors' work forms the substance of the book, and, as editors, we are the beneficiaries of their brilliance and kindness.

As much as we may have been personally energized to do this work, it is made more possible because of the support of our institutions—Ramapo College of New Jersey, Syracuse University, and Tulane University. We understand that we do not work in a vacuum, and it is through institutional support that we are able to do scholarly work. We are especially grateful for Tulane University's Department of Communication, the Asian Studies Program, and the Yang Won Sun Foundation for sponsoring a hybrid symposium titled "Racial Translocalism and the Reception of Korean Popular Culture," which was held in New Orleans on the Tulane University campus in November 2022. The symposium provided a valuable opportunity for contributors to share their work and strengthen the arguments of their chapters. We also hope that it will prove to have been a fertile space for new connections. Despite the proliferation of "Korean Wave" research, there has been relatively little work that examines reception with a critical lens, considering questions of how racial, ethnic, and national difference matter in fans' and audiences' transnational reception of Korean media.

We also wish to thank Mike Baccam, the acquisitions editor at the University of Washington Press, for his faith in the project and for championing it. His support has been energizing, and it helps provide the conditions for us to feel comfortable to do our best work. Publishing with the University of Washington Press is not only an honor, but it has been a pleasure.

Finally, we would be remiss if we did not thank our families. Our families have our deepest gratitude for providing us the space to do our work and the emotional support that is necessary for any intellectual work. The life of the mind is built on the bedrock of interpersonal connections.

KOREAN POP CULTURE BEYOND ASIA

Introduction

••••••

DAVID C. OH AND BENJAMIN M. HAN

It is not hyperbolic to say that South Korean media industries' rise as a hub of global media production has been explosive. It was only in the mid-1990s that South Korea (hereafter, Korea) began to invest substantially in its media industries. Following decades of authoritarian rule, President Kim Young-sam, the first democratically elected president, famously recognized the export value of cultural products when he learned that it would require the overseas sales of 1.5 million Hyundai automobiles to match the profits of *Jurassic Park* (1993; Shim 2006).[1] In less than three decades since, Korean media have developed an award-winning film industry that is critically well received around the globe, most visible in *Parasite*'s (2020) six Academy Awards. Before the Oscars, Korean cinema was already punching above its weight in major international film festivals, including Cannes and the Venice Film Festivals. In addition to critical successes, the film industry has been commercially successful in its domestic market as the only national cinema to regain a majority share of box office receipts after being dominated by Hollywood (Leong 2002).

Korean television programs have also spread across the globe, particularly in the Asia-Pacific region but also notably in Latin America and the Middle East. In the West, although Korean television has mostly appealed to niche tastes, the popularity of shows such as *Squid Game* (2021) and the US television industry's interest in Korea as source material for adaptations, including programs such as *The Good Doctor* (2017–present) and *The Masked Singer* (2019–present), portend increasing presence. Ju Oak Kim (2021) argues that this movement demonstrates the "Third Korean

Wave" when Korean media flows are a part of the mainstream in Western spaces, including the United States, which has been historically resistant to non-English-language media. Although we do not quite share Kim's optimistic interpretation, it is hardly debatable that Korean television is more present, even if its presence is frequently indirect, such as with adaptations. When the original shows are watched on digital platforms such as Netflix, Apple TV, and Rakuten Viki, it is not only, nor even mainly, diasporic or Asian American audiences watching. For instance, Viki.com, a site that hosts East Asian television and movies, claims that only 20 percent of its audience identifies as racially Asian (Gordon 2016). This cross-racial viewership has, for some fans, created interracial, intercultural intimacies, including heterosexual fantasies about romantically and sexually desirable Koreans. For dedicated women fans with the socioeconomic capital to travel, they seek idealized partners, thereby subverting Orientalized notions of Asian men's asexuality and undesirability (Lee 2020). After watching *Squid Game*, for instance, it was reported that some heterosexual women viewers tweeted their fetishistic desire to be slapped by Gong Yoo, who plays a minor role as the recruiter (Rosenberg 2021).

Less well known but increasingly visible are "webtoons," a portmanteau of "world wide web" and "cartoon" to describe the digital presentation of *manhwa* (comic books) for mobile devices, which scroll vertically as a single long page (Jeong 2020). With the webtoon industry's business model as an exhibition platform for aspiring artists and storytellers, it has reached globally situated audiences and has also become a space for non-Koreans to participate, replicating the storytelling structure and, in many cases, the expected aesthetics of the medium. Along with webtoons, Koreans are also important players in e-sports, producing games such as *PUBG* and *Lineage*. Gaming competitions have been part of the cultural mainstream, although reports of their popularity are sometimes exaggerated in the Western press. That said, it is true that e-sports are institutionally supported and mainstream. Indeed, the Korean multinational corporation, Samsung, set up the first World Cyber Games in Seoul in 2000, and Korean corporate sponsors and athletes have been a conspicuous presence. For example, Lee Sanghyeok, known as Faker, is widely considered the top e-sports athlete because of his four League of Legends World Championships (Bencomo 2023).

Perhaps, most notably, Korean popular music, K-pop, is now commonly known around the world. With the viral popularity of Psy's "Gangnam Style," which once held the record for the most viewed YouTube video, and the chart-topping popularity of BTS and its well-known fandom called ARMY, Korean music is an important part of the tapestry of popular music worldwide. In some Asian countries, K-pop is embedded in mainstream music culture and enjoys cultural capital, yet outside the region, particularly where Whiteness and Westernness are valorized as hegemonic norms, K-pop fans are disciplined for their musical tastes as well as cross-cultural and cross-racial interests (Lee, Lee, and Park 2020; Lyan 2023). Even still, there are numerous news reports of fans in the United States camping for tickets to see their favorite artists, performances at music festivals such as Coachella and Lollapalooza, and major exhibitions such as KCON, a K-pop music festival that visits multiple continents. Indeed, it recorded attendance of more than one hundred thousand for its LA show in 2019, the last year it was held before COVID-19, and ninety thousand in its first year after the pandemic restrictions were lifted (Benjamin 2022).

Although this transnational movement of Korean media, often called the "Korean Wave," is important to study, we are more interested in the transnational reception of Korean media than we are in its transnational circulation. Early studies of the Korean Wave focused on cultural policy from a political economic perspective, and later manuscripts and edited collections have centered on the textual qualities of Korean popular culture that allow for its transnational mobility with a robust area of work focused on Korean media's hybridity (Ryoo 2009; Shim 2006; Anderson 2020). Hybridity usually refers to the incorporation of Western elements that are already familiar because of the dominance of Western, particularly US, cultural flows. For instance, Myoung-Sun Song's (2019) book examined the ways "underground" rappers incorporated the global flows of hip hop into the local cultural terrain and music scene. In addition to genres and texts, scholars have claimed that hybridity is also expressed in the body. Sun Jung (2011) argues that masculinity as a construct is presented in hybrid, flexible ways that are broadly and commercially appealing. Although transnational reception is critically important at the other end of the Korean Wave, there have been few collections solely dedicated to it. Although theoretically interesting, these studies can only remark on the qualities of texts while making theoretically based assumptions about how users *actually* interpret,

Introduction

value, and incorporate Korean media into their lives. That said, there have been a handful of collections that have included some reception studies, but there has only been one other collection with its predominant focus on transnational audience reception (Jin, Yoon, and Min 2021). It is in this gap that this book is situated. In particular, this book builds on this work with its focus on the cross-racial, transnational reception of Korean popular culture. We assert the importance of understanding the complexities of actual reception practices while centering race as a major discursive standpoint, particularly in the "West" and in postcolonial nations.[2] Even for countries not directly involved in the Western project of colonization, the current neocolonial arrangement of the globe means that Western ideas about difference seep into their discursive terrains.

With the counterflows of Korean media into the West and its attendant movements around the globe, audiences encounter and negotiate transnational, symbolic meanings encoded in these texts. Because meanings are produced at the site of reception (Ang 1990), it is important to understand how Korean media are received by overseas audiences, whose lived experiences are racially and culturally different from the Korean texts they are consuming. It is to this purpose that this book is situated—to examine how racial difference matters in the reception of Korean media. Even for diasporic Asians outside of Asia, their everyday lives are situated within dominant cultural spaces that are racially marginalizing, and it is from this local site of meaning-making that Korean texts are transnationally encountered. These transnational encounters fuel more interest, investment, and expansion of Korean texts. For instance, KCON, the multi-day Korean culture "conference," includes Korean food and cosmetics, so-called K-food and K-beauty, and is highlighted by K-pop artists, who travel internationally and meet fans who would otherwise only be able to experience fandom through digital screens. KCON started in Los Angeles only in 2012 and has expanded to multiple cities across the world, including, but not limited to, Mexico City, Paris, Abu Dhabi, Tokyo, and Bangkok (KCON n.d.). Recently, BTS's multi-day concerts in Los Angeles sold out in pre-sale prior to general admissions sales, angering much of its fandom (Belmis 2021). Although BTS is the most dramatic example, there are frequently reports of tickets being sold out quickly when K-pop artists such as Blackpink make international stops on their world tours.

Oh and Han

Fan interests have also resulted in the study of the Korean language as the fastest growing foreign language major in the United Kingdom, although it still lags far behind other languages in raw numbers (R. Hall and Otte 2021). In the United States, because of fan interests, Korean and Japanese are the only foreign language majors that are experiencing growth with enrollments falling in other foreign languages (Flaherty 2018). Interests in Korean popular culture have also greatly benefited tourism, including romantic tourism (Lee 2020). Although non-Asian women fans' heterosexual romantic interests do not overturn existing racialized romantic and sexual desire, it does at least complicate them.

As Korean media move beyond North and Southeast Asia, its reception is necessarily cross-racial. Even when encountered by racialized Asian fans, the context of reception happens within different racial systems. In other words, Korean American fans receive Korean cultural texts within the context of a US articulation of White supremacist racial logics as well as White supremacy's gendered, class, religious, and heteronormative meanings. The purpose of this book, then, is to understand how *racial difference* matters in the uses and reception of Korean popular culture either as the primary focus of analysis or as context with other intersectional identities. It is for this reason that the book does not include the important contributions of scholars, such as Koichi Iwabuchi and Doobo Shim, who study intra-racial, cross-cultural reception of Korean media across Asia because, for example, Japanese, Malaysian, and Pakistani fans are racially Asian. A critically centered book on intra-Asian audience reception would make an important contribution to studies of the Korean Wave, but it is conceptually different and would require a different theoretical framework.

The book makes an intentional move toward critical analysis rather than some common approaches that valorize cultural affinities, such as cultural proximity or counterflows. By centering race, we take up calls by scholars in fields such as communication who have argued that race is central to the study of the discipline even as it is often trivialized by it (Flores 2018). Likewise, we assert that race cannot be neglected in the study of transnational audience reception. As intersectional scholars, we are committed to understanding how race plus other social identities matter in the transnational, cross-racial reception of Korean media. As Du Bois ([1903] 1989) argues, race continues to mark a fundamental division in the United

Introduction

States, and this remains true today despite claims of post-racialism (Omi and Winant 1994; Bonilla-Silva 2010). The difference is that racism takes the more "genteel" form of post-racialism by denying structural inequality and reducing racism to individual prejudice (Prashad 2001, 38). Denials of racism often coexist with fascination in the racial other.

Without critical intervention and analysis, Koreaphilia is too easily assumed to be a one-way form of soft power that challenges US racial logics as a counter-hegemonic force. This should be complicated because, as scholars of race point out, racial interest can co-mingle with exoticism and even fear and hatred (Yousman 2003; Bow 2022). At the same time, we should also be attentive to how audiences of color and other historically marginalized groups encounter Korean media as an alternative to dominant racial formations in US media texts and industries. Identifying across racial difference can be liberating, allowing users to construct transnational, transcultural affinities (Han 2017). As one of the few media industries produced outside of the West to be received widely, Korean media have intervened as an important counterflow that disrupts White-centered flows of cultural imperialism, liberating new imaginative possibilities and affective investments. Yet a critical analysis does not romanticize or simplify counter-hegemonic possibilities; instead, it will understand that even counter-hegemonic racial possibilities are located within the larger field of dominant racial discourses (S. Hall 2003). The purpose of this book, then, is to take race seriously as an intersectional identity that matters in the transnational reception of Korean mediated flows. To do this, we argue that all transnational audience reception is local and, as such, that all cross-racial local meanings are filtered through the prism of race, a concept we call "racial translocalism."

Bringing together scholars who study race and Korean popular reception, this book adds to what is called Korean Wave studies. We, however, do not use this term in our writing but rather the more generic description of transnational audience reception of Korean media. Although it is wordier, we wish to avoid the branding around the Korean Wave as well as to disarm its implied suggestion of a sort of Korean media exceptionalism. We recognize that Korean media are notable for their scale and counterflows, but we believe it is important theoretically to place them in context with other mediated counterflows and reception that are complicating the near

Oh and Han

unidirectionality of North–South flows that marked much of the twentieth century. Historically, Korean media flows may well be exceptional in this present moment because of their magnitude, but, theoretically, they are in dialogue with other media flows, such as the increased interest in Spanish-language telenovelas from Latin America, Indian cinema, and Hong Kong martial arts and action movies. The branding can in some cases lead to celebratory explanations of the Korean Wave as "soft power."

As critical scholars, it is our hope as editors to place into dialogue scholars who consider the ways the reception of Korean popular culture simultaneously reifies and challenges the West as the dominant referent as well as how fans and audiences ambivalently make sense of Korean popular culture through their locally embedded and specific cultural standpoints. Fans, like all audiences, poach meanings from popular culture in ways that can be transgressive but that can also reify domination (Jenkins 1992). A goal, then, is to understand the cross-racial complexities in the reception of Korean media abroad that do not merely indulge nor dismiss the resistive potential of cross-racial reception and that is attentive to the ways in which this reception can reinforce hegemonies at home and can import the mediated hegemonies of Korean society. Toward that end, our work features leading scholars and emerging scholars of transnational audience reception of Korean media, who empirically examine cross-racial reception digitally and in person.

Many existing studies on the Korean Wave have employed political economy and textual analysis as a primary means to explore the transnational popularity of K-dramas and K-pop, but we are interested in how audiences, listeners, and fans negotiate Korean popular culture in their specific localized contexts. As Sonia Livingstone writes, "[Audience] research should conceptualise 'audiences' as a relational or interactional construct, as a way of focusing on the diverse set of relationships between people and media forms" (1998, 14). More specifically, instead of inquiring into the meaning of texts, we are interested in research that seeks to understand "how texts are located and understood as part of, indeed as agents in, the practices of people's daily lives" (Livingstone 1998, 14). It is instructive to very briefly untangle audience reception studies and fan studies as this introduction and the contributions to the book shift between these fields. We make a distinction between fans and what John Fiske (1992) calls

Introduction

7

ordinary viewers and what Henry Jenkins (1992) refers to as spectators. Largely, the difference is in degree rather than type (Fiske 1992). Fans are highly active readers, who often produce fan texts and who join together in a community of shared taste (Jenkins 1992). Fans also develop their own self and collective identities based on their media consumption—for example, identification as a "Bunny," the name of the NewJeans fandom, or ARMY, the name of the BTS fandom (J. L. Sullivan 2020). Fans, then, blur boundaries between reception, or the consumption and interpretation of a text, and production, or the creation of a text. In this way, fans demonstrate emotional investment, and their practices challenge dominant culture distinctions between the text and the reader (Fiske 1992). In contrast, audience reception encompasses fan reception and the readings of spectators, some of whom have only minimal interests in a text. Because of the nature of the spectator's relationship to a text, audience reception more often considers ways audiences enact agency to actively resist media texts (Miller 2010; Lewis 1991; Ang 1990; S. Hall 1999). Audience reception is interested in the social uses of media and meaning-making about a text (Ang 1990), whereas fan studies is interested in the participatory culture of fans (Jenkins 1992).

Therefore, moving away from the "media effects" tradition that assumes "passive audiences," who are acted upon by media (Lewis 1991), the "active audiences" approach of reception analysis recognizes the audience's agency and complicity in the circulation of meaning. One limitation to either approach, though, is that scholars have historically used a nation-centered orientation to fan and audience reception. However, as is demonstrative with Korean mediated flows, the consumption of popular culture as a cultural practice increasingly accrues meaning across national borders. As Adrian Athique reminds us, "The growing attention paid to transnational media consumption in contemporary audience studies is particularly valuable in that it recognizes the simultaneous mobility of media content and its audiences beyond a strictly national framework" (2016, 11). However, we are also keenly aware that the study of transnational reception often elides other critical elements that constitute culture.

For this book, we center our examination on racial difference to explore cultural practices that further considers race and racism as central to transnational popular cultures as symptoms of "global connectivity and a

Oh and Han

greater awareness of cultural diversity" (Athique 2016, 5). Furthermore, as Bertha Chin and Lori Morimoto remind us, "A strict focus on the trans/national aspects of even geopolitical border-crossing fandoms runs the risk of overshadowing other contexts—popular cultural, racial, sexual, gender, class, and so on—that inform both a diversity of fan practices globally, as well as diversity within fandoms themselves" (2015, 175–76). Hence, our focus on the transnational reception of Korean popular culture through the lens of racial difference underscores the significance of intersectional identifications in the meaning-making process.

More significantly, as the book centers on the issues of racial difference and reception, it enables us to redirect attention from existing theoretical concepts to more empirically grounded research, which provides a micro-level-oriented analysis of how Korean popular culture is being integrated, appropriated, and subverted in different geopolitical contexts. Additionally, the study of Korean popular culture exemplifies the counterflows of media and media culture from other nations that have been considered peripheral centers of cultural production in the past (D. C. Oh 2021), thereby challenging the dominant West/East binary while renewing interest in theories of media/cultural imperialism and hybridity. For instance, while scholars have used the phrase "platform imperialism" (Jin 2013, 2015; Srnicek 2017) to characterize Netflix as a dominant global streaming platform, it simultaneously enables counterflows of popular culture from other national markets. Moreover, the study of Korean popular culture prompts us to rethink how Western modernity is no longer a dominant referent for the rest of the world. The emphasis on transnational reception underscores "Asia as Method" (Chen 2010) while offering new theoretical frameworks that challenge Western theories of audience reception and fandom.

Moreover, such concepts as geo-linguistic region (Sinclair 1999), cultural proximity (La Pastina and Straubhaar 2005), and transcultural affinity (Han 2017) have been coined to better capture the nuances of how media and popular culture from different nations travel across borders and find transnational appeal. For example, Joseph Straubhaar's (2021) concept of cultural proximity has been widely adopted to explore how perceived cultural similarity facilitates the movement of and identification with popular culture produced in a different national culture. While multiple layers of

Introduction

identification inform cultural proximity, it aims to provide a totalizing view of the transnational reception of popular media and culture without considering the nuances and specificities of audiences' local contexts and everyday lived experiences. Therefore, by directing our focus to the question of reception, we are interested in not merely the circulation of Korean popular culture but also what happens when it arrives at different contact zones; in other words, we are interested in the interaction.

By studying the transnational reception of Korean popular culture in different geopolitical contexts, the book does not offer a celebratory view of how Korean media are empowering marginalized communities in a reductive sense, but it instead considers the complexities and contradictions in the form of cacophonies and tensions in the act of reception. This provides a more nuanced analysis of how audiences and fans negotiate popular culture into their lived social, cultural, and racial experiences. For instance, transnational reception studies can help us better understand how K-pop as both a foreign and global cultural commodity not only is integrated into localized political contexts but could also engender social ruptures and new cross-racial alliances in the context of rising anxieties around neoliberal capitalism in the Global South. For example, in 2019, amid the growing anti-government protests in Chile, an official government document circulated online in which the Ministry of the Interior blamed K-pop for inciting local demonstrations and civil unrest. This example illustrates how K-pop as a global cultural form at the point of contact is integrated into a localized political context in Latin America. Reception studies can, in this case, probe Chileans' ambivalent appropriation of Korean popular culture to confront neoliberal reform; to resist Eurocentric masculinity rooted in Whiteness, which derides indigeneity as part of Chile's racial identity; and to assert itself as the nation becomes more multicultural (Diaz Pino 2021). Racial difference in reception analysis enables an investigation into the ways Korean popular culture contributes to social movements, evidenced by K-pop fans' activist support of the Black Lives Matter movement, which also resisted hegemonic structures of Whiteness.

Korean popular culture studies that incorporate racial difference as a critical element of reception enables an exploration of global and local entanglements. However, transnational reception studies are not merely about the tensions between the global and the local but also about affec-

Oh and Han

tive intimacies and resonances between different racial, ethnic, gender, and class groups. Additionally, reception allows us to explore the invisible structures of power and agency operating at the point of contact. Hence, racial difference also allows us to discuss how Korean popular culture could reproduce Orientalist imaginaries in its global reception as it contributes to the racialization of Asians as exotic and perpetual foreigners, embedded in the politics of visibility and invisibility that continue to govern domesticated Asian diasporic bodies around the world. Lastly, the book's concentration on racial difference and reception problematizes existing literature and discussion that credit the government as the agent responsible for the globalization of Korean popular culture. While the government has contributed to the development of the Korean cultural industry in terms of finances, infrastructure, and soft power, we argue that reception is integral to transnational Korean media and popular culture. Thus, we need more scholarship that shifts away from top-down institutional studies of Korean popular culture to audience studies that consider the micropolitics and cultural specificities of reception.

Racial Translocalism

The central tie that binds the book's chapters is that transnational reception of Korean media texts happens through the locally specific racial standpoint of audiences. We call this *racial translocalism* in order to emphasize that transnational media texts are indigenized within the local culture of the audience and that the local culture of the audience is experienced through audiences' racial standpoints, which are themselves intersectionally situated. In other words, audiences of Korean media make sense of transnationally received media through their own racially situated standpoints within local cultures. By making this intervention, we affirm audience reception's emphasis on the local, which emphasizes a bottom-up approach to understanding meaning-making about Korean texts and which avoids celebratory accounts of top-down power and influence. For Western reception and postcolonial nations imprinted with the racial logics of Western colonialism, we argue that the local reception of transnational media is racially informed; thus, we call this racial translocalism. Transnational audience reception studies must consider intersectional racial meanings that value

Introduction

racial awareness rather than reify post-racial elisions. We do not share Hyeri Jung's (2017) optimistic assertion that K-pop brings fans together into a shared sense of "woori-ness," or "we-ness," that dissolves racial and cultural boundaries. Rather, we argue that while fans come together in a cosmopolitan project, their specific racial identities matter in reception practices and in intra-fandom hierarchies. Even as these largely digital fandom communities are deterritorialized, their local sites of reception and their everyday meaning-making still very much inform their cultural interpretations and experiences within fandom.

Across the West, race is one of the primary constructs through which difference is understood. White supremacist racial logics that were constructed to justify colonialism (Pieterse 1992) and the racial formations of settler colonies (Omi and Winant 1994) are not a historical relic but a historical legacy that is deeply intertwined into the structures of society, cultural thought, and habits of being. Even in postcolonial states outside of the West, these racial logics are pervasive and become internalized ambivalences (Fanon [1952] 2008). Racial logics pervade social thought, and racial standpoints shape perspectives. They matter in the reception and uses of transnational texts because the interpretation and uses of texts are made to fit local racial frameworks. In order to make this latter point, we situate this theoretical work in critical transculturalism, counterflows, and existing transnational audience reception studies, particularly the studies that deal with racial difference.

Considering the relationship between transnationalism and hybridity, Marwan Kraidy argues that hybridity is a "lopsided articulation" (2005, 149) that is structured through global institutions, which largely favor the West but are received through the agency and meaning-making processes of audiences. This understanding continues to position hybridity from the perspective of the globally marginalized, but it is less optimistic and, as we believe, a more realistic understanding of the limits of hybridity's liberatory potential. It is at this point that we must consider hybridity that is created when there are mediated counterflows. That is, what happens when media outside the historically dominant centers of the West flow from the periphery against the current toward the center?[3] The difference, then, from the perspective of critical transculturalism is that in these cases, media are arriving from places of diminished global strength but yet have

Oh and Han

enough cultural legitimacy and power to arrive. When it does, power does not evaporate; the Western site of reception is, of course, still a place of racialized global dominance.

Then, in the case of transnational Korean media flows, the question is what kind of hybridity, if any, emerges when the receiving culture is more powerful than the sending culture. The existing literature on counterflows (outside of Korean Wave studies) suggests that hybridity is, at best, an ambivalent formation. These researchers point to the political economic structures that favor dominant flows (Thussu 2007), the minuscule reception of counterflows in the West (Xie and Boyd-Barrett 2015), the ideological accommodations that Global South media must make in order to find a place within the US mediascape (Samuel-Azran 2009), and the ideological disciplining that dominant media perform to undermine the reception of counterflows (D. C. Oh 2021). These studies, however, do not directly address hybridities that might form at the site of *reception*. Rather, they clarify that counterflows are structurally contained. Yet, even so, there are structurally enabled leakages such as the global popularity of *Squid Game*, which was made possible because of Netflix's exigence to find content after major US media had abandoned it for their own distribution platforms (e.g., Hulu, Disney+, and Apple+). For this reason, it is important to also turn to the transnational audience reception research to consider how racial difference matters in the reception of transnational Korean media.

It is nearly a truism in transnational audience reception studies that the transnational meanings of texts are interpreted through the local culture (Ang 1985). Texts are not read through the cultural codes of the originating site of production but through the cultural codes of the audience's local culture. Indeed, transnational texts are only meaningful to the extent that they matter in the local, everyday lives of their viewers (Morley and Robins 1995; Georgiou 2006). For second-generation racialized diasporas, oftentimes, the use and interpretation of "homeland" media reflect their positions of racial marginalization. Vicki Mayer (2003), for instance, demonstrates that second-generation Mexican American girls watched *Maria Isabel* (1997–1998), a Mexican telenovela, because they could project onto the lead character their own hopes for upwardly mobile integration. Their readings produced elisions in which they saw the protagonist's struggles as an Indigenous woman in Mexico as parallel to their own as racialized

Introduction

13

minorities in the United States. In studies of second-generation Desi Americans, Jigna Desai (2005) argues that watching Bollywood films creates a collective sense of belonging through shared viewing and dialogic interpretations that, sometimes, creates pan-South Asian identities that resist Western assimilation, and Meenakshi Gigi Durham (2004) claims that her second-generation Indian American participants produced "new ethnicities" through their identifications and disidentifications with both US and Indian media. For diasporic reception of transnational Korean media, David Oh (2015) claims that second-generation Korean American youth's reception of "homeland" media provides resistive symbolic material to construct identities, but the media also act as key cultural markers to discipline intra-ethnic boundaries.

Outside studies of diasporas, research on other Asian Americans' reception of Korean media is still inchoate. The research that exists argues that for East Asian American viewers, Korean media are understood in a pan-ethnic framework (Ju and Lee 2015). They view it as part of a pan-East Asian identity that is defined in opposition to the perceived moral excesses of US television—sex, partying, drugs. Viewing provides comfort and legitimation in a White supremacist society that devalues Asian Americans by showing assertive Asian characters with whom they identify and by seeing their subjectivities reflected (Ju and Lee 2015). Similarly, Asian Canadian fans "consumed racial affinities of K-pop and thus sought a positive reaffirmation of their Asian identities and responded to the White dominant mediascape" (K. Yoon 2017, 2358). For queer Asian Americans, K-pop additionally provides a desirable Asian American identity that accepts male androgyny and gender fluidity (Kuo et al., 2022). In this way, Asianness is not constructed as antithetical to queer identities but constitutive of it. Thus, Asian (North) American fans receive Korean popular culture through an intersectional, pan-Asian framework that provides symbolic legitimation. Their racialization, the flattening of ethnic specificity, is reworked in order to act as a space to find meaning across multiple East Asian cultures. Thus, instead of flattening ethnic difference, Asian American identity is patched from specific East Asian cultures into a pan-ethnic tapestry (Park 2008).

For non-Asians, they consume transnational media in ways that are culturally legible and purposeful within the site of the local culture. For instance, Sunaina Maira (2005) argues that White American suburban youths'

Oh and Han

consumption of the electronic dance music style known as Goa trance (because of its origins in the Indian state of Goa) is a means by which they could imagine themselves as belonging to globalized, racialized Otherness. White users are not consuming Goa trance to be like Indians but rather to validate their own sense of self as cosmopolites who have the authority and power to consume difference. For transnational fandoms, however, there is some evidence that White, Western consumptive power is moderated by the elevation of the cross-racial fan object of desire, which produces the possibility of a more even hybrid identification (D. C. Oh 2017b). However, this should not be interpreted to assume that Orientalist fascination does not drive some White fans' interests (Maliangkay 2013). Perhaps because of these dual impulses—Orientalist desire and elevation of fan object— some heterosexual women fans produce fantasies and desires of idealized romance with Korean men, which can lead to, in some more resourceful cases, romantic tourism by economically mobile White women (Lee 2020). In addition to the powerful meanings attributed to transnational texts and fandoms, it is an ambivalent formation with White women's assertion of racial and economic capital to live their romantic/sexualized fan desires.

Through their local racial lens in their home countries, White women fans, even those who are disciplined and mocked as "Koreaboos" and "weeaboos," fans who are understood to be overinvested in Korean and Japanese popular culture, respectively, do not transform their views of masculinity in ways that challenge White and Western hegemonic masculinity but rather produce an alternative, feminized masculinity that is also desirable; thus, the counterflows even for fandoms are still interpreted within their local cultural worldviews (Lee, Lee, and Park 2020). Nissim Otmazgin and Irina Lyan (2013) find that, at least in Israel, fans act as "cultural missionaries" to localize Korean popular culture for their social networks in order to generate interest that, in turn, legitimates their fan interests. This may, however, be more possible in Israel because US and North American fans generally hide their fan interests and speak in coded language to find others because of the severity of cultural stigma (Lee, Lee, and Park 2020). For White Western audiences, then, the reception of Korean media is an ambivalent articulation of power that is mediated by global arrangements and local meanings, which is one of the reasons for its disproportionate heterosexual women fandom beyond Korea's shores.

Introduction

15

The reasons White Europeans in Eastern Europe engage with Korean media and their meaning-making are quite different, however, as their local experiences are marked by their exclusion from the West and their nations' economic development. Eastern European fans' interests are described less as individual desires for legitimation but instead as hopes for their nations, which have been disadvantaged because of the Cold War and their previous alignment with the Communist Bloc (S. Yoon 2016). For Eastern European fans, Korea, through its media, is understood as a space for progressive, modern possibilities. For instance, Polish fans of K-pop tend to be particularly progressive, expressing support for and reading queer possibilities that are less available in their local site of reception (Trzcińska 2020). "For Eastern European fans, Korean media stimulate a desire to construct new nations, which they believe were lost in the course of socialism and capitalist reconstruction under the guidance of the West" (S. Yoon 2016, 222). As such, White fans' experiences and their view of themselves in relationship to Korean media are shaped differently by available meanings and hardships in their home countries.

Regrettably, there is much less research on Black fans or audiences anywhere, whether in the West or across the Global South. In David Oh's (2017a) study of Black American YouTubers who create K-pop reaction videos, he concludes that Black fan creators perform polycultural identities, a form of hybridity that does not merge together into a new identity formation but rather asserts an identity with multiple lineages—Black American and Korean—as a way of asserting a global, cosmopolitan Black identity. This articulation claims Black American belonging while also not being bound by essentialist determinations of Black American fan interest (Anderson 2007). This is a resistive assertion within the White supremacist racial logics of their local culture as it claims both their historically racialized identities as well as a transnational connection to Korean texts, celebrities, and culture that is also racially marginalized and stigmatized in its transnational movement. In another study, Wonseok Lee and Grace Kao (2021) argue that Black fans were instrumental in leveraging their fan activities with their activism for Black Lives Matter. This conclusion connects to the many thought pieces about K-pop fan activism that emerged in response to organized efforts to support Black Lives Matter. As such,

Oh and Han

local racial standpoints matter in fan use, interpretation, and affective commitments to Korean popular culture.

For Mexican fans, at least in the capital of Mexico City, their fan experiences are quite different. Finding a community of like-minded fans was perceived as the primary benefit of their fan practice (Vogel 2019). There was no particular desire to want to be Korean or live in Korea; rather, they took pride in how they could contribute to a global project, which K-pop signified, as advocates, creators, and fans (Vogel 2019). Studies of Latin American audiences in other countries also demonstrate the local meanings imputed on K-pop that make it more culturally resonant. For instance, Xanat Vargas Meza and Han Woo Park argue that "Hispanic countries are culturally predisposed to accept it because of the special emphasis on the dance feature" (2015, 1350). Another reason for its reception, which is gendered across Latin America, is a rejection of the sexual objectification and violence seen in various Latin American media systems; this makes the representations of tender masculinity in Korea more desirable (Ko et al. 2014). But apart from these reasons, racially translocal reception is also aspirational as it is constructed in part to join a global project through K-pop participation while resisting the Western-led, neoliberal global order (Humphreys 2021). These aspirations discipline fans into neoliberal self-improvement as their favorite idols are admired for their hard work and perseverance under exploitative contracts with entertainment companies, but they also provide space to resist Western neoliberalism because of the idols' emphasis on love—within the idol groups and for their fans. Loving their idols and loving one another in community call individualism into question in favor of mutual support.

Yet, as Laura-Zoë Humphreys (2021) notes, fans see their K-pop fandom as not diminishing but renewing their *cubanidad*. Similarly, Benjamin Han argues that Latin American fan labor is culturally specific to their nations of reception. This allows fans to draw themselves into transcultural fandoms that are engaged with "cross-cultural communication and identification, which further expands into cultural values and virtues, despite the transcultural fandom's peripheral global status as a subculture" (2017, 2251). These affective affinities produce imagined hopes for their own societies to modernize; the interest is in an exoticized Korea not to sample but to

Introduction

incorporate in their lives in order to produce new hopeful possibilities. Comparatively, research on Latinx *diasporic* audiences of Korean media is rare. The only study about which we are aware is Chuyun Oh's (2020) performance ethnography of K-pop cover dancers, which focused on two cases—Chinese American and Mexican American women. Comparatively, the Mexican American dancer's fan experience was resource deficient; she struggled alone as her fan practice was isolated and devoid of the capital resources that studio spaces and training provide.

Clearly, the power differentials of race matter globally and locally. Those whose societies have more global power or who are positioned with racial privilege within their societies will receive Korean popular texts with the habits of Whiteness. These habits insist on claiming space (S. Sullivan 2006), including within fandoms, and transracially consuming in order to gain pleasure through the act of taking and oftentimes claiming expertise about the other (hooks 1992). For people of color in the West, reception will have more complications. Korean media can provide symbolic resources that allow departures from White-dominated global media, but fans may also exert power over Korea and its cultural logics as well as over fans from the Global South by claiming their geopolitical superiority. Likewise, White fans from Eastern Europe may claim power over the texts, fans of color, and Korea(ns) because of the elevated status of Whiteness, but they may also view their own nations as less modern, creating ambivalences in these power relations. As the chapters demonstrate, there are important complications and nuances in transnational audience reception of Korean media that demonstrate that power operates through global, intersectional racial logics. This affirms Kraidy's (2005) claims of unevenness in hybridity.

Yet we must be careful to not overstate the case of reception. Indeed, Kraidy's focus on critical transculturalism is largely from the perspective of structures and texts. Hybridity is produced through reception, but it is still structured, including by texts. As cultural studies theorists claim, meanings are generated at the intersection of text and reception (S. Hall 1999; Ang 1990). Thus, we do not mean to emphasize reception and the limiting structures of race in reception at the expense of the texts and the cultural codes embedded in them. Texts matter because they provide the symbols that are used and interpreted; they constrain the possible meanings that can be drawn. As Douglas Kellner (1995) claims, media culture provides raw materials through which people construct identities and meanings. In the previous discussion of the literature, it is clear that texts provide new possible desires that can be taken up and meaningfully incorporated into audiences' lives, so we recognize that Korean media have become an influential site of global media production and that its influence means there is wider distribution, recognition, and reception. Its global power is a necessary condition of meaning-making as the text must be received, and its global power is encoded through the production and cultural codes in the texts, but the meanings of transnational texts become diluted and changed as they move, being received and transformed by local audiences in ways that fit their racial and cultural logics. Instead of the Korean Wave, which connotes that transnationalism sweeps across and indelibly changes a culture as a tidal force, perhaps it should be better understood as a tributary or a confluence when two bodies of water merge—the interaction between the Korean Wave and the cultural waters of transnational reception.

Chapter Summaries

The chapters in this book are organized around two central themes, as captured in the two section titles: "Transcultural Affinity, Excess, and Contradiction" and "Intersectional Connection and Imaginaries." The first section situates *transnational affinity* at the locus of analysis as it traverses racial, ethnic, and gender boundaries to explore the question of audience reception through the lens of joy, Koreanness, appropriation, audibility, and neoliberal capitalism. In particular, this thematic section highlights how racial standpoints in specific local contexts are the lens through which fans and audiences engage in meaning-making processes in their consumption of K-pop and Korean television. Affinity includes fan joy in reception and sharing, exoticizing and colonial desire to possess Koreanness through racial transformation, the pleasure in consuming "wholesome" Korean romance and in condemning its perceived vices, the ambivalence in being aligned with K-pop for Asian American musicians, and the hope that is provided through Korean popular culture of non-Western modernity.

The second section emphasizes *transnational imaginaries*. This section centrally examines audience's imaginative play, desires, and fantasies as they interact with Korean popular culture in their lives. These imaginaries are

Introduction

19

processed through intersectional racial and ethnic standpoints that include gender, religion, region, and class. Imaginaries involve (mis)readings of texts, the use of humor to consider different temporalities, heterosexual women fans' desired Korean romantic partners to imagine heterosexual love outside of what fans interpret as toxic masculinity in their home nations, Muslim fans' ambivalence toward K-pop's "appropriations," and TikTok edits to fantasize queer possibilities. The second section also shifts the analytical focus to more regions of the world, including Europe, North America, the Middle East, and Latin America, to explore the critical role that racial translocalism plays in the reception of Korean popular culture across different geographical spaces.

In the first chapter, Crystal S. Anderson explores Black K-pop fans and non-fans in YouTube reaction videos. In a case study of Lauryn Sneeze, a YouTuber and fan, and matriarchs in her family, who are not fans of K-pop, Anderson argues for "Black joy" in cross-racial fan reception as a critical framework. This is an important intervention that challenges popular narratives of Black-Korean tension. Instead, Anderson argues that these reactions subvert essentialized understanding of authenticity that tends to erase both Black and Korean cultures by offering alternative modes of cross-racial engagement. The chapter examines K-pop beyond the frameworks of neoliberal capitalism and fan studies that often ignore fans of color and confine them to a political function.

In chapter 2, Min Joo Lee uses online ethnography of popular sites such as TikTok and Instagram to explore how fans who claim that they have already become or plan to become Korean negotiate the boundaries of Koreanness. Focusing on controversial "transracial" fans, Oli London and Xiahn Nishi, Lee uses an intersectional feminist and critical race lens to argue that claims of transracialism reinforce Western postcolonial discourses of masculinized superiority that justified colonial possession. For Koreans on the peninsula and across the diaspora, their transracial appropriation, mired in gendered racist logics, produce bewilderment and anger, further demonstrating their lack of interest in real Korean communities and their ability to possess the Asian body through becoming the Asian person, a version of self-corporeal colonial desire.

In chapter 3, Woori Han analyzes internet discourse to understand Anglophone viewers' global reception to the reality dating show *Single's Inferno*

Oh and Han

(2021–present). Using critical transculturalism as a framework, she demonstrates audiences' unexpected interest in the show's "wholesomeness" but also their judgment of its perceived racism and sexism. Viewers responded favorably to the show's less sensationalistic, "dramatic" interpretation of the island dating reality show compared to its UK and US counterparts, but at the same time, in moments in which the text provokes ideological *dis*pleasure, viewers assert Western discursive frameworks to criticize and dominate the text as well as, in some cases, Korean culture for its sexism and racism. These assertions of domination over the text as well as viewing pleasure and preference ambivalently produce hybridity that is infused with a Western cultural common sense. As such, Han demonstrates that Western transnational audiences' viewing objectifies Korean media for Western pleasure—to relieve frustrations at "sensationalism" that avoids naming sexism and patriarchy in Western texts and to assert Western superiority by overtly naming sexism and patriarchy in Korean texts.

In chapter 4, Donna Lee Kwon examines how the global popularity of K-pop has impacted the racialized reception of Asian American musicians through the lens of audibility. Drawing on the theories of racial abjection and triangulation, Kwon argues how K-pop reinforces the acceptability of Asians that retains their perpetual foreignness and abjectness while introducing Korea-based understandings of race, ethnicity, and gender, manifested in beauty aesthetics and colorism. The case studies of St. Lenox (Andrew Choi), Eric Nam, and Audrey Nuna illustrate how Asian American artists as subjects of reception negotiate the racial boundary to claim their artistic identities.

In chapter 5, Laura-Zoë Humphreys investigates how Cuban fans engage with Korean media to imagine parallel modernity that had emerged from colonial domination. This functions not only as a space for imaginative possibility but also as a reminder of Cuba's geopolitical economic realities. Yet the admiration for Korean popular culture is also marked by disidentification with Korea's embrace of neoliberal capitalism and Korean media's treatment of Cuba as an exotic locale trapped in time. Additionally, Humphreys illustrates how the admiration for Korea reinforced fans' anti-Black, class-based disparagement of reggaeton. As such, the chapter points to the contradictions and complexities of transnational fandom in Latin America when race, class, geopolitics, and soft power converge with one another.

Introduction

In chapter 6, Moisés Park combines both reception and textual analysis to examine the representation of Easter Island, also known as Rapa Nui and Isla de Pascua, in Seo Taiji's music video "Moai" (2009). Park explores how Chileans and Rapa Nui negotiate the racialized meanings encoded in the music video that contribute to the Latin Orientalist imaginary. In doing so, the chapter argues that Anglo-hegemonic structures rooted in messianic neoliberalism and exceptionalism are prevalent in Korean popular culture, further engendering internalized racialization and othering of Chile, which is often dismissed in the global imaginary of K-pop. However, because audiences are linguistically unable to decode the Korean lyrics, they primarily engage with the video's visual representation.

In chapter 7, Irina Lyan explores the role of transracial fantasies of being or becoming Korean among Israeli Hallyu fans. Drawing on theories of ethnic and racial humor and transracial carnivalesque performance, Lyan posits an argument for "minority capital" in jokes that claim "I was probably Korean in a previous life" or "I feel part Korean." Noting her participants' humorous discourses of past belonging, present crossing, and future romantic fantasies, their utterances communicate sincere desires for transnational, transracial connection that uses humor to transgress what is permissible. This brings Israeli fans closer to the subject of their fandom while maintaining the boundaries between their own and others' negotiation of racial identity.

In chapter 8, Rebecca Chiyoko King-O'Riain examines how Latina, Black, and White fans in the American Midwest and Black and White fans in Ireland use K-dramas as an emotional space to cope with their non-hegemonic identities and racialized translocal contexts. Drawing on ethnographic fieldwork, the chapter illustrates how the fans situated in different geopolitical contexts consume K-dramas to seek an alternative form of masculinity. She further argues that K-dramas enable fans to imagine global mobility in order to escape from their everyday lived experienced rooted in exclusion and toxic masculinity.

In chapter 9, Young Jung uses different K-pop case studies to examine how global fans respond to the appropriation of religious practices and imagery, particularly those of Islam. Focusing on the question of cultural appropriation and adaptation, Young explores how international K-pop fans' religious identities intersect with their racial and ethnic identities to produce conflicting meanings about the commodification of Islamic culture. Young

Oh and Han

further explores how cultural conflicts between the K-pop industry and fans illustrate the complex dynamics of pan-ethnic fandom and solidarity.

In the final chapter, Julia Trzcińska and David C. Oh explore how Anglophone fans from around the world (international fans, or "I-fans") on TikTok use Todrick Hall's song "Both" to construct K-pop fan videos that fetishize idols as attractive for their gender fluidity. The chapter analyzes the fan-produced TikTok videos and fans' online comments and reactions to imagine K-pop as a space for queer expression and K-pop idols as exemplars of idealized gender fluidity. Stripping K-pop idols of the cultural contexts of their performance, Trzcińska and Oh problematize queer I-fans' empowerment of their own queer identities through K-pop. Through the edits, I-fans remove K-pop idols' agency to express their own gender and sexual identities and substantiate racial stereotypes of Asian masculinity. This points to the complexities of transnational reception in which I-fans' empowering queer play can reify racialized gender stereotypes and normalize whose identities can be manipulated for whose pleasure.

Notes

1. We follow the Korean convention of listing the person's family name before their personal name. The exception is when the individual has a Western first name, e.g., Kim Junho and John Kim. We also use the individual's choice of romanized spelling for their name. For people who are not public figures or authors with names in the public domain, for people whose romanized name is unknown, and for common nouns, we use the Revised Romanization of Korean System to convert Korean language names and words into English.

2. "The West" as a conceptual category is contentious. We define the West as inclusive of advanced industrial nations, which have a legacy of colonial domination, including settler colonialism, that builds its moral justification upon White supremacy.

3. We recognize the problematic nature of this spatial metaphor, particularly in a world that is a three-dimensional sphere rather than a two-dimensional map. We also understand it as problematic because the West is not always located in the geographic West—for example, Australia. The flows also, of course, go toward the South, following one other major spatial metaphor of Global North and Global South. We only use this spatial metaphor of West and East because of the predominance of the West as a discursive formation.

Introduction

References

Anderson, Crystal S. 2007. "The Afro-Asiatic Floating World: Post-Soul Implications of the Art of Iona Rozeal Brown." *African American Review* 41 (4): 655–65.

————. 2020. *Soul in Seoul: African American Popular Music and K-pop*. Jackson: University Press of Mississippi.

Ang, Ien. 1985. *Watching Dallas: Soap Opera and the Melodramatic Imagination*. Translated by Della Couling. London: Methuen.

————. 1990. "The Nature of the Audience." In *Questioning the Media: A Critical Introduction*, edited by John Downing, Ali Mohammadi, and Annabelle Sreberny-Mohammadi, 155–65. Newbury Park, CA: Sage Publications.

Athique, Adrian. 2016. *Transnational Audiences: Media Reception on a Global Scale*. Cambridge: Polity Press.

Belmis, Victoria Marian. 2021. "ARMYs in Dismay as BTS' Concert Tickets Sold Out Even before Going on Sale!" *Korea Portal*, October 10, 2021. http://en .koreaportal.com/articles/50742/20211010/armys-dismay-bts-concert-tickets -sold-out-even-before-going.htm.

Bencomo, Brian. 2023. "A Legendary Career: Faker's Results at Worlds and MSI." *Nerd Street*, October 2, 2023. https://nerdstreet.com/news/2024/5/faker-skt-t1 -league-of-legends-worlds-msi.

Benjamin, Jeff. 2022. "KCON 2022 Wraps with 90,000 Attendees at Los Angeles K-Pop Festival." *Billboard*, August 23, 2022. https://www.billboard.com/music /concerts/kcon-2022-los-angeles-review-1235129547/.

Bong, Joon-ho, dir. 2020. *Parasite*. Seoul: CJ Entertainment.

Bonilla-Silva, Eduardo. 2010. *Racism without Racists: Color-Blind Racism and Racial Inequality in Contemporary America*. 3rd ed. Lanham, MD: Rowman and Littlefield.

Bow, Leslie. 2022. *Racist Love: Asian Abstraction and the Pleasures of Fantasy*. Durham, NC: Duke University Press.

Chen, Kuan-Hsing. 2010. *Asia as Method: Toward Deimperialization*. Durham, NC: Duke University Press.

Chin, Bertha, and Lori Hitchcock Morimoto. 2015. "Introduction: Fan and Fan Studies in Transcultural Context." *Participations: Journal of Audience and Reception Studies* 12 (2): 174–79.

Desai, Jigna. 2005. "Planet Bollywood: Indian Cinema Abroad." In *East Main Street: Asian American Popular Culture*, edited by Shilpa Davé, LeiLani Nishime, and Tasha G. Oren, 55–71. New York: New York University Press.

Diaz Pino, Camilo. 2021. "'K-pop Is Rupturing Chilean Society': Fighting with

Globalized Objects in Localized Conflicts." *Communication, Culture and Critique* 14 (4): 551–67. https://doi.org/10.1093/ccc/tcab047.

Du Bois, W. E. B. (1903) 1989. *The Souls of Black Folk*. New York: Bantam Books.

Durham, Meenakshi Gigi. 2004. "Constructing the 'New Ethnicities': Media, Sexuality, and Diaspora Identity in the Lives of South Asian Immigrant Girls." *Critical Studies in Media Communication* 21 (2): 140–61. https://doi.org/10.1080/07393180410001688047.

Fanon, Frantz. (1952) 2008. *Black Skin, White Masks*. Translated by Charles Lam Markmann. London: Pluto Press.

Fiske, John. 1992. "The Cultural Economy of Fandom." In *The Adoring Audience: Fan Culture and Popular Media*, edited by Lisa A. Lewis, 30–49. London: Routledge.

Flaherty, Colleen. 2018. "L'oeuf ou la poule?" *Inside Higher Ed*, March 18, 2018. https://www.insidehighered.com/news/2018/03/19/mla-data-enrollments-show-foreign-language-study-decline.

Flores, Lisa A. 2018. "Towards an Insistent and Transformative Racial Rhetorical Criticism." *Communication and Critical/Cultural Studies* 15 (4): 349–57. https://doi.org/10.1080/14791420.2018.1526387.

Georgiou, Myria. 2006. *Diaspora, Identity and the Media: Diasporic Transnationalism and Mediated Spatialities*. Cresskill, NJ: Hampton Press.

Gordon, Diane. 2016. "Korean Drama Gets American Twist with Viki's 'Dramaworld.'" *Variety*, April 17, 2016. https://variety.com/2016/digital/news/dramaworld-premiere-viki-chris-martin-sean-dulake-1201755291/.

Hall, Rachel, and Jedidajah Otte. 2021. "Interest in Anime and K-pop Drive Boom in Korean and Japanese Degrees." *Guardian*, December 29, 2021. https://www.theguardian.com/education/2021/dec/29/interest-anime-k-pop-drive-boom-korean-japanese-degrees.

Hall, Stuart. 1999. "Encoding, Decoding." In *The Cultural Studies Reader*, 2nd ed., edited by Simon During, 507–17. New York: Routledge.

———. 2003. "The Whites of Their Eyes: Racist Ideologies and the Media." In *Gender, Race, and Class in Media: A Text-Reader*, 2nd ed., edited by Gail Dines and Jean M. Humez, 89–93. Thousand Oaks, CA: Sage Publications.

Han, Benjamin. 2017. "K-Pop in Latin America: Transcultural Fandom and Digital Mediation." *International Journal of Communication* 11: 2250–69. https://ijoc.org/index.php/ijoc/article/view/6304.

hooks, bell. 1992. *Black Looks: Race and Representation*. Boston: South End Press.

Humphreys, Laura-Zoë. 2021. "Loving Idols: K-pop and the Limits of Neoliberal Solidarity in Cuba." *International Journal of Cultural Studies* 24 (6): 1009–26. https://doi.org/10.1177/13678779211024665.

Jenkins, Henry. 1992. *Textual Poachers: Television Fans & Participatory Culture.* New York: Routledge.

Jeong, Jaehyeon. 2020. "Webtoons Go Viral? The Globalization Processes of Korean Digital Comics." *Korea Journal* 60 (1): 71–99. https://doi.org/10.25024/kj.2020.60.1.71.

Jin, Dal Yong. 2013. "The Construction of Platform Imperialism in the Globalization Era." *TripleC* 11 (1): 145–72. https://doi.org/10.31269/triplec.v11i1.458.

———. 2015. *Digital Platforms, Imperialism and Political Culture.* New York: Routledge.

Jin, Dal Yong, Kyong Yoon, and Wonjung Min. 2021. *Transnational Hallyu: The Globalization of Korean Digital and Popular Culture.* Lanham, MD: Rowman and Littlefield.

Ju, Hyejung, and Soobum Lee. 2015. "The Korean Wave and Asian Americans: The Ethnic Meanings of Transnational Korean Pop Culture in the USA." *Continuum: Journal of Media & Cultural Studies* 29 (3): 323–38. https://doi.org/10.1080/10304312.2014.986059.

Jung, Hyeri. 2017. "Transnational Media Culture and Soft Power of the Korean Wave in the United States." In *The Korean Wave: Evolution, Fandom, and Transnationality,* edited by Tae-Jin Yoon and Dal Yong Jin, 225–43. Lanham, MD: Lexington Books.

Jung, Sun. 2011. *Korean Masculinities and Transcultural Consumption: Yonsama, Rain, Oldboy, K-pop Idols.* Hong Kong: Hong Kong University Press.

KCON. "About Us." n.d. Accessed December 30, 2021. https://www.kconusa.com/about-us/.

Kellner, Douglas. 1995. *Media Culture: Cultural Studies, Identity and Politics between the Modern and the Postmodern.* London: Routledge.

Kim, Ju Oak. 2021. "The Korean Wave and the New Global Media Economy." In *The Routledge Handbook of Digital Media and Globalization,* edited by Dal Yong Jin, 77–85. New York: Routledge.

Ko, Nusta Carranza, Song No, Jeong-Nam Kim, and Ronald Gobbi Simões. 2014. "Landing of the Wave: *Hallyu* in Peru and Brazil." *Development and Society* 43 (2): 297–350. https://www.jstor.org/journal/deveandsoci.

Kraidy, Marwan M. 2005. *Hybridity, or the Cultural Logic of Globalization.* Philadelphia: Temple University Press.

Kuo, Linda, Simone Perez-Garcia, Lindsey Burke, Vic Yamasaki, and Thomas Le. 2022. "Performance, Fantasy, or Narrative: LGBTQ+ Asian American Identity through Kpop Media and Fandom." *Journal of Homosexuality* 69 (1): 145–68. https://doi.org/10.1080/00918369.2020.1815428.

La Pastina, Antonio C., and Joseph D. Straubhaar. 2005. "Multiple Proximities between Television Genres and Audiences: The Schism between Telenovelas'

Global Distribution and Local Consumption." *Gazette* (Leiden, Netherlands) 67 (3): 271–88. https://doi.org/10.1177/0016549205052231.

Lee, Jeehyun Jenny, Rachel Kar Yee Lee, and Ji Hoon Park. 2020. "Unpacking K-pop in America: The Subversive Potential of Male K-pop Idols' Soft Masculinity." *International Journal of Communication* 14: 5900–5919. https://ijoc.org/index.php/ijoc/article/view/13514.

Lee, Min Joo. 2020. "Touring the Land of Romance: Transnational Korean Television Drama Consumption from Online Desires to Offline Intimacy." *Journal of Tourism and Cultural Change* 18 (1): 67–80. https://doi.org/10.1080/14766825.2020.1707467.

Lee, Wonseok, and Grace Kao. 2021. "'Make It Right': Why #BlackLivesMatter(s) to K-pop, BTS, and BTS ARMYs." *Journal of the International Association for the Study of Popular Music* 11 (1): 70–87. https://doi.org/10.5429/2079-3871(2021)v11i1.7en.

Leong, Anthony C. Y. 2002. *Korean Cinema: The New Hong Kong.* Victoria, Canada: Trafford Publishing.

Lewis, Justin. 1991. *The Ideological Octopus: An Exploration of Television and Its Audience.* London: Routledge.

Livingstone, Sonia. 1998. "Relationships between Media and Audiences: Prospects for Audience Reception Studies." In *Media, Ritual and Identity*, edited by Tamar Liebes and James Curran, 237–55. London: Routledge.

Lyan, Irina. 2023. "Shock and Surprise: Theorizing the Korean Wave through Mediatized Emotions." *International Journal of Communication* 17: 29–51. https://ijoc.org/index.php/ijoc/article/view/18460.

Maira, Sunaina. 2005. "Trance-Formations: Orientalism and Cosmopolitanism in Youth Culture." In *East Main Street: Asian American Popular Culture*, edited by Shilpa Davé, LeiLani Nishime, and Tasha G. Oren, 13–31. New York: New York University Press.

Maliangkay, Roald. 2013. "Defining Qualities: The Socio-Political Significance of K-pop Collections." *Korean Histories* 4 (1): 3–14.

Mayer, Vicki. 2003. *Producing Dreams, Consuming Youth: Mexican Americans and Mass Media.* New Brunswick, NJ: Rutgers University Press.

Miller, Toby. 2010. *Television Studies: The Basics.* London: Routledge.

Morley, David, and Kevin Robins. 1995. *Spaces of Identity: Global Media, Electronic Landscapes and Cultural Boundaries.* London: Routledge.

Oh, Chuyun. 2020. "Identity Passing in Intercultural Performance of K-pop Cover Dance." *Journal of Intercultural Communication Research* 49 (5): 472–83. https://doi.org/10.1080/17475759.2020.1803103.

Oh, David C. 2015. *Second-Generation Korean Americans and Transnational Media: Diasporic Identifications.* Lanham, MD: Lexington Books.

Introduction

———. 2017a. "Black K-pop Fan Videos and Polyculturalism." *Popular Communication: The International Journal of Media and Culture* 15 (4): 269–82. https://doi.org/10.1080/15405702.2017.1371309.

———. 2017b. "K-Pop Fans React: Hybridity and the White Celebrity-Fan on YouTube." *International Journal of Communication* 11: 2270–87. http://ijoc.org/index.php/ijoc/article/view/6307.

———. 2021. "Disciplining Transnational Popular Culture's Counter-Flows on *Family Guy*." In *The Routledge Handbook of Digital Media and Globalization*, edited by Dal Yong Jin, 129–36. New York: Routledge.

Omi, Michael, and Howard Winant. 1994. *Racial Formations in the United States: From the 1960s to the 1990s*. 2nd ed. New York: Routledge.

Otmazgin, Nissim, and Irina Lyan. 2013. "Hallyu across the Desert: K-pop Fandom in Israel and Palestine." *Cross-Currents: East Asian History and Culture Review* 9: 68–89.

Park, Jerry Z. 2008. "Second-Generation Asian American Pan-Ethnic Identity: Pluralized Meanings of a Racial Label." *Sociological Perspectives* 51 (3): 541–61. https://doi.org/10.1525/sop.2008.51.3.541.

Pieterse, Jan Nederveen. 1992. *White on Black: Images of Africa and Blacks in Western Popular Culture*. New Haven, CT: Yale University Press.

Prashad, Vijay. 2001. *Everybody Was Kung Fu Fighting: Afro-Asian Connections and the Myth of Cultural Purity*. Boston: Beacon Press.

Rosenberg, Amanda. 2021. "So You Want Gong Yoo to Slap You. Now What?" *Vulture*, October 1, 2021. https://www.vulture.com/article/squid-game-gong-yoo-thirst-watch-next.html.

Ryoo, Woongjae. 2009. "Globalization, or the Logic of Cultural Hybridization: The Case of the Korean Wave." *Asian Journal of Communication* 19 (2): 137–51. https://doi.org/10.1080/01292980902826427.

Samuel-Azran, Tal. 2009. "Counterflows and Counterpublics." *Journal of International Communication* 15 (1): 56–73. https://doi.org/10.1080/13216597.2009.9674744.

Shim, Doobo. 2006. "Hybridity and the Rise of Korean Popular Culture in Asia." *Media, Culture and Society* 28 (1): 25–44. https://doi.org/10.1177/0163443706059278.

Sinclair, John. 1999. *Latin American Television: A Global View*. Oxford: Oxford University Press.

Song, Myoung-Sun. 2019. *Hanguk Hip Hop: Global Rap in South Korea*. Cham, Switzerland: Palgrave Macmillan.

Srnicek, Nick. 2017. *Platform Capitalism*. Cambridge: Polity Press.

Straubhaar, Joseph. (2021). "Cultural Proximity." In *The Routledge Handbook of Digital Media and Globalization*, edited by Dal Yong Jin, 24–33. New York: Routledge.

Sullivan, John L. 2020. *Media Audiences: Effects, Users, Institutions, and Power*. 2nd ed. Thousand Oaks, CA: Sage Publications.

Sullivan, Shannon. 2006. *Revealing Whiteness: The Unconscious Habits of Racial Privilege*. Bloomington: Indiana University Press.

Thussu, Daya Kishan. 2007. "Mapping Global Media Flow and Contra-Flow." In *Media on the Move: Global Flow and Contra-Flow*, edited by Daya Kishan Thussu, 11–32. London: Routledge.

Trzcińska, Julia. 2020. "K-Pop Fandom as a Left-Wing Political Force? The Case of Poland." *Culture and Empathy* 3 (3–4): 119–42.

Vargas Meza, Xanat, and Han Woo Park. 2015. "Globalization of Cultural Products: A Webometric Analysis of Kpop in Spanish-Speaking Countries." *Quality and Quantity* 49: 1345–60. https://doi.org/10.1007/s11135-014-0047-2.

Vogel, Erica. 2019. "K-pop in Mexico: Flash Mobs, Media Stunts, and the Momentum of Global Mutual Recognition." In *Pop Empires: Transnational and Diasporic Flows of India and Korea*, edited by S. Heijin Lee, Monika Mehta, and Robert Ji-song Ku, 55–71. Honolulu: University of Hawai'i Press.

Xie, Shuang, and Oliver Boyd-Barrett. 2015. "External-National TV News Networks' Way to America: Is the United States Losing the Global 'Information War'?" *International Journal of Communication* 9: 66–83. http://ijoc.org/index.php/ijoc/article/view/2752.

Yoon, Kyong. 2017. "Cultural Translation of K-pop among Asian Canadian Fans." *International Journal of Communication* 11: 2350–66. http://ijoc.org/index.php/ijoc/article/view/6303.

Yoon, Sunny. 2016. "East to East: Cultural Politics and Fandom of Korean Popular Culture in Eastern Europe." *International Journal of Media and Cultural Politics* 12 (2): 213–27. https://doi.org/10.1386/macp.12.2.213_1.

Yousman, Bill. 2003. "Blackophilia and Blackophobia: White Youth, the Consumption of Rap Music, and White Supremacy." *Communication Theory* 13 (4): 366–91. https://doi.org/10.1111/j.1468-2885.2003.tb00297.x.

Introduction

PART I

......

Transcultural Affinity, Excess, and Contradiction

1

······

The Road to Fandom

Joy and Black "Fans" in K-pop

······

CRYSTAL S. ANDERSON

After a nearly two-year hiatus, Black YouTube creators and K-pop fans Cortney and Jasmine returned with a new video on their channel, 2MinJinkJongKey. The channel includes abbreviated versions of the names of all five members of the K-pop group SHINee. Cortney and Jasmine started the channel to react to K-pop music in 2012. In one of their earliest videos, they introduced viewers to the channel and their joyous and infectious style. They explicitly stated that the channel would not indulge in "serious" commentary about K-pop and promised energetic fan reactions (2MinJinkJongKey 2012). As K-pop fans of only one year, they introduced the channel, interspersing fancam video from the 2011 SM Town concert in New York. The "family" concert put on by major Korean agency SM Entertainment, SM Town featured many of the artists on the label, and these Black fans were excited to see them all. Proudly identifying themselves as fangirls, they end the video lip-syncing to K-pop girl group Miss A's "Goodbye Baby" with a bit of choreography. For the next ten years, Cortney and Jasmine uploaded over nine hundred raucous K-pop reaction videos. In doing so, they represent Black fan engagement in a way rarely seen in mainstream media, a kind of engagement fueled by joy at just being a fan.

While Black fans like Cortney and Jasmine continue to generate a wide variety of user content on other sites, media outlets tend to focus on their racial identity rather than their fan behavior. Despite being part of the diverse fandom of K-pop, Black K-pop fans are hypervisible in stories about racial topics and K-pop. Media almost exclusively associate Black fans with negative racial experiences and frequently call on them to speak as authorities on racial issues when they arise in fandom. Using the work of Black cultural studies scholars, this chapter reveals the complexity around Black engagement with transnational Korean media by centering the role of Black joy in the interplay between Black K-pop fans and non-fans in YouTube reaction videos. These videos show how Black K-pop fans, motivated by joy, function as cultural translators and curators for non-fans and talk about K-pop beyond its racial implications. Non-fans experience joy in the videos, challenging perceptions that general Black audiences are hostile to transnational Korean media. This range of constructions of Black audiences represent a broader kind of cross-racial engagement, challenging approaches from fan studies that reduce fans of color to a monolith and approaches from neoliberal capitalism that reduce them solely to economic actors. As a result, this chapter expands our consideration of racial translocalism by focusing on the specific ways that Black audiences engage transnational Korean media.

Media Constructions of Black K-pop Fans

Media coverage featuring Black K-pop fans tends to render them hyper-visible around issues of race. Their opinions commonly focus on tensions and cultural theft between Black culture and K-pop. For example, John Yoon and Mike Ives published a story in the *New York Times* about Crush, a K-pop artist who was accused of avoiding Black fans' hands during a concert performance. After providing context for the artist's career, the story turns to Black fans for their take, including an African American schoolteacher in South Korea who said "skipping over the Black fans seemed unlike him, but it didn't seem like it was unlike K-pop" and a Black South African teacher in South Korea who "struggled to reconcile her enjoyment of K-pop with what she sees as its creators' insensitivity toward other cultures" (Yoon and Ives 2022). These sources imply that the K-pop industry is rife with cultural appropriation and problematic dynamics toward race in general and Blackness specifically. This theme is echoed in an op-ed by Natasha Mulenga (2020) for *Teen Vogue*: "It's valid to ask Korean pop and hip hop artists to use their platforms to bring awareness [to] Black Lives Matter, because K-pop has a fraught history with cultural appropriation."

Anderson

The K-pop community is not immune to the racial dynamics that permeate the larger culture. Incidents around race do happen. However, these media pieces fail to provide comprehensive contexts for such incidents. Without additional perspectives, such stories suggest that such conclusions are shared by the majority of Black fans.

Media also feature Black fans as authorities about other racial topics in relation to K-pop. As a result of raising awareness online in the wake of the racial reckoning initiated by the death of George Floyd, Black fans experienced hostility and harassment online. Black K-pop fans function as witnesses to racially inflected treatment by other K-pop fans. Their fan behavior is contextualized by such treatment: "Black K-pop fans have been gaslit by members of their own fandoms when they dare to raise real concerns. That's caused a lot of dedicated Black fans to leave fandoms or fade into the background" (Mulenga 2020). Other stories, such as Elizabeth de Luna's (2020) piece for the *Guardian*, position Black K-pop fans as authorities who determine what counts as cultural appropriation. Still other stories focus on Black fans' response to racist imagery from Korean culture (Wong 2017). Again, there is no justification for online harassment. However, it is difficult to find stories about Black K-pop fans having anything other than negative online experiences in K-pop fandom. Media tends to focus on Black voices only when racially inflected issues are in play.

Black fans' frequent association with racial conflict through hypervisibility is particularly relevant to discourses about transnational Korean media because of the narrative of conflict between Black Americans and Korean immigrants that also traffics in negative perceptions of Black people. The narrative of Black-Korean conflict is invoked to describe tensions between the two groups in American cities in the 1980s and 1990s. Sources for the tensions range from perceptions about economic favoritism toward Korean merchants, differing cultural values, and conflicting economic interests (Nopper 2014; Joyce 2003). As Nancy Abelmann and John Lie argue, this narrative of conflict "reifies both African Americans and Korean Americans" and pits two historically underrepresented groups against each other (1995, 149). Negative stereotypes emerge from the conflict and impact how members of the two groups view each other. For example, when some Korean rappers draw from mainstream US hip hop, they also draw on negative stereotypes: "When talking about the differences between American and

The Road to Fandom

Korean hip hop, artists first noted language (how we say) and this naturally led to the differences in lyrical content (what we say). Based on sociocultural differences, what 'we said'—or are able to say—differed greatly. For many artists, American hip hop dealt with themes of 'thurr, women, money, and drugs'" (Song 2019, 36). This preoccupation with material pursuit, criminal activity, and misogyny informs Korean perceptions of African Americans. Song quotes Naachal of the Korean hip hop group Garion, who explains how Black-Korean dynamics within the United States influence perceptions of African Americans in Korea: "People thought of hip hop music as 'freely expressing one's opinion.' Whose opinion? The opinion and stories of American 'gangsters.' Hip hop became understood as music that was done by gangsters. This was how people perceived hip hop in 1996, 1997 and 1998. . . . Now this was right after the 1992 Los Angeles Riots, so it was a time when Koreans' perceptions of Black people were the worst" (2019, 15). The narrative of conflict shapes Korean perceptions of Black people. When media routinely feature Black commentary that only points out racial conflict, this continues to link Black people with only one kind of perspective, one that distances them from transnational Korean media.

When Black fans are front and center in media about race, they are invisible in discussions about the appeal of K-pop. Black fans fall to the background or are perceived as outsiders and interlopers, despite being part of K-pop's diverse and global fanbase. By being simultaneously rendered hypervisible and invisible, Black fans become restricted by Whiteness in the media space in the United States. Racial translocalism also suggests that local contexts can be shaped by other, dominant racial identities. Reflecting such racial dominance, mainstream media representations fail to recognize Black K-pop fans as authorities on and appreciators of K-pop. Black K-pop fans remain largely invisible in a fandom largely experienced digitally despite their overall presence and influence on online platforms (Luckie 2021; Fox, Zickuhr, and Smith 2009).

Black Audience Reception in YouTube Reaction Videos

While media construe Black fans as a monolith in stories on racial topics, Black cultural studies scholars explain the impact of such hypervisibility and offer alternatives. Toni Morrison explains why centering Black identity

Anderson

on negative racial experiences is problematic and identifies the ways that discourses and descriptions of Black people and their behavior reduce their experiences: "It would seem that to continue to see a race of people, any race of people, as one single personality, is an ignorance of gothic proportions. An ignorance so vast, so public, a perception so blind and blunted, imagination so bleak that no nuance, no subtlety, no difference among them can be ascertained" (Portland State University et al. 1975). When media only solicit the voices of Black K-pop fans on issues of race, the representation of Black K-pop fans are reduced to a monolith. Morrison further explains the consequences of focusing only on racism and the harm it visits on Black people: "It's important, therefore, to know who the real enemy is, and to know the function, the very serious function of racism, which is distraction. It keeps you from doing your work. It keeps you explaining over and over again your reason for being" (Portland State University et al. 1975). Racism comes to define Black experiences to the exclusion of other forces.

In the case of Black K-pop fans, the focus on racism diminishes the ability to grant Black fans a multitude of experiences, especially on social media, which provides a landscape where Black users exercise the freedom to construct complex identities. André Brock argues that "the construction of online identity is in many ways analogous to Du Bois' 'double consciousness.' Our online persona is the uneasy reconciliation of offline multiplicity and online fixity" (2012, 538). Given that K-pop is largely experienced online by foreign fans, it stands to reason that Black fans who use online spaces to expand their identities have experiences beyond racial harassment. The heterogeneity of Black identity makes its way to Black fandom. Rebecca Wanzo (2015) suggests that "Black fandom can thus be both counter to white hegemony and normative in its adherence to projects that treat Black people as representative of US culture instead of outliers.... Black intellectuals routinely talk about their intense pleasure, disgust or investments in popular representations of Black people." In other words, Black fans, like other fans, have a range of experiences in fandom. In order to complicate Black fan experiences, we need to allow Black fans to reclaim the affective aspect of fan identity. Mark Duffett defines fans as people "with a relatively deep, positive emotional conviction about someone or something famous, usually expressed through a recognition of style or creativity" (2013, 18). One way to examine the "positive emotional conviction" of Black fans is to

The Road to Fandom

recognize the Black joy they experience as fans. Delineating a theorization of joy that stretches from gospel artist Shirley Caesar to philosopher Cornel West to rapper Nicki Minaj, Jessica H. Lu and Catherine Knight Steele note that Black joy inscribes complexity in the online space where users "celebrate Black life in ways that challenge mainstream media's attempts to fix Black people and Black life into a position of death and despair; assert Black people as fully human, capable of experiencing and expressing a full, dynamic range of emotion; and capture, share and circulate expressions of Black life without concern for the white gaze" (2019, 829). Rather than being distinct from it, Black joy is a significant part of Black experience and forms its own critical lens as scholars have explored its impact in political philosophy, romance films, and pedagogy (Stewart 2021; Drake 2019; Williams 2022). Black joy is particularly relevant in disrupting the narrative of Black-Korean conflict by positing an alternative where Black people can appreciate transnational Korean media. Therefore, Black joy is a concept that expands our perception of the Black audience experience beyond conflict, racism, or discrimination.

Using this critical lens from Black cultural studies that reveals diverse Black experience, this chapter further examines the role that joy plays in the interplay between Black K-pop fans and non-fans in YouTube reaction videos. Reaction videos function as a gauge for how audiences respond to content. Yeran Kim notes that "reaction videos on YouTube are a significant form of cultural practice through which one can see how, in a global context of the digital mediascape, a certain genre of culture consumed in private spaces and made available using sequential processes of popular networks of intermission—production, distribution, and consumption—emerges as a particular collective form of fandom culture" (2016, 333).

K-pop reaction videos sometimes feature the presence of non-K-pop fans, and the interplay between fans and non-fans provides an extra dimension to the commentary. The reaction video is typically produced by a K-pop fan, someone who "loves with intensity, repeatedly watches a film or television show, follows a creator or performer without fail, and constantly discusses beloved texts with friends, family and strangers" (Wanzo 2015). It is the K-pop fan who organizes the viewing of videos by non-fans, fills in gaps in knowledge, provides context and seeks opinions from the non-fan. Yet fans are not the only consumers of cultural production in the reaction video. A non-fan is someone who may not have the kind of devotion exhibited by a fan but is still aware of the cultural production. Jonathan Gray notes that being a non-fan "is considerably more open and nebulous a category and practice, involving considerable flow in and out of different viewing positions" (2003, 74). Non-fans add to the conversation despite lacking the preferences, predisposition, or bias for the fan object that guide the opinions of fans. Not only are non-fans "the comfortable majority," their engagement with the fan object is "part of a common language, as are many of their events and characters, and these texts grow through media talk to something more than just the moment(s) of viewing. . . . All of these programmes *mean* something to many of us, regardless of how little we watch them" (Gray 2003, 76). Thus, the interplay between fans and non-fans in K-pop reaction videos prefigure the dynamics between the niche and general audiences of cultural production and provide the opportunity to see how Black audiences engage with transnational Korean media.

YouTube features a subgenre of K-pop reaction videos that focus on reactions by someone who is perceived as distanced from the subject matter. Reactors may be from a different genre of music or performing art, as in classical musicians react to K-pop or professional dancers react to K-pop videos. Such videos emphasize their outsider status, as opposed to K-pop fans, who would approach the reaction video with more knowledge and established preferences. These videos draw upon the identity of the reactor. When reactors are Black, they may be perceived as outsiders, but they function as fans. Michael Grant-Smith constructed an entire YouTube channel around the premise "that it's unexpected for African Americans to listen to K-pop" and hopes to "help make Koreans see beyond their stereotype of Black people as cartoon gangsters, and dispel the false notion that Africans can't be into K-pop" (Wong 2017).

A series of reaction videos by Black YouTuber Lauryn Sneeze offers a unique interplay between a Black K-pop fan and non-fans. Initial searches for "reaction videos by Black K-pop fans" brings back results of many videos. In these videos, individual or groups reacting to K-pop videos emerge. I identified several Black YouTubers with a series of reaction videos that featured non-K-pop fans. Within this group, there were two Black YouTubers that reacted to K-pop videos with members of their family, but only Lauryn's videos featured multiple generations of non-fans. I reviewed

The Road to Fandom

39

nineteen of Lauryn's videos that spanned two years and performed a thematic analysis that revealed common themes and behavior, the analysis of which reveals dimensions of Black fan identity and engagement with transnational Korean media. Lauryn's channel was established to react to K-pop music videos. Located in the United States, she joined YouTube in February 2012. She identifies herself as a fan of multiple groups, but her ultimate group is BTS. While her channel is small with a little over five thousand subscribers, it is unique because it features reactions by two generations of non-K-pop fans in her family, thereby allowing the viewer to get a greater variety of reactions and approximate the general audience who may engage with K-pop. Lauryn reacts with her aunt (Aunt Danielle) and her mother as well as with a group that includes her mother, aunt, and grandmother, Nana Joy.

Sometimes it may be difficult to confirm the racial identity for Black YouTubers. As David Oh (2017) notes, determining the racial identity of such reactors is imperfect unless the YouTubers self-identity, and often the determination of the identity of uploaders relies on visuals. However, such identification can be bolstered by the recognition of what Brock sees as Black cultural discourse in the form of signifyin', which "is the articulation of a shared worldview, where recognition of the forms plus participation in the wordplay signals membership in the Black community" (2012, 533). While the identification of the YouTube reactors may be ambivalent, the use of Black cultural discourse strengthens the probability that the reactors identify as Black. Lauryn exhibits behavior and discourse that marks her as a Black YouTuber. She self-identifies as Black on her other social media. Her Instagram features pictures with hashtags including #blackgirl, #blackgirlmagic, #blackgirliskillingit, #blackgirlfashion, and #blackgurl. Other hashtags reinforce Lauryn's Black identity, such as #aggiepride, #hbcupride, and #hbculove. "Aggie" refers to the mascot for North Carolina A&T University, a historically Black university in the United States. HBCUs is an acronym for historically Black colleges and universities, referring to institutions of higher learning in the United States originally founded to serve African American students during the segregation era when they were barred from many White colleges. Since that time, these institutions have created a rich tradition of collegiate Black culture: "The embrace of historically Black colleges has been influenced by concerns about racial

Anderson

hostility, students' feeling of isolation in predominantly White schools and shifting views on what constitutes the pinnacle of higher education" (Green 2022).

While some Black fans feature critical content on their channels, Lauryn's reaction videos with her non-fan family exude the kinds of joyful behaviors we attribute to fans in general. Lauryn happily identifies as a fan and explains that she chooses videos she likes. Unlike a review video, which would seek to evaluate the video by pointing out pros and cons, Lauryn explains to her non-fan family that she hopes they will like the videos she shares. By doing so, Lauryn establishes the non-critical function of the videos. They are for fun. Byrd McDaniel distinguishes the reaction video from other kinds of content, describing it as a "creative act" where reactors "narrate, sensationalize, and exaggerate the feeling of listening to popular music," thereby turning "private music consumption into a public performance that can be tagged, shared, and archived" (2021, 1625).

In the interplay between Lauryn and her family, Lauryn functions as a cultural translator. Lauryn explains how K-pop fandom works and the promotional cycle of a group, including debuts and comebacks (Sneeze 2019a). Lauryn also explains the unique elements of K-pop idol groups. For example, she explains the structure of NCT, a group from one of the influential Korean entertainment agencies, SM Entertainment. Using the metaphor of a bank with branches, Lauryn explains that subunits of the group have different functions: NCT 127 focuses on promotions in South Korea; WayV focuses on promotions in China; NCT Dream features younger members; and NCT U changes its members based on the concept of the song (Sneeze 2020a). Lauryn also provides historical context and industry knowledge about the artists. In introducing the group EXO, Lauryn explains SM Entertainment's position in the Korean music industry and the reasons behind the changing personnel of the group. Lauryn notes how the political dynamics between China and South Korea impact the way the Chinese members participate in the group (Sneeze 2019a). Such explanations show not only that Lauryn is a well-versed Black fan but that she explains to her family members how the Korean context informs the K-pop industry.

Lauryn's explanations also make Korean culture visible by highlighting the way that Korean social norms inform the perceptions of and dynamics

The Road to Fandom

between Korean artists. Lauryn explains to Nana Joy the beauty standards in Korea, including the value placed on features like double eyelids (Sneeze 2020c). She also explains the negative feedback that Hwasa, a member of the group Mamamoo, received as a result of being curvier than the average Korean woman (Sneeze 2019c). She reviews the Korean names of positions of members in groups, such as *maknae* (막내), or the youngest member of the group. Lauryn explains how Korean relationship norms govern the dynamics between members of groups, such as *hoobae* (후배), a title for someone younger, and *sunbae* (선배), a title for someone older. Lauryn's references to Korean culture and language shape her family's perception of Korean popular culture as distinctly Korean.

Lauryn also acts as a curator, tailoring listening sessions for her mom, Aunt Danielle, and Nana Joy. She chooses specific videos that correspond to their preferences, selecting more complicated, concept-driven videos for her Aunt Danielle, while focusing on videos with "less going on" for Nana Joy. Lauryn explains that K-pop fandom is made up of a combination of multi-fans, or fans who like multiple groups, and solo fans, those who only like one artist. While Lauryn identifies her ultimate group as BTS, a group that also contains her bias, she also identifies herself as a multi-fan on her YouTube channel. Drawing on that knowledge, she is able to provide context for a variety of K-pop artists she presents to the family, from currently popular acts such as BTS, Blackpink, TWICE, and Monsta X to acts that may be lesser known in the United States but are popular within K-pop circles, such as SHINee. As a curator and cultural translator, Lauryn functions as a fan with knowledge beyond racial issues. Duffett notes that fans "can be distinguished by their off-by-heart knowledge of their text and their expertise both about it and any associated material" (2013, 21). Because of the upbeat tone of the video, Lauryn appears thrilled to share her knowledge with her family, exuding Black joy in a way that is often absent from media portrayals of Black fans. Lauryn's role as a cultural translator and curator represents a negotiation with monoracial norms similar to those discussed in Irina Lyan's contribution to this volume, envisioning her beyond the identity of activist often used to characterize Black fans.

Black joy also underscores the reactions by Aunt Danielle and Nana Joy, non-fans who function as a Black general audience. Sometimes, Black non-fans express the same critiques about K-pop they pick up from fans,

Anderson

focusing on what they perceive as common racially problematic elements of K-pop and concluding that K-pop overall is racist. In contrast, Lauryn's family members are open to Lauryn's information and visibly enjoy the experience. No one ridicules the appearance of the members. Lauryn's mom, Aunt Danielle, and Nana Joy point out members they like, songs they appreciate, the styling of the artists, and the overall appearance in the K-pop music videos. In doing so, they function as a general audience willing to recognize Korean culture as a complex entity. Lauryn's family also draws parallels between Korean and Black artists. Their familiarity with Black cultural production allows them to make these comparisons. Aunt Danielle compares the choreography of K-pop artist Lay with choreography by Usher and Chris Brown (Sneeze 2020a). Both Usher and Chris Brown are Black R&B artists known for their vocals and choreography who achieved fame in the early 2000s. However, Nana Joy compares the choreography in a BTS video to that of Michael Jackson and Prince, also known for their vocals and choreography but whose biggest hits occurred in the 1980s and 1990s (2020b). Both Aunt Danielle and Lauryn's mom recognize elements of Nikki Minaj in the rap bridge in a Blackpink music video (Sneeze 2021). These varying responses suggest that Black non-K-pop fans associate elements of K-pop with aspects of Black culture with which they themselves are familiar and like. These videos show Black people enjoying K-pop, which counters the media representations that largely represent criticism of K-pop.

When Lauryn's family encounters racially related content, they tend to have a more nuanced response informed by context. For example, when Lauryn (2019b) points out box braids on one of the members of the group Blackpink in a music video, Aunt Danielle said she did not even notice (Sneeze 2019b). Box braids are a braiding style commonly associated with and worn by Black women, yet Aunt Danielle did not take umbrage at a Korean woman wearing box braids. The use of the hairstyle did not even register for her as something she should be upset about. This contrasts with the perception of some Black K-pop fans who view such styles as appropriation. Kay Sesoko (2021) argues that the K-pop industry's very use of Black hairstyles rises to the level of cultural appropriation and blames the K-pop industry for the negative response to Black hair: "[K-pop idols] can have dreadlocks or braids for about a month and then never have to do

The Road to Fandom

43

them again. However, many K-pop fans do not have the option of treating their hairstyle as a temporary fashion trend. They can't change who they are. Many cultures feel that their culture is appropriated when used as a fashion trend to make money. This is because when they embrace their culture, it is not accepted. They are disrespected, mocked, and insulted for it." While the natural hair texture is what grows out of a person's head, Black people can change their hairstyles and the texture of their hair. Black people are not required to wear their hair in Black hairstyles such as braids, locks, and cornrows; they choose to. Sesoko's critique is really about negative reactions to Black hairstyles often from dominant forces in Western cultures. The House of Representatives of the US Congress (H.R. 2116, 117th Cong. [2022]) found that "people of African descent are deprived of educational and employment opportunities because they are adorned with natural or protective hairstyles in which hair is tightly coiled or tightly curled, or worn in locs, cornrows, twists, braids, Bantu knots or Afros" and that misinterpretation of federal civil rights laws allows "employers to discriminate against people of African descent who wear natural or protective hairstyles even though the employment policies involved are not related to workers' ability to perform their jobs." Black people are not subject to discrimination by the Korean entertainment agencies. Aunt Danielle's lack of concern around the presence of braids shows a different, less visible yet viable reading of appropriation in K-pop.

Other conversations between Lauryn and her family regarding appropriation reflect a more nuanced and comprehensive perspective brought by a different generational view. When Lauryn does broach the discourse in K-pop fandom around music appropriation, she acknowledges that some fans complain that the K-pop industry and idols "steal" from Black culture, failing to acknowledge the source of the cultural production they "appropriate." She also explains that interviews show that idols often give credit to Black artists and music (Sneeze 2019b). For many Black Americans, the accusation of cultural theft is informed by a history in which White Americans introduced Black music to the mainstream in the 1950s and 1960s without acknowledging the Black originators. However, to accuse K-pop artists of this kind of appropriation erroneously casts Koreans in the role of White people within a distinctly US racial context when talking about transnational Korean media. It fails to recognize that experiences of

Korean immigrants resemble the treatment of African Americans in the segregation and post-segregation eras. It ignores the political and cultural relationship between the United States and South Korea, a relationship in which South Korea does not occupy a dominant subject position (Anderson 2020, 116). Such dynamics also call to mind Min Joo Lee's chapter in this volume, which examines how appropriation is often framed by the historical impact of Whiteness. Lauryn's family's reaction to such charges of appropriation is informed by their generational experience. In one of Lauryn's (2020c) reaction videos, Nana Joy sees such use of Black culture as raising the bar in terms of performance. She also opines that they do not rely on a victimization discourse epitomized by "the white man holding me back." Instead, they promote the development of creativity. Nana Joy evokes a perspective that recognizes discriminatory treatment but also supports improvement and pursuit of excellence despite obstacles. In doing so, she reflects a different mindset around the discourse of cultural appropriation. Nana Joy's response also echoes Rebecca Chiyoko King-O'Riain's findings, as presented in this volume, about the ways that audiences experience transnational Korean popular culture through their own lived experiences. Rather than view the K-pop artists as cultural thieves, Nana Joy aligns them with Black artists in striving to make high-quality performances. Overall, these reaction videos challenge the reductive ways that the local culture can restrain perceptions of Black fans by providing a range of expressions by Black fans and non-fans. Race operates in several different ways that impact reception, thus expanding racial translocalism's focus on the local context.

Challenges to Representations of Monolithic Black Audiences

Black fan reaction videos embody a broader kind of cross-racial engagement with transnational Korean media. In fan studies, even though Black fans exist, White fans are perceived as the default fan, no matter the fandom. In a study of the concept of the fan in media industries, Mel Stanfill finds that "representations of fans imagine them overwhelmingly as white people" (2018, 311). Oh notes that "K-pop fan reaction videos of White English-speaking fans, in particular, are theoretically interesting because their videos are an articulation of discourse that fits within global racial logics

The Road to Fandom

still structured and advanced by Whiteness" (2017, 5). Shifting the lens to Black fans can change our conclusions. When fan studies constructs Black fans as authorities, it is largely related to Black cultural production. It rarely grants them the same kind of authority in other fan spaces. Stanfill observes that "African Americans often feel an expectation that they will show up to support Black media to prove that they sell and stake a claim that such stories are important" (2018, 308). As a result, Black fans are rarely seen as authorities outside of fandoms that revolve around Black cultural objects.

Black reaction videos also destabilize tendencies to view Black fans as a monolith. They expand how we perceive Blackness in social media fan spaces. By revealing expressions of joy in engaging with a different culture, Lauryn's videos show that not only can Black fans be fans, but they can also be fans of things outside of Black culture. They do not always have to grapple with politics, economics, and appropriation. Recognizing the Black joy in Black fan experiences disrupts an identity defined solely by struggle. Incorporating Black joy into a fan studies lens recognizes the affective aspect of Black fandom. Wanzo (2015) suggests that we place "a particular identity at the center of the reading or interpretative practice—and explore the possibility that a different kind of fan, as well as different issues of concern to fans, might be visible if we focus on African Americans." Doing so gets us away from the binary perspective in which Black fans only function as nodes for conflict and recognizes different ways that Black audiences engage with transnational Korean media. Moreover, Anna Lee Swan notes that "these YouTubers are not white, the racial group with the most power in the United States, and are not Korean, and thus embody a fan identity that does not reify stereotypical assumptions of dominance in the transnational community" (2018, 560). Black K-pop fans therefore diversify perspectives on the fan object.

The interplay between Black fans and non-fans of K-pop also challenges approaches from neoliberal capitalism, a common interpretative frame for transnational Korean media. Sangjoon Lee identifies globalization as a major interpretative frame in English-language scholarship used to examine Korean cultural production, which "has accelerated the cross-border movement of capital, commodities, and people" and is "perceived as an economic experience encircling such trends as economic liberalization, deregulation, and the heightened mobility of capital, commodities, services

Anderson

and labor around the world" (2018, 10–11). Some scholars have applied an economic-based approach to transnational Korean media because they view cultural production like K-pop as commodities. John Lie notes, "South Korea's twentieth-century history of creative destruction and the cultural amnesia that surrounds it account at least in part for the country's ability to succeed in the ruthless competition of global capitalism, including the culture industry and K-pop. . . . The culture industry in general and popular music in particular have little concern for continuity or history for its own sake. The ultimate principles remain market demand and popular consumption; the pursuit of profit valorizes planned obsolescence and the fabrication of the next blockbuster" (2014, 120). Rather than viewing K-pop as cultural expression, Lie sees it solely as a product, reducing the artists involved in the creation of the music to mere cogs in a machines and fans to only consumers.

However, Lauryn's reaction videos challenge this approach by reintroducing the human factor. Duffett notes that "to see fandom as primarily about consumption is to forget, first, that fans like things for free, and second, that they are always *more than* consumers. They are more than buyers and their transactions are pursued with a cultural interest that goes beyond merely practicing the process of buying" (2013, 21). Fans may participate in a globalized economy, but they also derive meaning from other fan practices. Lauryn's YouTube videos reflect an emotional rather than an economic engagement with K-pop. Moreover, the neoliberal approach to transnational Korean media ignores the very emotional experience that Black fans are denied by media coverage. Because neoliberal capitalism focuses on economic systems and not the people who produce or who are impacted by productions, it misses the way neoliberal capitalism disrupts the experiences of people of color. If it does not recognize people of color, then it would not recognize the distinct ways in which Black K-pop fans engage with K-pop as global cultural production beyond mere consumption.

The interplay between Black fans and non-fans of K-pop represents just one manifestation of cross-racial engagement with transnational Korean media. Lauryn's videos highlight the need to recognize Black joy in the ways that Black people engage with Korean popular culture, going beyond casting Black fans only as racial spokespersons. Black fans function as curators and cultural translators, while Black non-fans prefigure a more general

The Road to Fandom

audience open to engagement with transnational Korean media. Recognizing the interplay between Black fans and non-fans counters reductive media representation. By disrupting the reductive impulses of fan studies and approaches grounded in neoliberal capitalism, this chapter expands racial translocalism by examining how Black fans negotiate a variety of meanings related to transnational Korean media. These fans operate within a specific localized context, one informed by a complex and nuanced Black culture and history. This localized context brings depth to our consideration of engagements with transnational Korean media in the West.

References

Abelmann, Nancy, and John Lie. 1995. *Blue Dreams: Korean Americans and the Los Angeles Riots*. Cambridge, MA: Harvard University Press.

Anderson, Crystal S. 2020. *Soul in Seoul: African American Popular Music and K-pop*. Jackson: University Press of Mississippi.

Ashe, Bertram D. 2007. "Theorizing the Post-Soul Aesthetic: An Introduction." *African American Review* 41 (4): 609–23.

Brock, André. 2012. "From the Blackhand Side: Twitter as a Cultural Conversation." *Journal of Broadcasting and Electronic Media* 56 (4): 529–49. https://doi.org/10.1080/08838151.2012.732147.

De Luna, Elizabeth. 2020. "'They Use Our Culture': The Black Creatives and Fans Holding K-pop Accountable." *Guardian*, July 20, 2020. https://www.theguardian.com/music/2020/jul/20/k-pop-black-fans-creatives-industry-accountable-race.

Drake, Simone. 2019. "The Marketability of Black Joy: After 'I Do' in Black Romance Film." *Women, Gender, and Families of Color* 7 (2): 161–81. https://doi.org/10.5406/womgenfamcol.7.2.0161.

Duffett, Mark. 2013. *Understanding Fandom: An Introduction to the Study of Media Fan Culture*. New York: Bloomsbury.

Fox, Susannah, Kathryn Zickuhr, and Aaron Smith. 2009. "Twitter and Status Updating, Fall 2009." Pew Research Center, October 21, 2009. https://www.pewresearch.org/internet/2009/10/21/twitter-and-status-updating-fall-2009/.

Gray, Jonathan. 2003. "New Audiences, New Textualities: Anti-fans and Non-fans." *International Journal of Cultural Studies* 6 (1): 64–81. https://doi.org/10.1177/1367877903006001004.

Green, Erica L. 2022. "Why Students Are Choosing H.B.C.U.s: '4 Years Being Seen as Family.'" *New York Times*, June 11, 2022. https://www.nytimes.com/2022/06/11/us/hbcu-enrollment-black-students.html.

Issar, Siddhant. 2021. "Listening to Black Lives Matter: Racial Capitalism and the Critique of Neoliberalism." *Contemporary Political Theory* 20: 48–71. https://doi .org/10.1057/s41296-020-00399-0.

Joyce, Patrick D. 2003. *No Fire Next Time: Black-Korean Conflicts and the Future of America's Cities.* Ithaca, NY: Cornell University Press.

Kim, Yeran. 2016. "Globalization of the Privatized Self-Image: The Reaction Video and Its Attention Economy on YouTube." In *Routledge Handbook of New Media in Asia,* edited by Larissa Hjorth and Olivia Khoo, 333–42. London: Routledge.

Lee, Sangjoon. 2015. "Introduction. A Decade of Hallyu Scholarship: Toward a New Direction in Hallyu 2.0." In *Hallyu 2.0: The Korean Wave in the Age of Social Media,* edited by Sangjoon Lee and Abé Mark Nornes, 1–27. Ann Arbor: University of Michigan Press.

Lie, John. 2015. *K-pop: Popular Music, Cultural Amnesia, and Economic Innovation in South Korea.* Oakland: University of California Press.

Lu, Jessica H., and Catherine Knight Steele. 2019. "'Joy Is Resistance': Cross-Platform Resilience and (Re)Invention of Black Oral Culture Online." *Information, Communication and Society* 22 (6): 823–37. https://doi.org/10.1080/1369118X .2019.1575449.

Luckie, Mark S. 2021. "Black People Build Social Media, but We're the Least Protected across Platforms." *Ebony,* March 1, 2021. https://www.ebony.com/life /how-big-tech-wins-on-the-backs-of-black-people/.

McDaniel, Byrd. 2021. "Popular Music Reaction Videos: Reactivity, Creator Labor, and the Performance of Listening Online." *New Media and Society* 23 (6): 1624–41. https://doi.org/10.1177/1461444820918549.

Mulenga, Natasha. 2020. "Why K-pop Stars Must Keep Speaking Up about Supporting Black Lives Matter." *Teen Vogue,* June 5, 2020. https://www.teenvogue .com/story/k-pop-stars-speaking-up-black-lives-matter.

Nopper, Tamara K. 2014. "Revisiting 'Black-Korean Conflict' and the 'Myth of Special Assistance': Korean Banks, US Government Agencies, and the Capitalization of Korean Immigrant Small Business in the United States." *Kalfou* 1 (2): 59–86. https://doi.org/10.15367/kf.v1i2.33.

Oh, David C. 2017. "K-pop Fans React: Hybridity and the White Celebrity Fan on YouTube." *International Journal of Communication* 11: 2270–87.

Ohlheiser, A. W. 2020. "How K-pop Fans Became Celebrated Online Vigilantes." *MIT Technology Review,* June 5, 2020. https://www.technologyreview.com /2020/06/05/1002781/kpop-fans-and-black-lives-matter/.

Omolade, Tiwa. 2021. "When Black K-pop Fans Are Terrorized Online, Who Listens?" *Refinery 29,* March 24, 2021. https://www.refinery29.com/en-us/2021 /03/10180347/black-k-pop-fans-doxxed-harassed-cyber-bullying.

The Road to Fandom

Portland State University, Toni Morrison, Primus St. John, John Callahan, Susan Callahan, and Lloyd Baker. 1975. "Black Studies Center Public Dialogue, Part 2." Oregon Public Speakers Collection, May 30, 1975. https://pdxscholar.library .pdx.edu/orspeakers/90.

Sesoko, Kay. 2021. "3 Things the K-pop Industry Needs to Know about the Cultural Appropriation of Hairstyles." *Kpopmap*, July 30, 2021. https://www .kpopmap.com/3-things-the-kpop-industry-needs-to-know-about-the -cultural-appropriation-of-hairstyles/.

Sneeze, Lauryn. 2019a. "My Aunt and I React to K-POP!!! | (BTS, iKON, STRAY KIDS, GOT7, EXO, Katie, Whee In)." February 5, 2019. YouTube video, 1:08:52. https://youtu.be/789EQnN-Bbw.

———. 2019b. "My Aunt and I React To K-Pop! | BTS and BLACKPINK | Part 1." May 18, 2019. YouTube video, 19:40. https://youtu.be/ZRFTYc6cu6o.

———. 2019c. "My Aunt and I React to K-Pop! Part 2 | ATEEZ, EVERGLOW, MAMAMOO, & HWASA | KPOP REACTION!!!" May 21, 2019. YouTube video, 27:36. https://youtu.be/MUrTU1jioDQ.

———. 2020a. "MY MOM & AUNT REACT TO KPOP pt. 2 | NCT 127, MONSTA X, LAY | NON KPOP FANS REACT | KPOP REACTION." April 18, 2020. YouTube video, 23:00. https://youtu.be/DSeqkDavJac.

———.2020b. "MY GRANDMA REACTS TO KPOP pt. 1 | BTS | NON KPOP FAN REACTION | BTS REACTION." April 22, 2020. YouTube video, 20:08. https://youtu.be/T9O7XQ6Wljs.

———. 2020c. "MY GRANDMA REACTS TO KPOP pt. 2| SEVENTEEN, ASTRO, EXO | NON KPOP FAN REACTION | KPOP REACTION!" April 23, 2020. YouTube video, 24:29. https://youtu.be/CGxlDOTcShk.

———. 2021. "My WHOLE Family Reacts to K-Pop Pt. 3 | BLACKPINK, NCT 127, STRAY KIDS, BTS, SUPERM, KAI | REACTION!" March 19, 2021. YouTube video, 38:15. https://youtu.be/ZHMO2O97gAo.

Song, Myoung-Sun. 2019. *Hanguk Hip Hop: Global Rap in South Korea*. Cham, Switzerland: Palgrave Macmillan.

Stanfill, Mel. 2018. "The Unbearable Whiteness of Fandom and Fan Studies." In *A Companion to Media Fandom and Fan Studies*, edited by Paul Booth, 305–17. Hoboken, NJ: John Wiley and Sons.

Stewart, Lindsey. 2021. *The Politics of Black Joy: Zora Neale Hurston and Neo-Abolitionism*. Evanston, IL: Northwestern University Press.

Swan, Anna Lee. 2018. "Transnational Identities and Feeling in Fandom: Place and Embodiment in K-pop Fan Reaction Videos." *Communication, Culture and Critique* 11 (4): 548–65. https://doi.org/10.1093/ccc/tcy026.

2MinJinkJongKey. "Our KPop Life/Sm Town NYC Experience." February 26, 2012. YouTube video, 7:11. https://youtu.be/jEuzNFwodCs.

Wanzo, Rebecca. 2015. "African American Acafandom and Other Strangers: New Genealogies of Fan Studies." *Transformative Works and Cultures* 20. https://doi.org/10.3983/twc.2015.0699.

Williams, Michelle Grace. 2022. "'They Never Told Us That Black Is Beautiful': Fostering Black Joy and Pro-Blackness Pedagogies in Early Childhood Classrooms." *Journal of Early Childhood Literacy* 22 (3): 357–82. https://doi.org/10.1177/14687984221121163.

Wong, Sterling. 2017. "Black K-pop Fans Come Out of the Closet." *Daily Beast*, updated April 14, 2017. https://www.thedailybeast.com/black-k-pop-fans-come-out-of-the-closet.

Yoon, John, and Mikes Ives. 2022. "A K-pop Star Didn't High-Five Black Fans. Was It Racism?" *New York Times*, October 19, 2022. https://www.nytimes.com/2022/10/19/arts/music/crush-racism-kpop.html.

2

······

Between Appreciation and Appropriation

Race-Transitioning among Hallyu Fans

······

MIN JOO LEE

Appropriation of East Asian cultures and identities by non-Asians has become a "cool" online trend. On TikTok, YouTube, Instagram, and other user-generated websites, users upload makeup tutorials that supposedly make them look Asian, express their desires to be reborn as one, or even claim to have already become Asian through their consumption of Asian popular culture. As Irina Lyan discusses in her chapter in this volume, fans sometimes say that they were Korean in their previous life, and Koreans sometimes tell foreigners, "I thought you were a real Korean" to compliment their Korean pronunciation. Although some fans and Koreans may use the identity of Korean lightheartedly, in this chapter, I examine graver ways in which some fans appropriate Korean identity and culture. Even though these fans' actions resonate with yellowface, the historical Hollywood practice of non-Asian actors performing Asian characters, the two practices are slightly different. The early Hollywood rendition of yellowface consisted of White actors donning exaggerated facial makeup and performance to portray Asian characters. The White actors did not desire to become Asian. However, the twenty-first-century version of yellowface is complicated by the claim that the individuals participating in it admire Asian cultures and therefore are supposedly appreciating them, even aspiring to become Asian.

The rise in popularity of Asian aesthetics, identity, and culture can be attributed to many cultural influences, one of which is the rise in the transnational popularity of Korean popular culture. Individuals from different parts of the world consume Korean popular culture and become avid fans of it in a phenomenon known as Hallyu. However, some Hallyu fans are dissatisfied with simply consuming Korean popular culture; they desire closer connection with it and a sense of belonging within it. Hence, they appropriate Korean identity and culture. Their behaviors raise certain questions: Can one become Korean simply by claiming it as a part of one's identity? What is the difference between appropriation and appreciation?

In this chapter, I critically examine the media discourses and social media posts of two White Hallyu fans: Oli London and Xiahn Nishi. They are Hallyu fans from the United Kingdom and Brazil, respectively, who toe the boundary between appreciation and appropriation of Korean masculinity. Both underwent cosmetic surgery to alter their facial features to embody their exoticized understanding of how Korean faces look. Their decision to undergo cosmetic surgery to "look Korean" results in a near-permanent embodiment of cultural appropriation. In their case, cultural appropriation is not just a temporary performance or action but also a perpetual embodied state of being. In that regard, I suggest that even though they claim to appreciate the nation and its people, they assert their White privilege to create an essentialized image of Korean culture and people that they disseminate around the world through their (social) media appearances.

I selected London and Nishi as case studies for this chapter because they are the most infamous transracial individuals; they appeared in Korean news media as well as in news media around the world, including in the United States, Brazil, and the United Kingdom. I use critical race theory to examine ten Instagram posts and two news interviews from Nishi and twenty Instagram posts, ten Twitter posts, and fifteen TikToks from London. Furthermore, I searched for Oli London–related reaction videos on YouTube, ranked the videos based on viewership, and used purposive sampling to select the top ten videos featuring Koreans and Asian Americans reacting to London's social media posts. In the following sections of this chapter, I critically analyze these data to parse the fine line between fans' appreciation and appropriation of Korean culture and identity.

Between Appreciation and Appropriation

53

Appropriation and Appreciation

What is appropriation? How is it different from appreciation? According to LeRhonda Manigault-Bryant, appropriation is "this very fluid exchange of culture that happens among human beings. . . . But the way that we think about it, especially now, is that it refers to taking someone else's culture—intellectual property, artifacts, style, art form, etc.—without permission" (quoted in Brucculieri 2018). However, Brian Morton (2020) challenges this definition by arguing that permission should not be the framework through which to distinguish between appropriation and appreciation. After all, as Morton says, most cultures do not have representatives who can give permission to outsiders to use their culture. To have such a system would create its own problems of intra-cultural power hierarchy regarding matters of whom is given the authority to dictate the nation's cultural boundaries. Furthermore, such practices would result in essentializing the culture by making its borders and membership unreasonably strict.

I agree with Morton that appropriation and the outrage surrounding it has more nuanced power dynamics that cannot be explained through the notion of permission. I contend appropriation occurs when the act reifies historical and current existing power dynamics of race and national hierarchies. In other words, the outrage surrounding cultural appropriation is not simply about the act of outsiders trying to become insiders to a culture or identity they were not born into. As a case in point, on social media, a significant number of non-Korean Asian Hallyu fans of different nationalities use hashtags such as #wannabeKorean and #Korean or more specific hashtags such as #pinoytoKorean to voluntarily adopt Korean culture and identity as their own. However, none of them gained as much media attention and notoriety as the two White social media influencers Oli London and Xiahn Nishi, who garnered Korean, as well as international, limelight as White Europeans (London being from the United Kingdom and Nishi being from Brazil but being of German heritage) appropriating Korean masculinity. I suggest the outrage and accusations of appropriation aimed against them by ethnic Koreans and diasporic Asians are fueled by the unique positionality of Whiteness and White supremacy in a Korean/Asian historical context, which these two social media influencers ignore in their attempts to "become Korean."

Lee

I find Jason Baird Jackson's (2021) definition of appropriation useful because it factors history and intergroup power hierarchy to differentiate appropriation from other forms of intercultural encounters, such as acculturation and assimilation. According to Jackson, cultural exchange can only be defined as "exchange" when the two cultures involved are relative equals in power, who are engaging with each other without coercion. In contrast, acculturation, assimilation, and appropriation occur among groups with relative power imbalance. Acculturation is multidirectional; despite the power imbalance, both cultures are changed by each other. In that regard, compared to assimilation or appropriation, its outcome is less skewed in favor of one party over the other. However, assimilation and appropriation are mono-directional: "In assimilation, a powerful group imposes aspects of its culture on an economically, politically, and/or demographically weaker target group. In a framework of appropriation, in contrast, the powerful group takes aspects of the culture of the subordinated group, making them its own" (Jackson 2021, 87).

The objective of assimilation is the incorporation of the *people*—the cultural outsiders—into the dominant culture. The objective of appropriation is not the people, but the incorporation of certain aspects of an outside *culture* into the culture of a more powerful nation (Han 2019; Heyd 2003; Hladki 1994; Matthes 2016). During appropriation, the people of that culture are marginalized because their culture is treated as disembodied. The appropriators claim to embody the "authentic" version of the culture and profit from such self-promotion, whereas the people who originally belonged to that culture are deprived of financial opportunities and rights to define the authenticity of their own culture (Heyd 2003). Appropriation fosters misrecognition of the culture and its people. In the process of appropriation, the culture becomes essentialized and stereotyped, and then such stereotypes become disseminated around the world (Lalonde 2021; Han 2019). The key problem of cultural appropriation is that the appropriators usurp the authority and the authenticity of the appropriated cultures and people, often under the guise of appreciation.

However, appreciation of a culture is based on one's desire to understand and accept differences between cultures and to contextualize such differences (Howard 2020). In other words, the key difference between appropriation and appreciation is one of attempting to erase the differ-

Between Appreciation and Appropriation

ence between cultures through absorption versus accepting the difference between one's culture and that of the other, respectively.

As a disclaimer, I am not the ultimate authority in dividing Hallyu fans into appreciators versus appropriators. C. Michelle Kleisath claims that "scholars enjoy a privileged vantage point in the sense of access to multiple points of view, but also in the sense of comfortable distance from painful lived experiences [of cultural appropriation experienced by the research subjects]" (2014, 107). However, I find that while I do have the privilege, as a scholar of Korean culture, of observing multiple points of view about appropriation and analyzing them through critical theoretical frameworks, as a Korean, I am a subjective "insider" regarding the issue at hand.

Who Is Korean? What Is Korean Culture?

Definitions of Korean and Korean culture are central to the controversy surrounding the legitimacy, or lack thereof, of foreign Hallyu fans' claims to Korean identity and culture.[1] At first glance, they may seem like commonsense terms that can be easily defined. However, determining who or what belongs within or outside boundaries of Korean and Korean culture is complex.

The concept of Korean culture is in flux; disputes about the Koreanness of cultural products such as K-pop and Korean food constantly arise (Choi 2011; H.-E. Lee 2006; Rawnsley 2014; Sik 2006). Likewise, the boundary of Korean as an identity is constantly changing and dependent upon aspects such as one's place of residency, citizenship, and race. For instance, historically, Korean media discourses about ethnic Koreans living abroad oscillated between treating them as foreigners versus creating the term *overseas Korean* (재외동포) to bring them into the boundary of the nation (Joo 2012). Similarly, throughout the nation's history, mixed-race Koreans, especially those born to foreign men and Korean women, were treated as subhuman foreigners polluting the "pure" Korean identity (N. Y. Kim 2014). However, recently, due to the declining birth rate and the resultant imperative for the country to embrace multiracialism, the media and the government reversed course and began calling mixed-race Koreans positive symbols of the nation's bright future (Jun 2014; N. H.-J. Kim 2014; Oh 2020). In these ways, the sociopolitical and media discourses significantly

Lee

influence whether one is accepted or excluded from the boundaries of Korean.

For the purpose of this chapter, I abide by the legal definition of Korean identity. This definition is imperfect and stricter than the cultural definitions, which include a broad spectrum of people with Korean heritage. Nonetheless, I find the strict legal definition helpful to juxtapose against the superficial meaning of Korean identity that some Hallyu fans mobilize in their appropriation of it. The Korean Nationality Act defines those who meet at least one of the following criteria as Korean: a person whose parents are citizens at the time of one's birth or a person who is born in the Republic of Korea but whose parents are unknown or are nationless subjects (Korea Legislation Research Institute 1976). Foreigners with parents who are non-Koreans can become Korean through (1) marriage to a Korean, (2) adoption by Korean parents (only in the case of children), or (3) by meeting all of the following requirements: being a domicile of Korea for five or more consecutive years; being twenty years or older; being of good behavior; having sufficient property or ability to secure livelihood; and having no nationality or promising to forfeit his or her current foreign nationality within six months after acquiring Korean nationality (Korea Legislation Research Institute 1976). Exceptions to these rules are made for foreigners who made, or are expected to make, significant contributions to the nation. The legal definition of Korean focuses on one's familial connection, residence in the Korean peninsula, behavior, income, and national loyalty.

In contrast to the legal definition of Korean, the Hallyu fans' definition of it focuses solely on Korean popular culture. For instance, some fans assume that K-pop idols, who are foreign nationals, are Korean or have become so by virtue of being a K-pop ("Korean" pop) idol. For instance, in a comment thread on one K-pop YouTube video, a viewer remarked, "How to act Korean: be born Korean." In a rebuttal to the comment, another person said, "hmm. . . . but Lisa from Blackpink is from Thailand and she CAN act like a Korean." This comment generated other responses, such as "OMG she really is Thai! This whole time I thought she was Korean woooow" (S. Kim 2022). These comments garnered thousands of "likes" by other fans. This impromptu conversation points to the paradox of some Hallyu fans' popular culture–centered definitions of Koreanness, whereby a foreign celebrity's behaviors and identity are interpreted as Korean by

Between Appreciation and Appropriation

virtue of her working within the Korean popular culture industry. What kind of Korean identity does a Hallyu fan embody if the fan models one's appropriation of Koreanness after Lisa, a Thai woman, who they mistakenly believe to be Korean? In this case, can the fan's embodiment of Koreanness actually be defined as Korean, or is it some other form of hybrid identity?

Hallyu is a hybrid culture. Since the early 2010s, scholars critically examining it have questioned whether, and to what extent, it is culturally Korean (Lie 2012; Choi 2011; K. H. Kim 2021). While they agree that Hallyu is culturally hybrid and not "purely" Korean, all of them differ on what they mean by "Korean culture" and why they view Hallyu as culturally hybrid. Some scholars point to Confucian ideologies as the root of Korean culture, while others point to traditional folk songs and performances dating back to hundreds of years ago as true symbols of Korean culture (Teo Kia Choong 2005; M. J. Lee 2021; Demelius 2021). They argue that Hallyu's deviation from such ideologies and performances indicates that it is not "purely" Korean. These scholars' debates demonstrate that the boundaries of Korean culture and Korean are hard to define, even for experts of Korea.

Therefore, perhaps it is unsurprising that the Hallyu fans who were inspired by Korean popular culture to want to become Korean do not have clear-cut definitions of what that entails. Being unable to clearly define what Korean and Korean culture mean in itself is not condemnable. However, the problematic practice lies in how some fans cross the boundary between appreciation and appropriation as they make up their own definitions of what Korean culture is and what it means to be Korean while ignoring how their actions perpetuate historical power hierarchies.

Changing Appearances through Cosmetic Surgery to "Look Korean"

Xiahn Nishi garnered widespread media attention in 2014 as a White Brazilian man of German heritage who underwent cosmetic surgery to "look Korean." However, perhaps predicting the criticism from Koreans, in interviews, Nishi downplayed his choice to have the surgery. For instance, in an interview with a Korean news agency, he said, "Deep down, I may have wanted to become Korean, but when I was at the Brazilian plastic surgeon's office, I didn't ask for a Korean face, I asked for Asian eyes" (Y.-h.

Lee

Kim 2014). He claimed that he only underwent cosmetic surgery once to temporarily have "Asian eyes." However, further news reports indicated that he underwent cosmetic surgery approximately ten times to make himself look "perfectly" Korean (YTN News 2014) and that he consulted with numerous doctors because he could not find one who was willing to perform surgery on his eyes to remove his epicanthic fold, the crease between one's eyes and eyebrows (Hoh 2014).

The shape of one's eyes are mired in a long history of racism, xenophobia, and White saviorism. In the West, the presence, or lack thereof, of a natural epicanthic fold has long symbolized the difference between East Asians and White people and even between friends and foes. During World War II, racist posters circulated among the Allied powers informing their citizens on ways to distinguish between the "friendly" Asians and the "enemy" Japanese. *Life* magazine described the former as "more frequently having epicanthic folds," whereas the latter were described as having "less frequent epicanthic folds" (Miles 2012). The US military pamphlet at the time described "friendly" Chinese as having eyes "set like any Europeans' or Americans'," whereas Japanese were marked as the Other by having eyes "slanted towards his nose" (US Army 1942). The double eyelid surgery, to create epicanthic folds on East Asian eyes, was first introduced in Korea by a US military doctor, during the aftermath of the Korean War, as a life-affirming pathway to modernization for Koreans, whom these doctors believed looked anti-modern and dimwitted due to their eyes (S. H. Lee 2016). However, Nishi appropriates the "Asian eyes" with disregard for how this trait of Koreans/Asians has been marked as negative, marking their "Otherness" and as needing to be fixed by White Westerners. Nishi's disregard for the historical resonance of his actions makes his surgical procedure appropriation rather than appreciation of supposedly Korean aesthetics.

Nishi trivializes the racial motivations behind his cosmetic surgery and justifies his aesthetic choice through the discourse of self-love: "I think I look handsomer like this. Maybe some people think it's not but I think it is," and "I've always been shy but now I'm more happy, more confident with myself" (Hoh 2014). After his cosmetic surgery, he posted many highly stylized photos of himself on social media that make him look like a K-pop idol. For instance, in one of his photos, he has dyed platinum blond hair and is wearing a light blue button-up shirt. He is hugging a stuffed horse and looking into the camera while puckering his lips. In other photos, he either stares intently into the camera with puckered lips or stares off to the side in feigned nonchalance, which are poses that were popular among male K-pop idols in the early 2010s. Granted, his poses and style are not unique to male K-pop idols (some Japanese and Chinese idols do it as well), but I attribute his photographic inspiration to that of the male K-pop idols because of the resounding Korean influence that runs throughout his social media page, such as numerous photos of him wearing *hanbok*, the nation's traditional attire, and others where he is at a Korean restaurant, eating fried chicken and soju, a popular food and drink combination among young Koreans.

While Nishi frames cosmetic surgery as a necessary choice to find his happiness, his neoliberal discourse of "choice" regarding beauty is closely connected to Whiteness's appropriative ability that is not permitted for non-White individuals. He asserts that his choices only affect him and argue that his desires are tightly entwined with his own happiness and well-being. By claiming his racial "choice" only affects his own well-being, he excuses himself from the broader historical resonance of his actions and their ramifications for Koreans.

However, when Koreans make those same choices (e.g., cosmetic surgery and following makeup trends), Western feminists and media accuse them of being oppressed by the patriarchal culture of lookism and desires to look White (Chang and Thompson 2014; Stewart 2013). The K-pop idols undergoing a weight-loss diet and cosmetic surgery as well as wearing certain outfits deemed to be hypersexual are issues that feminists and fans from outside of Korea often criticize as problematic. For instance, a cursory Google search of the key words "K-pop diet" summons English-language newspaper articles criticizing K-pop idols for perpetuating what the articles describe as "extreme" and "shocking" diets, while the key words "K-pop plastic surgery" typed in the search engine summons op-eds and blog posts describing the practice as fueled by "obsession." On various fan forums, Hallyu fans condemn cosmetic surgery and diet practices by posting comments filled with sympathy, such as "I know it's the Korean culture, but it's sickening just imagining what they go through on a daily basis."[2] The K-pop idols' and the women's claims that they are pursuing their happiness through their beauty regimen are met with Western feminists' sympathy at

Lee

how supposedly brainwashed they are with misogynistic values and how they need to be "saved" (S. H. Lee 2016). Furthermore, some Western feminists criticize Asian people as hating themselves and trying to look White (Hoang 2015). These Asians' supposed attempts to embody Whiteness are conceived as pathological desires that need to be cured by White saviors.

Nishi draws parallels between Koreans' supposed desires to look White and his surgery to have "Asian eyes" by claiming that when he was an exchange student in Korea, he saw "many people change their original look with make-up and look completely different so I think it's the same with [my] surgery" (Hoh 2014). However, they are not the same in terms of their appropriative power. First, a majority of Korean, and Asian women at large, undergoing cosmetic surgery or applying skin-whitening products are not trying to be White (Holliday and Elfving-Hwang 2012). As Jeaney Yip, Susan Ainsworth, and Miles Tycho Hugh (2019) claim, Asian women's beauty regimen centers on the "pan-Asian beauty ideal" rather than their idealization and appropriation of Whiteness. Nishi's assumption that Koreans want to become White is presumptuous and premised on the idea of White superiority that neglects the possibility that perhaps Whiteness is not as desired in Korea as it is in the West. In his attempts to justify his appropriation, Nishi misrepresents the nation's culture and its people's actions by analyzing them through the framework of White superiority.

Furthermore, a non-White Asian supposedly trying to become White and a White cis-man trying to look Asian are mired in different historical contexts, making the latter much more appropriative than the former. Black, brown, and mixed-race people who attempted to "choose" their own race, either temporarily or permanently, to escape from racism and segregation have historically faced legal ramifications and violent retaliation from White supremacists (Harris 1993). Yet the appropriative power of Whiteness granted White Westerners the power to claim their racelessness (Bell 2021) to "try on" different races at their whim through minstrelsy and yellowface. Historically, the White performers donning blackface and yellowface could profit from their performance, while the same opportunities did not arise for folks of color performing Whiteness (Lemons 1977). Similarly, in the twenty-first century, Nishi's appropriation of supposedly Korean aesthetics gives him opportunities such as being asked to be a model for a South American apparel company selling Asian clothes (Hoh 2014).

Between Appreciation and Appropriation

61

Instead of Asian models, Nishi, the cross-racial subject who appropriates Koreanness, is offered profitable opportunities. However, since 2021, his limited media appearance and lack of interaction with his followers on social media make his appropriative power relatively less impactful than that of Oli London, who grabbed global media attention around the same time as Nishi did and continues to shock the digital sphere by engaging in increasingly controversial activities.

Becoming Jimin: Reinterpretation and Appropriation of Korean Masculinity

Oli London is a White British social media influencer who is infamous for undergoing multiple cosmetic surgeries to look like Jimin, a member of the K-pop idol group BTS. At the time of writing, London identifies as a gender non-binary Korean. According to their social media profile, they use the "pronouns: they, them, Korean, and Jimin."[3] "Korean" and "Jimin" are proper nouns that respectively indicate nationality and the name of one of the members of BTS. By appropriating proper nouns as pronouns, London undermines the legitimacy of the Korean identity as well as that of Jimin. Instead of identities that are connected to legitimacy founded on government-defined legal definitions, they become pronouns that anyone can claim.

Rather than stopping at simply emulating Jimin, London usurps Jimin's authenticity and claims to be the "authentic" and legitimate version of Jimin, in a practice typical of appropriators who claim to be more authentic than the inhabitants of the appropriated culture. For instance, under one of the photos uploaded on their Instagram page, London comments, "Jimin who?"[4] The photo is of London posing as if a paparazzi caught them by surprise as they are exiting a skyscraper. They are wearing a neon pink jumper, and their hair is dyed platinum blond and styled with a center part like Jimin's. By asking "Jimin who?" London asks the viewers whether they can distinguish between the "original" Jimin and London in the photo. The question connotes that London's mimicry of Jimin is so complete that there is no difference between the "original" and London. They are asking the viewers, who are you going to call Jimin? Through this social media post and many that resemble it, London appropriates Jimin's

Lee

identity. The response to this post was mixed. While it received 9,411 likes, the comments were resoundingly negative, with some leaving comments such as "I appreciate that you like Jimin but you shouldn't do this he is trying to be himself and you are trying to copy" and "You are a copyJimin" and others posting frowning face and puking emoji.

Beyond claiming to be Jimin, London essentializes Korean masculinity and perpetuates racist stereotypes in their attempts to appropriate it. For example, London announced in 2022 that they are planning on undergoing penis reduction surgery to become "fully Korean" (Song 2022). In the interview, London said that they recently found out that Korean men's average penis size is 3.5 inches (8.9 centimeters) and that they are planning on going to Thailand to have their penis reduced to become "100% Korean." London added that they hoped that "Koreans are not offended" by this news. However, Koreans were offended. In the comment section to the Korean-language news of London undergoing penis reduction surgery to become "fully Korean," many used profanities and questioned London's mental state, with one commenter saying, "What the hell. There are crazies everywhere" (Song 2022).[5] The most popular comment under the news article said, "Korean men's average is not 8.9 centimeters, it's 12 centimeters. 8.9 centimeters would bring shame upon the country. The government needs to step in; the Korean embassy in the UK needs to correct this influencer's assumption that Korean men have small penis."

Through the announcement about the penis reduction surgery, London achieved two outcomes. First, they implied their penis size is bigger than that of an average Korean by announcing that they will have to *reduce* their penis size as opposed to simply announcing that they will *alter* it. Second, the supposedly small Asian penis, in comparison to that of White men, has historically been a way to queer and emasculate Asian men (Nguyen 2014), and London perpetuated such narratives through their widely publicized announcement. Historically, in the West, Asian masculinity has been maligned as effeminate, nonvirile, and queer (Chong and Kim 2021; Nemoto 2008; Nguyen 2014; Wong et al., 2012). London, who appropriates Korean masculinity to "become Korean," does so in ways that perpetuate these stereotypes rather than in ways that problematize White heteronormative masculinity. They essentialize Korean masculinity without considering the diverse array of masculinities and penis sizes among these men.

Between Appreciation and Appropriation

63

Furthermore, I view London as appropriating Korean masculinity rather than appreciating it because of how London perpetuates the historical power dynamic through which Korean masculinity was used to prop up White masculinity. During and after the Korean War, White masculinity has been formative in shaping Korean masculinity. White men, represented by US soldiers stationed in Korea after the Korean War, asserted their hypermasculinity through their sexual prowess. Some of the soldiers had indiscriminate sex with both Korean female sex workers and gay men in Seoul in places they nicknamed "Hooker Hill" and "Homo Hill" (Schober 2014). Meanwhile, Korean men were desexualized and emasculated as cuckolded bystanders who could only observe while foreign men had sexual access to Korean women and men. Such comparative subjugation of Korean masculinity by White men continued long after the Korean War. During the Vietnam War, Korean soldiers served as the "surrogates" of the US soldiers to carry out violent acts on their behalf (J.-k. Lee 2009). Even in the twenty-first century, some young Korean men still believe they are emasculated and desexualized by White men, which affects their self-esteem and performance of masculinity (Schober 2014; M. J. Lee 2020). Hence, the outcry related to London appropriating and queering Korean masculinity is not only about Koreans' attempts to safeguard the national boundaries from outsiders but also about the paradox of a White man appropriating Korean masculinity for the purpose of self-affirmation while ignoring how White masculinity and Korean masculinity were historically pitted against each other to affirm the former's supposed dominance over the latter.

Although London's actions are by and large condemned, London also has more than five hundred thousand followers on Instagram who regularly like their social media posts. How did they garner such popularity? How do they legitimize their racial "transition"? London claims to be a non-binary Korean who will help the Korean LGBTQ community. Furthermore, they use transgender communities' discourse of body dysmorphia to garner sympathy from the public about their urge to racially transition from a White British person to a Korean. For instance, in a news interview, London claims to feel trapped in the wrong body:

So, I feel the only way of really comparing this is with someone that's transgender, and I mean no offense to the transgender community, this is just how I would explain it, as someone that feels like they are born in the wrong body. So, for the last nine years I felt like I've been trapped. Since I lived in Korea [for one year], I feel like I identify as Korean. Everything about the culture is me. I feel at home now. I don't feel judged. I feel like Korean people accept me. I feel like I have the look now. So, it's been a very difficult journey, but I just feel like it's how I felt inside, and I just felt trapped. (London 2021)

I cannot verify London's claims that "Korean people accept" them. However, if true, it highlights London's privilege as a White Westerner, because not many queer Koreans are able to find such acceptance among other Koreans (M.-A. Cho 2011). Their "acceptance" in Korea as a gender non-binary, self-proclaimed Korean is predicated on Koreans interpreting London as a foreigner, who would not fundamentally disrupt Korean gender norms through their queer identity. In other words, even though London claims to have now become "fully" Korean, they are still being viewed as foreign. For instance, in a video where three cosmopolitan Korean YouTubers review Oli London's social media posts, upon hearing London claim in a video clip that their identity as a non-binary Korean is going to help empower the Korean LGBTQ community, one of the YouTubers shouts incredulously, "He's not even Korean!" while another remarks, "Out of all the people, Oli London coming out as a non-binary Korean is not going to help Korean LGBTQ people. This is entitlement. He's just out of his mind" (DKDKTV 2021). They do not accept him as Korean, and they argue that his claim to a non-binary Korean identity is detrimental to the nation's LGBTQ movement. These YouTubers are not the only Koreans voicing their concern and rejecting Hallyu fans who attempt to appropriate Korean culture.

Reception from Koreans and Korean Diaspora

Many Koreans express concern for the fans who appropriate their culture and identity. For instance, a Korean grandmother in her eighties said, "If I were their mother, I would feel so bad. I feel so bad for them. They used to look fantastic! They used to look fine before the surgeries" (ReacThing 2020). She expresses concern for their mental health and that of their parents. Two Korean men, reacting to London's social media posts, begin

Between Appreciation and Appropriation

by attempting to understand and sympathize with them.[6] For instance, the two men say, "He's weird but I feel like he really loves our culture. At least he's doing what he likes." They express some appreciation at the length that London would go to appropriate Korean culture and identify such acts as signs of their dedication. However, as the men watch more videos of London, near the end of their reaction video, one of the men switches from speaking in mild tones in English to an angry tone in Korean and says, "진짜 너무 할말이 없어. 아니 진짜 갑자기 화가나, 나는" (I have no words. I'm suddenly very angry). However, they conclude the video by expressing concern about London's mental well-being and looking directly at the camera to leave a message to London: "Whenever you visit Korea, just hit me up. We can hang out and I think we can help each other out." Similar to the grandmother's reaction video, the overriding emotion in these two men's reaction video is that of concern rather than anger.

Even those who express a sense of anger brush their feelings aside by saying that, ultimately, the fans are doing what they love with their lives and that others should leave them be. For instance, a Korean YouTuber who regularly posts videos of public figures who committed socially harmful acts equates the negative outcomes of London's appropriation to that of a con man.[7] However, after listing the offenses that London committed, such as sexually suggestive touching of a life-size cardboard cutout of Jimin and using Japanese and Chinese aesthetics in his music videos that were intended to commemorate Korean culture, the YouTuber concludes his video by saying, "I don't really have much to say because they are doing what they want to do with their lives, but I can't help feeling that they are going too far." These Korean YouTubers view fans appropriating Korean culture and identity as just harming their own and their family's well-being as opposed to creating negative consequences for Koreans.

Diasporic Koreans and Asians in the West, however, express more anger than concern toward London and Hallyu fans whom they view as appropriating Asian culture and identity. For instance, an Asian American social media influencer going by the name Sherliza Moé posted numerous videos criticizing Oli London and other White Hallyu fans who appropriate Korean identity. In one video, she says, "How convenient, and what a f—— privilege to jump to another race, just like that without getting actual backlash. . . . All the big news media are almost sympathetic to him, which

I don't understand! I have a huge problem with [London] because you can't just change your race!" (2021). A Korean diasporic YouTuber named Ben Kim also uploaded multiple videos related to the topic, and in his videos, he can hardly speak because he is so angry.[8] He turns red, stutters, swears, and takes long pauses between his sentences because he is too angry to verbally express himself. These diasporic Koreans and Asians express more anger toward the race-transitioning Hallyu fans than resident Koreans. The slightly different reactions of resident Koreans and of the Korean/Asian diaspora raises the question: If resident Koreans are not offended by Xiahn Nishi and Oli London, can their actions still be defined as appropriation?

The difference in opinion between Asians living in Asia and diasporic Asians regarding cultural appropriation and politics of race has been well documented in other scholarly works on appropriation. For instance, Jackson (2021) examines the Qipao prom dress controversy that arose in the United States when a non-Chinese White woman wore a Qipao to her prom. He observes how Chinese Americans expressed anger at having their traditional outfit appropriated but that a majority of resident Chinese felt honored that a non-Chinese person loved their culture. He attributes the different reactions to the different experiences the two groups have; diasporic Asians have to live with hegemonic White supremacy and the negative impacts of appropriation on a daily basis, whereas the resident Asians can distance themselves from the appropriators and surround themselves with others in their nation who can affirm one another's identities.

Just because resident Asians do not express vehement anger about cultural appropriation does not mean they approve of these acts. As Young Jung and Donna Lee Kwon examine in their respective chapters in this volume, the question of who has the right to express their offense at cultural appropriation is a complex issue. Furthermore, just because some resident Koreans appear to "approve" foreigners appropriating their culture does not mean that the act is acceptable or uncondemnable. Resident Koreans do not have more authority than the Korean diaspora to grant permission to fans to appropriate the culture. Furthermore, appropriation does not center on permission; it is related to the historical national and racial power dynamics between the appropriator and the appropriated. Despite Xiahn Nishi's and Oli London's claims that they appreciate Korean culture, their actions are closer to appropriation than appreciation because of the

Between Appreciation and Appropriation

67

historical power dynamic that they perpetuate through their actions and because they choose to essentialize Korean culture and identity rather than consider their multifaceted nature.

Conclusion

Is there a solution to appropriation? According to Morton, "the way forward [from debates on appropriation] isn't to pursue a dream of staying within our lanes" (2020, 92). I agree with Morton that the answer to appropriation is not for everyone to stop exploring and interacting with other cultures. However, can there be a way for foreigners to appreciate Korean culture and even become Korean without essentializing or appropriating the nation's identity and culture? In my view, yes. For instance, John Linton's (Korean name In Yo-han) family lived in Korea for four generations, originally coming from the United States. Linton's grandfather participated in Korea's anti-colonial movement during the Japanese colonial period; his father participated in the Korean War; and John Linton himself participated in the Korean democratization movement and, as a doctor, introduced and normalized ambulances in Korean hospitals (Kang 2021). Due to having contributed to Korean modernization, the government awarded him Korean citizenship. He is fluent in Korean, underwent Korean military training, and is married to a Korean woman. Although he can claim to be Korean legally and culturally, when he makes media appearances, while expressing his deep love for Korea, the country where he was born and raised, he also acknowledges the privileges he experienced as a person who is not ethnically Korean.

Appropriation is the embodiment of a decontextualized and essentialized version of another culture. Kris Sealey argues that "the white person who attempts to shed her white identity becomes blind to the racial privilege that she cannot opt out of, and therefore runs the risk of perpetuating the very structural racisms against which an ally ought to fight" (2018, 27). The appropriative power of Whiteness is closely connected to structural racism and White supremacy. London and Nishi justify their appropriative behaviors as appreciation for Korea, self-affirmation, and self-love as opposed to acts that are mired in the historical power hierarchy between Korea and the West. However, their claims to Korean culture and identity

Lee

are inextricably entwined with the role that Western White men (and women) played throughout history, and continue to play, in shaping Korean discourses of gender, race, and beauty.

Notes

1. In this chapter, I use the term *foreign* to refer to those who are not ethnically or legally Korean.

2. For the full context of the discussion that fans were having, please visit Imtryinjennifer, "Kpop Idols Messaging with Eating Can Be Very Damaging," r/kpopthoughts, n.d., Reddit, https://www.reddit.com/r/kpopthoughts/comments/pjl4u6/kpop_idols_messaging_with_eating_can_be_very/.

3. The original Tweet is no longer available on X (formerly Twitter); see Oli London (@OliLondonTV). Recently, Oli London has renounced his track record of claims to being transracial and gender non-binary and became an outspoken proponent of gender essentialism.

4. For the original Instagram post, see @londonoli (Oli London), https://www.instagram.com/londonoli/.

5. I am responsible for translating the comments from Korean to English.

6. The original video is no longer available on YouTube: "Korean Guys Reacting to Oli London," uploaded by JKTV, September, 11, 2021, length unknown.

7. The original video is no longer available on YouTube: "Facts You Didn't Know about Oli London," uploaded by @user-lq7ydıbt7z date uploaded, length unknown.

8. The original video is no longer available on YouTube but is available on TikTok: uploaded by skz08_bts07, March 27, 2022, TikTok, 1:39, https://www.tiktok.com/@skz08_bts07/video/7079820499831885061.

References

Bell, Marcus. 2021. "Invisible No More: White Racialization and the Localness of Racial Identity." *Sociology Compass* 15 (9): e12917. https://doi.org/10.1111/soc4.12917.

Brucculieri, Julia. 2018. "The Difference between Cultural Appropriation and Appreciation Is Tricky. Here's a Primer." *HuffPost*, February 7, 2018. https://www.huffpost.com/entry/cultural-appropriation-vs-appreciation_n_5a78d13ee4b0164659c72fb3.

Chang, Juju, and Victoria Thompson. 2014. "South Korea's Growing Obsession with Cosmetic Surgery." *ABC News*, June 20, 2014. https://abcnews.go.com

/Lifestyle/south-koreas-growing-obsession-cosmetic-surgery/story
?id=24123409.

Cho, Hong Sik. 2006. "Food and Nationalism: Kimchi and Korean National Identity." *Korean Journal of International Studies* 46 (5): 207–29. https://doi.org /10.14731/kjis.2006.12.46.5.207.

Cho, Min-Ah. 2011. "The Other Side of Their Zeal: Evangelical Nationalism and Anticommunism in the Korean Christian Fundamentalist Antigay Movement since the 1990s." *Theology and Sexuality* 17 (3): 297–318. https://doi.org/10.1179 /tas.17.3.xx56t21243207121.

Choi, Yun-Jung. 2011. "The Globalization of K-Pop: Is K-Pop Losing Its Korean-ness?" *Situations* 5: 61–67.

Chong, Kelly H., and Nadia Y. Kim. 2021. "'The Model Man': Shifting Perceptions of Asian American Masculinity and the Renegotiation of a Racial Hierarchy of Desire." *Men and Masculinities* 25 (5): 674–97. https://doi.org/10 .1177/1097184X211043563.

Demelius, Yoko. 2021. "Thinking through Community Spirit: Zainichi Koreans in Post-Korean Wave Japanese Communities." *Japanese Studies* 41 (1): 93–112. https://doi.org/10.1080/10371397.2021.1893673.

DKDKTV. 2021. "Koreans React to OLI LONDON Being Korean/Jimin." July 21, 2021. YouTube video, 23:03. https://youtu.be/pMZzoziRM2w.

Han, Hsiao-Cheng. 2019. "Moving from Cultural Appropriation to Cultural Appreciation." *Art Education* 72 (2): 8–13. https://doi.org/10.1080/00043125.2019 .1559575.

Harris, Cheryl I. 1993. "Whiteness as Property." *Harvard Law Review* 106 (8): 1707–91. https://doi.org/10.2307/1341787.

Heyd, Thomas. 2003. "Rock Art Aesthetics and Cultural Appropriation." *Journal of Aesthetics and Art Criticism* 61 (1): 37–46.

Hladki, Janice. 1994. "Problematizing the Issue of Cultural Appropriation." *Alternate Routes: A Journal of Critical Social Research* 11: 95–119.

Hoang, Kimberly Kay. 2015. *Dealing in Desire: Asian Ascendancy, Western Decline, and the Hidden Currencies of Global Sex Work*. Oakland: University of California Press.

Hoh, Amanda. 2014. "Brazilian Man Undergoes Surgery to Look Asian." *Sydney Morning Herald*, June 2, 2014. https://www.smh.com.au/lifestyle/brazilian-man -undergoes-surgery-to-look-asian-20140602-zrv8n.html.

Holliday, Ruth, and Joanna Elfving-Hwang. 2012. "Gender, Globalization and Aesthetic Surgery in South Korea." *Body and Society* 18 (2): 58–81. https://doi.org /10.1177/1357034X12440828.

Howard, Karen. 2020. "Equity in Music Education: Cultural Appropriation versus

Cultural Appreciation—Understanding the Difference." *Music Educators Journal* 106 (3): 68–70. https://doi.org/10.1177/0027432119892926.

Jackson, Jason Baird. 2021. "On Cultural Appropriation." *Journal of Folklore Research* 58 (1): 77–122.

Joo, Rachael Miyung. 2012. *Transnational Sport: Gender, Media, and Global Korea*. Durham, NC: Duke University Press.

Jun, EuyRyung. 2014. "Tolerance, *Tamunhwa*, and the Creating of the New Citizens." In *Multiethnic Korea? Multiculturalism, Migration, and Peoplehood Diversity in Contemporary South Korea*, edited by John Lie, 79–94. San Francisco: Institute of East Asian Studies.

Kang, Young-Koo. 2021. "'최초의 구급차' 와 '제2의 구급차'" ["First ambulance" and "second ambulance"]. *Hankook Ilbo*, July 5, 2021. https://www.han kookilbo.com/News/Read/A2021070216300002325.

Kim, Kyung Hyun. 2021. *Hegemonic Mimicry: Korean Popular Culture of the Twenty-First Century*. Durham, NC: Duke University Press.

Kim, Nadia Y. 2014. "Race-ing toward the Real South Korea: The Cases of Black-Korean Nationals and African Migrants." In *Multiethnic Korea? Multiculturalism, Migration, and Peoplehood Diversity in Contemporary South Korea*, edited by John Lie, 211–43. Berkeley, CA: Institute of East Asian Studies.

Kim, Nora Hui-Jung. 2014. "Korea: Multiethnic or Multicultural?" In *Multiethnic Korea? Multiculturalism, Migration, and Peoplehood Diversity in Contemporary South Korea*, edited by John Lie, 58–78. Berkeley, CA: Institute of East Asian Studies.

Kim, Sunny. 2017. "KOREAN REACTS: CRINGY KOREABOOS." August 31, 2017. YouTube video, 7:38. https://youtu.be/4sqVBKfMJ1E.

Kim, Young-hyun. 2014. "한국인처럼 성형수술한 브라질 남자, 그 이후" [Epilogue of the Brazilian man who underwent cosmetic surgery to look Korean]. *Yonhap News*, June 6, 2014. https://www.huffingtonpost.kr/2014/06/06 /story_n_5457463.html.

Kleisath, C. Michelle. 2014. "The Costume of Shangri-La: Thoughts on White Privilege, Cultural Appropriation, and Anti-Asian Racism." *Journal of Lesbian Studies* 18 (2): 142–57. https://doi.org/10.1080/10894160.2014.849164.

Korea Legislation Research Institute. 1976. Nationality Act. In *02-2110-4121*, edited by Ministry of Justice. Seoul: Korea Legislation Research Institute.

Lalonde, Dianne. 2021. "Does Cultural Appropriation Cause Harm?" *Politics, Groups, and Identities* 9 (2): 329–46. https://doi.org/10.1080/21565503.2019.1674160.

Lee, Hee-Eun. 2006. "Seeking the 'Others' within Us: Discourses of Korean-ness in Korean Popular Music." In *medi@sia: Global Media/tion in and out of Context*, edited by T. J. M. Holden and Timothy J. Scrase, 146–64. London: Routledge.

Lee, Jin-kyung. 2009. "Surrogate Military, Subimperialism, and Masculinity:

South Korea in the Vietnam War, 1965–73." *positions: east asia cultures critique* 17 (3): 655–82. https://doi.org/10.1215/10679847-2009-019.

Lee, Min Joo. 2020. "Transnational Intimacies: Korean Television Dramas, Romance, Erotics, and Race." PhD diss., University of California, Los Angeles.

———. 2021. "Branding Korea: Food, Cosmopolitanism, and Nationalism on Korean Television." *Situations: Cultural Studies in the Asian Context* 14 (1): 53–76. https://doi.org/10.22958/situcs.2021.14.1.003.

Lee, Sharon Heijin. 2016. "Beauty between Empires: Global Feminism, Plastic Surgery, and the Trouble with Self-Esteem." *Frontiers: A Journal of Women Studies* 37 (1): 1–31. https://doi.org/10.5250/fronjwomestud.37.1.0001.

Lemons, J. Stanley. 1977. "Black Stereotypes as Reflected in Popular Culture, 1880–1920." *American Quarterly* 29 (1): 102–16. https://doi.org/10.2307/2712263.

Lie, John. 2012. "What Is the K in K-pop? South Korean Popular Music, the Culture Industry, and National Identity." *Korea Observer* 43 (3): 339–63.

London, Oli. "'I Now Identify as Korean after Being Born in the Wrong Body' | This Morning." This Morning. July 6, 2021. YouTube video, 9:35. https://youtu.be/YvjdWEIzFwk.

Matthes, Erich Hatala. 2016. "Cultural Appropriation without Cultural Essentialism?" *Social Theory and Practice* 42 (2): 343–66.

Miles, Hannah. 2012. "WWII Propaganda: The Influence of Racism." *Artifacts Journal* 1 (6). https://artifactsjournal.missouri.edu/2012/03/wwii-propaganda-the-influence-of-racism/.

Morton, Brian. 2020. "All Shook Up: The Politics of Cultural Appropriation." *Dissent* 67 (4): 84–94.

Nemoto, Kumiko. 2008. "Climbing the Hierarchy of Masculinity: Asian American Men's Cross-Racial Competition for Intimacy with White Women." *Gender Issues* 25 (2): 80–100.

Nguyen, Tan Hoang. 2014. *A View from the Bottom: Asian American Masculinity and Sexual Representation.* Durham, NC: Duke University Press.

Oh, David C. 2020. "Representing the Western Super-Minority: Desirable Cosmopolitanism and Homosocial Multiculturalism on a South Korean Talk Show." *Television and New Media* 21 (3): 260–77. https://doi.org/10.1177/1527476418789895.

Rawnsley, Ming-Yeh T. 2014. "'Korean Wave' in Taiwan: The Cultural Representation of Identities and Food in Korean TV Drama, *Dae Jang Geum*." In *Reading Asian Television Drama: Crossing Borders and Breaking Boundaries,* edited by Jeongmee Kim, 215–38. London: IB Tauris.

ReacThing. 2020. "Korean in Her 80s Reacts to 'Oli London.'" February 25, 2020. YouTube video, 7:30. https://youtu.be/CVTO2YJ3Mdc.

Schober, Elisabeth. 2014. "Itaewon's Suspense: Masculinities, Place-Making and the US Armed Forces in a Seoul Entertainment District." *Social Anthropology* 22 (1): 36–51. https://doi.org/10.1111/1469-8676.12060.

Sealey, Kris. 2018. "Transracialism and White Allyship: A Response to Rebecca Tuvel." *Philosophy Today* 62 (1): 21–29. https://doi.org/10.5840/philtoday2018 29197.

Sherliza Moé. 2021. "WHITE Kpop Stan Changes Race to KOREAN." July 16, 2021. YouTube video, 15:00. https://youtu.be/MO2wN-FᴛᴠEk.

Song, Ju-sang. 2022. "BTS 지민 되려 성형한 인플루언서 '성기 축소 수술' 선언한 이유가 …" [The influencer who underwent cosmetic surgery to become BTS's Jimin announced he will undergo penis reduction surgery]. *Chosun Ilbo*, updated February 3, 2022. https://www.chosun.com/international /topic/2022/02/02/RFV74FRIWRAAZI63FPIKBM2GFE/.

Stewart, Dodai. 2013. "Plastic Surgery Means Many Beauty Queens, but Only One Kind of Face." *Jezebel*, April 25, 2013. https://jezebel.com/plastic-surgery -means-many-beauty-queens-but-only-one-480929886.

Teo Kia Choong, Kevin. 2005. "Old/New Korea(s): Korean-ness, Alterity, and Dreams of Re-unification in South Korean Cinema." *Contemporary Justice Review* 8 (3): 321–34. https://doi.org/10.1080/10282580500133128.

US Army. 1942. *How to Spot a Jap*. In *A Pocket Guide to China*. Washington, DC: US Government Printing Office.

Wong, Y. Joel, Jesse Owen, Kimberly K. Tran, Dana L. Collins, and Claire E. Higgins. 2012. "Asian American Male College Students' Perceptions of People's Stereotypes about Asian American Men." *Psychology of Men and Masculinity* 13 (1): 75–88. https://doi.org/10.1037/a0022800.

Yip, Jeaney, Susan Ainsworth, and Miles Tycho Hugh. 2019. "Beyond Whiteness: Perspectives on the Rise of the Pan-Asian Beauty Ideal." In *Race in the Marketplace: Crossing Critical Boundaries*, edited by Guillaume D. Johnson, Kevin D. Thomas, Anthony Kwame Harrison, and Sonya A. Grier, 73–85. Cham, Switzerland: Springer.

YTN News. 2014. "'한국인 되고 싶어서 …' 성형 10번 한 남자 / YTN" ["I wanted to become Korean …" A man who had ten cosmetic surgeries / YTN]. YTN, May 30, 2014. YouTube video, 1:14. https://youtu.be/u1-qYc _ldMM.

Between Appreciation and Appropriation

3

······

Korean Romance
for Wholesomeness and Racism?

The Transcultural Reception of the Reality
Dating Show Single's Inferno

······

WOORI HAN

Netflix Korea's dating show *Single's Inferno* (2021–present) epitomizes the counterflows in contemporary global television culture. Created by Korean cable channel JTBC as part of the channel's multiyear collaboration deal with Netflix, the show became the first Korean reality show to be distributed and released exclusively by Netflix. *Single's Inferno* was also the first Korean entertainment show to be ranked in the global top ten for non-English TV shows on the platform, coming in eighth in the second week of its release (December 27, 2021–January 2, 2022) and fourth in the following two weeks. The countries in which *Single's Inferno* ranked in the top ten are mostly Asian countries, including Singapore, Japan, Vietnam, Thailand, Taiwan, Malaysia, Qatar, Saudi Arabia, and South Korea, as well as the African country of Morocco. But the show also became a top ten TV show (English and non-English) in Canada in the week of January 3, 2022 (Netflix, n.d.). It made it onto the daily top ten TV list (English and non-English) on January 9, 2022, on Netflix US (#7) and Netflix UK (#8)—the two countries that are the originators of the globally successful reality dating shows *The Bachelor* (2002–present), *Too Hot to Handle* (2020–present), and *Love Island* (2015–present) (Flixpatrol, n.d.-a, n.d.-b). *Single's Inferno*'s original target audience was Korean viewers who enjoy reality dating shows.[1] This TV genre has recently been gaining more traction in South Korea (hereafter Korea) as well as among loyal fans in Asia of Korean entertainment shows. However, to the surprise of the producers, the show appealed to global audiences.

Aside from the fact that it has become a global hit, what makes *Single's Inferno* worthy of critical examination is that it manifests and complicates hybridity in the process of counter-media flows. As a reality show, *Single's Inferno* embodies the liminality and hybridity of the real and the unreal. For Western audiences, the reality expressed in the Korean reality show is complicated by unfamiliar Korean cultural conventions. I argue that global viewers' ambivalent emotional response to the Korea reality show creates a hybrid audience position that sits at the intersection of desires for nonsexual hetero-romance and soft masculinity and anxiety surrounding racial affect. In particular, this chapter examines how Western audiences fantasize heterosexual romance, aligning with and criticizing the notions of authenticity, Korean masculinity, and intimacy that are enacted in the show. Also, interrogating the controversy about whether *Single's Inferno*'s men candidates' preference for fairer-skinned women is White supremacist or Korean cultural preference, the chapter also shows how white-centered racism is constructed by Korean popular culture as an assemblage of affective and virtual qualities of cosmopolitanism, national identity, self-care, commodified beauty standards, and White supremacy.[2] Addressing these questions, this chapter argues that Korean media counterflows are marked by hybridity between accommodation/resistance, East/West, East/East, masculinity/femininity, White/Asian, and real/unreal.

Toward Conceptualizing Transcultural Hybrid Audience Positions

Cultural hybridity has gained political and cultural currency as postcolonial scholars have illuminated the ways in which the colonized negotiate with the dominant colonial power and culture (Bhabha 1994). Rather than being an imitation of the dominant colonial culture, hybridization by the colonized serves as a strategy for survival and for disrupting the dominant culture, just as queer people of color neither simply conform to nor resist dominant racist heteronormative power (Muñoz 1999). In this

Korean Romance

way, hybridity is created in what Homi Bhabha calls the "Third Space of enunciation" (1994, 37). David Oh similarly calls contemporary global popular culture a hybrid space where "the local culture is experienced and the global culture is received" (2017, 2272). It is a space where audiences, due to their lack of cultural and linguistic knowledge about the global culture, engage in a negotiated reading based on their local lived experience and then incorporate the meanings of the different cultural territories into their worldviews. However, the notion of hybridity does not negate the unequal, hierarchical nature of the imperial process. Rather, as Marwan Kraidy (2005) proposed the idea of lopsided articulation, hybrid formation can be unequally shaped by the West's institutional and infrastructural advantages over cultural influences. Even with the growing and diversifying counter-media flows moving from the East to the West (e.g., Japanese anime and K-pop), counter-media flows do not necessarily guarantee counter-hegemony. Commercial counterflows prefer free market capitalism, and dominant flows (from the West to the East and from the North to South) are also becoming stronger (Thussu 2007).

Nonetheless, counter-directional flows of ideas and goods can create new transcultural configurations, social relations, and identities (Thussu 2007). Transcultural identities and social relations are constructed and emerge particularly through a moment of emotional affinity forged in the contradictory and ambivalent "third space" between the local and the global. For example, Western and Japanese fans of anime, who are commonly known as *otaku*, have similarly experienced devaluation in their societies. The emotional affinity of devaluation among fans constructs a new transcultural subjectivity, "foregrounding the possibility that a fannish orientation may (at times) supersede national regional and/or geographical boundaries" (Chin and Morimoto 2013, 99). Benjamin Han (2017) similarly addresses Latin American fans' transcultural identification with K-pop, showing how the consumption of Korean culture allows fans to imagine a new social identity—internalizing K-pop idols' work ethic, dedication, and patience—that is not restricted by the dominant social hierarchies. Hyunji Lee (2018) presents another example of transcultural hybrid identity formation by showing how the transcultural flows of Korean dramas inspire new forms of global consciousness and cultural competency through which Western audiences understand cultural Others, thereby constructing

Western audiences' pop cosmopolitanism. This admiring of the received global Other provides an imagined space in which hybrid third meanings exist (Oh 2017).

However, the sharing emotional affinity is temporary and contingent on a particular context. In the chapter of this volume on Israeli K-pop fans, Irina Lyan argues that the fans' transracial identification and fantasies play an important role in negotiating their identity while maintaining the boundaries between their own and others' racial identity. Transcultural identification with Korean popular culture is a selective appropriation process, since global media are "received differently within the specific cultural framework formed by the political, economic and social contexts of each locality and by people of differing statuses depending on their gender, ethnicity, class, age, and other factors" (Iwabuchi 2007, 70). In the third space, audiences are forced to negotiate the tension between cultural domination and hybrid liberation. In counter-media flows from the East to the West, emotional affinity and transcultural identification among local audiences are refracted by the intersection of race and gender. In other words, in what the introduction of this volume refers to as racial translocalism, local audiences experience global culture through their racial standpoints that are intersected with and interdependent on other categories of gender and sexuality. For example, in his analysis of YouTube reaction videos of K-pop, Oh (2017) accounts for how White fans of Korean popular culture, because of the dominant White supremacy and anti-Asian racism in their local societies, rely on and reinforce post-racist color blindness despite their experience of being devalued as K-pop fans. Min Joo Lee (2020) argues that White women's erotic desires for Korean men, motivated by Korean dramas and by frustration with the sexually oriented dating cultures in their home countries, reinforce Orientalist stereotypes about Korean men's sexuality as passive and asexual and figuratively castrate Korean men.

Within this context, what does the hybridity generated by the global production and interpretation of Korean dating show *Single's Inferno*, as an example of a counter-media flow, look like? How are *Single's Inferno* and the emotional investments surrounding the show complicated by the dominant gender and race politics at the local level? *Single's Inferno* is an example of "a fusion formed out of adaption of [a global] media genre to suit local languages, styles, and conventions" (Thussu 2007, 18–19). While

Korean Romance

77

recruiting participants, Netflix and JTBC promoted the show as a hybrid formation of various global hit reality dating shows. With the headline "A Korean version of *Too Hot to Handle*? Netflix and JTBC create a reality show *Single's Inferno*," the show's press material stated that "the show will be as unbiased as *Love Is Blind* and more romantic than *Terrace House*" (S. Lee 2021). Indeed, similar to *Too Hot to Handle* (2020–), *Single's Inferno* was set on an isolated island in the heat of summer where scantily clad "sexy singles hoping to find love are marooned" (H. Jung 2022). While in *Too Hot to Handle*, Lana, a virtual host embodied in an assistant device similar to Alexa, summons the contestants and presents the rules, in *Single's Inferno* a voice resembling Lana's plays a similar role. Somewhat similar to *Love Is Blind* (2020–), *Single's Inferno* participants are not allowed to share (at least at the beginning of the show) personal information (e.g., occupation, age, education, and class background) that is critical to selecting a romantic partner. Like the Japanese show *Terrace House* (2012–20; and its Korean counterpart *Heart Signal*, 2017–present), *Single's Inferno* requires the participants to cook together in a circumscribed space and portrays the participants as relatively even tempered, collaborative, and respectful.

Single's Inferno also adapts the format of these global shows in order to navigate local Korean social cultural contexts, desires, and conventions. In their post-release interviews, *Single's Inferno* producers stated that although *Too Hot to Handle* was a reference in their recruitment video, the show should not and could not be "exactly the same" since "the pace of the relationships [in *Too Hot to Handle*] came as a culture shock for a lot of Korean viewers" who "tend to spend a lot of time building a relationship with" a romantic partner (H. Jung 2022). *Single's Inferno* utilizes Korean reality dating show conventions such as an emphasis on emotional connection *without* explicit depictions of sexuality. Netflix, defined by Korean laws as a telecommunications company, not as a broadcasting media company, does not fall under the Korea Communication Standards Commission that bans broadcasting companies from depicting sex as a marketable commodity or sensationalizing sexual intercourse (KCSC 2017). Nonetheless, to accommodate Korean viewers who are used to such standards, *Single's Inferno* follows the convention for the existing Korean reality dating shows. To compete with and differentiate itself from the existing and expanding world of dating reality shows—which includes both Korean shows such as *Transit Love* (2021–present), *I Am Solo* (2021–present), *Love after Divorce* (2021–present), *Change Days* (2021–present), *Love Catcher* (2018–present), and *Heart Signal*, as well as the aforementioned non-Korean shows—the *Single's Inferno* producers created a hybrid form that would appeal to local audiences and be adaptable for the global media.

The emotional affinity and hybrid positionality forged among deterritorialized audiences are complicated by "the paradoxical epistemology of reality television"—"viewers can regard the program as 'real' and 'not-real'" (Cloud 2010, 415). This is because "the sense of realism in which sameness and difference, closeness and distance, and reality and dreams delicately mix, elicits sympathy from viewers" (Iwabuchi 2007, 67). Media scholars articulate that reality TV is like "a laboratory experiment—a set-up that nonetheless can discover meaningful truth" (Cloud 2010, 417). Reality TV has employed apparatuses encouraging participants to express their emotions and claim the realness of such emotions, such as through confessions (Aslama and Pantti 2006). In many Korean reality TV shows, celebrity panels in a studio setting, who seemingly watch the same videos that ordinary viewers watch at home, bolster the idea that what is happening on-screen is real. The panels' seemingly genuine reactions to the videos (e.g., being surprised), despite being part of the show's production, add to authenticity of the show candidates' interactions. Thus, authenticity is not about whether what viewers watch is real or not but about the sincerity with which a show's candidates perform and how audiences respond to this sincerity (Cloud 2010). The perceived authenticity and performed sincerity are reinforced when such performances correspond to stereotypical social expectations. As Rachel Dubrofsky and Antoine Hardy (2008) point out in their analysis of the reality dating show *Flavor of Love* (2006–8), the more Black women participants avoid performing their stereotypical Blackness, the more they are thought to be self-undermining their authenticity.

Hybrid audience positions are also complicated by ambivalent audience reception—earnest investment in and detachment from reality shows. Viewers not only invest emotionally in TV shows, such as in the romantic arc of a reality show, but also actively mock and distance themselves from such shows. To address this seemingly contradictory audience reception, Dana Cloud (2010) proposes the idea of the "irony bribe" in her analysis of the dating reality show *The Bachelor*. An irony bribe is "a strategic mechanism of a cultural text that invites audiences to identify with the pleasure of the reaction against the taking seriously of a patently ideological fantasy," making audiences attached to the texts (Cloud 2010, 430). While similar to Ien Ang's (2007) ironic pleasure, the irony bribe is (un)intentionally driven and given by the text itself. Cloud (2010) argues that audiences' reflexive rejection of the silly TV show *The Bachelor*, which oscillates between "the unreal" and "real," does not challenge and instead ironically naturalizes the hegemonic worldview of the texts, such as heteronormativity. Similarly, in their analysis of *Dramaworld* (2016–21), a metatextual drama of Korean dramas, David Oh and LeiLani Nishime (2019) illustrate how parody and satire toward Korean drama clichés contribute to constructing the transnational fan as a White woman, helping her alternate between a superior and a horizontal relation to Korean culture.

Against the backdrop of the discussion above, my study examines how Western audiences' local lenses and hybrid subject formations are reproduced and complicated by appreciation and mockery of "real" Korean participants' heterosexual romantic interactions that oscillate between the real and the unreal as portrayed in *Single's Inferno*. I illuminate Western audiences' appreciation of the show's "genuine" portrayal of heterosexual romance while also focusing on their mockery of the show's candidates. This mockery is associated with audiences' attitudes toward Asian masculinity and their quick dismissal, based on dominant racial logics, of Asian logics of race. I argue that the dominant racist logic implicated in these ambivalent audience practices tends to reproduce stereotypical ideologies and emotions about Asian Others.

Methods

For this research, I analyzed online responses to the show. Given the important role played by online forums in creating a sense of community where deterritorialized and marginalized fans of Korean popular culture are encouraged to express their emotions, examining the reactions in online spaces is useful for understanding audiences' reception of the Korean show.

First, I collected Reddit posts (a total 2,933 posts as of July 2022) from four subreddits, each created for *Single's Inferno*'s first season's episodes 1 and 2, episodes 3 and 4, episodes 5 and 6, and episodes 7 and 8. Drawing on grounded theory (Strauss and Corbin 1990), I coded and analyzed the comments, and using NVivo, I first identified what topics and issues were the most frequently mentioned in the subreddits. These included the show's men participants' comments on white skin; the romance arc for participants Sehoon and Ji-Yeon from rejection to their final match; woman participant Ji-A's interactions with her two suitors; Asian/Korean romantic culture; the participants'—especially the women participants'—appearance; and rooting for favorite participants. I then read through a total 2,933 posts on these topics and collected 123 posts to analyze.

Second, in order to examine in-depth discussions of Koreans' white skin preference, one of the most controversial issues that the show generated, I collected and analyzed 275 replies to an article titled "Korean Dating Reality Show '*Single's Inferno*' Triggers Heated Discussion about 'Pale Skin' between International Viewers and Korean Netizens," published by allkpop (Sophie-Ha 2021). In the analysis that follows, I use excerpts and quotes from the two sources (Reddit and allkpop responses) but without specifying users' IDs or names to protect their anonymity.

The focus of my analysis is to examine racial discourses rather than to study racial bodies in a particular geographical location. Queer Black scholar E. Patrick Johnson (2003) argues that race is not an essential entity but rather performative practices—racial authenticity and boundaries are constantly reconfigured through cultural and bodily performance. For example, in online spaces such as Twitter (rebranded as X in 2023), Raven Maragh (2018) shows how Black Twitter users negotiate racial boundaries by performing and transgressing racial expectations in interactions with in-group members. In what follows, I will indicate how the subreddit users racially and ethnically self-identify whenever such self-identification is evident. However, following Johnson's and Maragh's discussions, my analysis is primarily about how such self-identification is part of discursive performance through which whiteness and Asianness are expressed and discussed in a way that reifies and reconstructs Koreanness, Asianness, and whiteness.

Korean Romance

Nostalgic Romance and Romantic Racism:
Ambivalence toward Asian Masculinity

Single's Inferno features "conventionally attractive" participants: six men and six women mostly in their twenties whose occupations include social media influencer, fitness model, cosmetic model, entrepreneur, and one college student (who later became a YouTuber). While flirting on an isolated island (named 지옥도, *jiokdo*, meaning inferno island) far from urban life and participating in competitive games for a prize, they exhibit their shirtless or bikini-clad fit bodies. This setting and the participants' personalities, which one of the celebrity panels pointed to as feeling like "a foreign show" instead of "a Korean dating show," are analogous to *Love Island* and *Too Hot to Handle*. However, Western audiences, including both old and new fans of Korean popular culture, did not want *Single's Inferno* to replicate the familiar Western format. Sharing the show's promotional news release on Reddit in April 2021, which introduced its concept as resembling *Too Hot to Handle* and *Love Island*, the fans of Korean popular culture on Reddit expressed concerns that the Korean show might "ride the trend of trashy western dating shows." However, when *Single's Inferno*'s first two episodes were released a few months later, their concerns were alleviated; one Reddit user said, "it's like *Heart Signal* but they're on an island."

Single's Inferno's first episode depicts the participants collaboratively working to cook rice and 된장국 (*doenjangguk*), soybean paste soup, and other side dishes using a pre-modern-style furnace; afterward, every participant placed an anonymized love letter in another participant's letter box, making the viewers and the participants guess who fancies whom. The second episode portrays the second day of their nine days on the island, when the men compete in a game for a small reward (having one-on-one brunches with two of the women) and each man participant selected one woman to accompany him to a Paradise hotel to stay the night together. While enjoying the show's sexualization of participants' bodies (the participants exercise every morning) by highlighting the men's shirtless muscular bodies and the women's round hips, which is a characteristic that defined *Love Island*, the Western viewers differentiated *Single's Inferno* from Western counterparts by emphasizing its Korean dating show characteristics: cooking together, having earnest conversations over dinner, sending an

Han

anonymous text message every night to a love interest, and guessing the identity of the sender, which are the staples of *Heart Signal.*

Here, this hybrid formation for *Single's Inferno* contributes to validate Western audiences' ambivalent positions toward reality dating shows and toward heterosexual romance—a combination of emotional attachment and distancing that reinforces their position of superiority over the show and reality shows in general. First, the Korean reality dating show provides Western audiences with a moment in which they can freely dismiss Western dating shows as "trashy" and "raunchy" while enjoying what they call the "wholesomeness" of the Korean dating reality show. *Too Hot to Handle's* sensational rules—which a feminist media critic has called "a conservative nightmare of a reality dating show" (Taylor 2020)—forbid participants from kissing or having sex with other participants. Violations are penalized in the form of deductions from the prize money. The show's apparatuses, such as a baptism-like ritual to be reborn out of a commitment-phobic life, lead the audiences to easily slut-shame the participants. One *Single's Inferno* viewer compared the show and *Too Hot to Handle*, writing that unlike "the other dating show when you saw naked people running around and doing something cringe like saying 'we can't touch' and then, touching each other," in *Single's Inferno* "they hang out, get to know each other, have drama here and there, and talk about their feelings." *Single's Inferno* viewers on Reddit often noted that they originally disliked dating shows that "turn out to be mostly superficial with people making out every five seconds." These viewers emphasized that *Single's Inferno* "is so different" and "refreshing" because it "capture[s] the small emotional moments and heartfelt exchanges between contestants very well." In particular, "doing group activities like cooking together, and hanging out together, instead of keeping themselves exclusively in little cliques like other reality shows," shows that participants "respect each other." Unlike Western shows such as *Jersey Shore* (2009–12), in which participants "seem to be very jealous and tend to fight a lot" for sensational impacts, *Single's Inferno* participants seem to "understand that they have to put an effort in order to win the person's heart or affection." This dismissal of Western reality shows and the differentiation of the Korean reality dating show from Western shows allowed the viewers to justify their love of Korean popular culture and reality shows in general, both of which are easily devalued in Western culture, and to further place themselves in a superior position. Here, my analysis does not intend to advocate for the audiences' celebration of wholesomeness in the Korean show. As discussed below, my focus is on how this reified celebration can produce racially homogenizing discourses, which are the flipside of racism that leads to positioning Korean dating culture and Korean masculinity as extremely patriarchal.

Second, the Western viewers' preference for Korean dating shows contributes to the viewers' ambivalent positions toward heterosexual romance and Asian culture. In making a contrast with *Too Hot to Handle*, one viewer wrote, "How on earth does the cast of *Singles Inferno* keep it in their pants?! ... I want to repeat I have mad respect for this and quite frankly wish that we were a little more reserved in the states." The audiences' respect and preference for nonsexual intimacy resonates with Western women's anxieties about sexual intimacy that have intensified in the post-#MeToo context. *Love Island* was criticized by an educator and a domestic abuse charity group in the United Kingdom for naturalizing having sex without consent and a man participant's emotional abuse toward women participants (Porter and Standing 2018). One teacher claimed that feminists must choose either the #MeToo movement or *Love Island* (Moss 2018). In their discussion of #MeToo discourses in popular culture, Rachel Dubrofsky and Marina Levina (2020) argue that consent is not simply about yes or no but about the gendered affective labor charged to women in negotiating between being sexually attractive and having unwanted sex. The women of *Single's Inferno*, however, do not seem to be pressured to engage in such toilsome affective labor, since the logistics of the Korean show do not allow sex. They are simply required to be sexually attractive enough to captivate the men of *Single's Inferno*; there is less concern about being forced to engage in unwanted sex to sustain their sexual appeal. This perception of a nonsexual environment helps Western women viewers aspire to safely identify with *Single's Inferno* participant Ji-A, who is courted by three men and is adept at dealing with all three without being slut-shamed. One viewer commented, "I want Ji-A's power. She is literally eating them [her suitors] up and spitting them out and they're falling for it."

Moreover, for some viewers, the "wholesome" Korean dating show evokes nostalgia for pure romance. This resonates with Western viewers' responses to other nonsexual Korean dating reality shows like *Heart Signal*, with comments such as "[the show] makes me feel young again" and "reliving middle school emotional train wreck only when watching that triangle." Similarly, *Single's Inferno* viewers commented that "only slight touching in these kinds of show[s] make[s] me feel alive." This nostalgic desire for the wholesome heterosexual romance represented by Korean popular culture positions contemporary Korean culture as the past of the viewers. This resonates with Sun Jung's (2011) study of middle-aged Japanese women's love for Korean Wave star Bae Yong-joon. She argues that Bae Yong-joon's body, embodying soft masculinity (e.g., politeness), becomes the site of Japanese women's retrospective desire for something that Japan's good old days symbolized and that contemporary Japanese men have lost.

Similar to Japanese fans' positioning of Korea as the past of Japan, *Single's Inferno*'s Western viewers also often distance themselves from Korean dating culture, in particular by implying that show participant Sehoon's persistent pursuit of woman participant Ji-Yeon is an example of unenlightened Asian culture. From the beginning, Ji-Yeon indirectly rejects Sehoon's persistent interest in her by avoiding several opportunities to converse with him one-on-one. Although Sehoon seems to accept Ji-Yeon 's rejection, in episode 7, he eventually chooses Ji-Yeon as the partner with whom he wants to go to a hotel, to everyone's surprise. Sehoon's decision is celebrated as manly (e.g., "a one-woman man"), "loyal," "admirable," "heroic," and "cool" by other participants, the celebrity panels, and some Reddit users. His performance of being his authentic self (he said, "I made this decision purely for myself") and of "a go-getter" masculinity (in Korean, 직진남 [*jikjinnam*]) meets and fails to meet the expectation of romance for Western viewers, thereby complicating the viewers' subject formation that leveraged nonsexual Asian intimacy and the reduced labor surrounding consent.

This go-getter masculinity by which women's agency seems to be dismissed has been racialized by some Asian viewers on Reddit who argue that this kind of performance is natural for Asian culture. One self-identifying Korean viewer wrote, "I know how persistent some Korean guys are, myself included." He even argued that "in Western society if a woman says no and don't show interest, it is 99% NO, but in Asian culture, if a woman says no, it doesn't necessarily mean no, it is 50/50." Although some Asian and non-Asian viewers criticized these comments as "gross generalization," other self-identifying Asian viewers agreed with the Korean viewer, saying "men's

Korean Romance

'never-give-up' attitude is widely accepted and respected in Asian culture." Although these self-identifying viewers might not actually be Korean, Asian, and non-Asian, my analysis is focused on how these discourses are produced by racialized performances—including racial self-identification and distancing from racial Others—that reproduce stereotypes. This kind of performance is evident in some US viewers who criticized this Asian cultural difference as betraying their expectation of nostalgic and pure romance in *Single's Inferno*. For these viewers, Sehoon's move and the panels' support for Sehoon are "cringeworthy," noting that Sehoon "comes off as a complete creep, [by] taking her to paradise when he knows she can't reject him [because of the rule of the show], that's just downright insane."

Some viewers realized that what they believed to be more romantic and ideal in the Korean dating show than in its Western counterparts could be problematic in terms of the aspect of getting consent. One self-identifying Western viewer made a contrast between "Western culture where consent is super important" and Korean culture, where "not that consent isn't respected but more so that Sehoon's perseverance and 'respectful pursuance' (or at least what they think lol) is admired." This cultural difference is often translated into a temporal gap: viewers' descriptions of Sehoon as "predatory," "egotistic," and a "manchild" are put in terms of a West that has developed enough to respect consent and a Korea that has not yet done so. This temporal account of Asian culture and Asian men's failure to respect women's feelings about relationships resonates with the controversy regarding Asian American comedian Aziz Ansari. A reportedly White woman accused Ansari of sexual misconduct, including his proceeding with sexual activities without noticing her discomfort. While appreciating the #MeToo movement, feminist scholars have pointed out that this controversy was underpinned by and reinforced the naturalization of Asian men's failure to enact a normative masculinity that recognizes (White) women's emotions and their struggle to balance being sexually attractive and avoiding unwanted sex, a masculinity that is celebrated as a norm in the post-#MeToo era (Dubrofsky and Levina 2020). As in Ansari's case, the Korean masculinity performed in *Single's Inferno* is reified as otherized, in association with Asianness.

Even though some of the Western and Asian viewers knew that *Love Island*'s men participants were notorious for being predatory toward women participants, they tended to attribute Sehoon's problematic behavior to Asian culture. Their attribution is supported by the self-identifying Asian and Korean audiences who approved of Sehoon's behavior. In this way, these *Single's Inferno* viewers' emotional detachment from the show and reflexive (partial) rejection of patriarchal ideas do not challenge but ironically naturalize the hegemonic worldview of Asianness and the temporal lags between America and Korea. Here the Korean culture and masculinity that are performed authentically in the reality show work to justify the Western viewers' superior position.

Interpreting Korean Whiteness: Oscillating between Anti-racism and the Dominant Racial Logics

What complicates global viewers' negotiated understanding of Korea and Korean popular culture are overlapping but different racial logics that are differentially arranged and employed in the local contexts and Korea. *Single's Inferno* provides an exemplary case. After the release of episode 1 in which men participants praised a woman participant's "white" skin, *Single's Inferno* and the participants were accused of being racist. In their casual conversation in a men-only tent about first impressions of each woman participant, Sehoon said of Ji-Yeon, "She seemed so white and pure." Sihun added, "Her skin is so fair. And I like people with that tone."[3] This conversation sparked debates among *Single's Inferno* viewers and K-pop fans across various online media platforms. More than ten TikTok videos were created, some of which gained three million views, to criticize the participants' comments. K-pop news site allkpop's article covering the issue attracted 275 replies. The show's subreddit was also filled with similar comments.

I argue that the global viewers who engaged with the debate constructed a hybrid audience position based on their different local logics of race and racism, providing valid critiques of dominant White supremacy but also often failing to disavow the fixity of whiteness and flattening the complexity of racism in Korea. In online debates around the issue, the viewers and K-pop fans tried to identify with and distance themselves from the dating show. Three juxtaposed points emerged in the online discussion: (1) denouncing Koreans' desires for Caucasian Whiteness; (2) Koreans' national/personal

Korean Romance

preference for paler skin, which has nothing to do with desiring Caucasian Whiteness but is a culturally grounded preference; and (3) Koreans' preference for fair skin as a mode of colorism. The viewers' discourses avow and disavow essentialized racial stereotypes and circumscribe and challenge racial authenticity through reiterating and transgressing dominant racial logics and appropriating inside knowledge about Korean culture. These racial discourses reveal that whiteness and desires for whiteness are historically contingent, culturally constructed, performative, and thus virtual—neither real nor unreal (Saraswati 2010) while also reifying whiteness as something that is always associated with Caucasian Whiteness and reconstructing Koreanness. In this process, the global viewers' seemingly divergent interpretations of *Single's Inferno* and Korean popular culture inadvertently converge to reveal and obscure the historical and complex ways in which whiteness is constructed.

First, some viewers claim that Korean men's preference for women with fair skin is about looking for someone resembling a Caucasian White woman. In talking about classic Korean beauty standards, one viewer on Reddit contended that Korean netizens "WORSHIP Caucasians that fit their beauty standards. . . . K-netizens would take offense to [comparing Korean stars with Olivia Hussey] just because 'you shouldn't compare just anybody to a top tier beauty like Olivia.'" A responder to the allkpop article also wrote, "we all know how Koreans look up to White people."

Second, disputing this equation of the Korean white skin preference with an aspiration for Caucasian Whiteness, other Reddit users pointed out how this preference is rooted in Korean history. One user wrote, "the preference for lighter skin goes back many centuries before Koreans were even exposed to people outside of Korea, China, and Japan." This user continued, "People with lighter skin were often associated with people either coming from an aristocratic or educated background which were viewed as superior." Their argument resonates with the point made by scholars that "paler skin has historically signified distance from agricultural labour, representing high-class status" (Holliday and Elfving-Hwang 2012, 75). This historically rooted, class-based white skin preference in Korea has been a beauty standard that did not arise out of the racist logics employed in Western countries. Scholars argue that the Korean colorist logics can be partly associated with and enact Korean people's neo-Confucian ethics that

Han

"advocated conformity as a virtue that measured social success by approximation to an elite class image" (Holliday and Elfving-Hwang 2012, 75). This shared preference signifying people's aspiration for upward mobility can be associated with constructing a white-skinned Korean as a national identity, as Mikiko Ashikari (2005) similarly argues about Japanese white skin preference. Such viewers' historical understanding can provide an opening for disavowing the association of desiring whiteness with desiring Caucasian Whiteness, further suggesting how the dominant association of race and skin color often imposes Caucasian White-centeredness. In other words, these viewers may be able to point out that "there is no real whiteness to begin with: whiteness is a virtual quality, neither real nor unreal" (Saraswati 2010, 18), potentially revealing that the White Race is also the result of colonial invention.

However, some viewers replaced the historical articulation of race/color and class/nation with essentialized cultural difference, claiming that "every country has its beauty standards and preferences." The reduction of Korean white skin preference to cultural difference in beauty leads to a dismissal of how the complex contemporary racial dynamics of globalization become implicated in the articulation of Korean whiteness. Here is where some K-pop fans and *Single's Inferno* viewers intervene in making a critical point about the Korean white skin preference beyond the local historical contexts. This group of people form a third type of response. This third response centers how the European and Anglo-American colonization experience, enduring White supremacy, and circulations of people and Korean popular culture across national boundaries affect people in the Global South and their understanding of Korean white skin preference. Drawing from this anti-colonial perspective, one allkpop website user wrote, "being fair and white was and is a European mindset. . . . It's not just a 'Korean' thing. It happens in India, the Philippines, the Caribbean . . . and well—the whole world." This argument resonates with Joanne Rondilla and Paul Spickard's (2007) articulation of whiteness as a colonial language. As another responder to the allkpop article commented, "people with light skin tended to be preferred more in jobs . . . and were seen as superior to those with darker skin" in their own country. In other words, for these viewers, the globally distributed Korean show's naturalization of white skin preference seems to reproduce colonial White supremacy.

Korean Romance

In particular, the Korean beauty industry's churning out of skin-whitening products has played a crucial role in facilitating the belief by people in the Global South that Korean society is remarkably colorist and racist. Many responders to the allkpop article urged viewers to look at the pervasive whitening creams in Korea, the K-beauty industry's export of such products, and tan-skinned K-pop woman stars wearing such creams to look pale. As beauty is an embodiment of personal and cultural identity expression, Korean skin-whitening cosmetics targeting the global market and their ads featuring Korean stars—ones who are particularly popular in Asia—with flawless, fair skin seem to represent Koreanness as desirable whiteness. Filipino and Thai cosmetic brands that utilize the word *Seoul* for their skin-whitening cosmetics are proof of this desirable Korean whiteness (Park 2020). In these ads, the Korean whiteness that flows into the Philippines and Thailand works as an alternative to objectionable Caucasian Whiteness that evokes European colonization for consumers in the Global South. However, this Korean whiteness also operates as an apparatus for reproducing colorist hierarchies. As white-skinned Korean women in the cosmetic ads "have easier access to transnational (visual) mobility," cosmopolitanism is defined by whiteness (Saraswati 2010, 27). Also, as Korea has emerged as a subempire in the Asian region, it has developed in its *nouveau riche* nationalism (G.-S. Han 2015) what Kim (2020) calls a tri-system of racism that privileges pure-blood Koreans over light-skinned migrants over dark-skinned migrants. In this system, "non-white multicultural subjects are stigmatized as a potential threat to the national identity and have to fight for a social inclusion" (Ahn 2015, 945). Some global fans on the allkpop website suggested that when Korean "society looks down on their darker skin neighbors in Southeast Asia," the Korean beauty standard's privileging of whiteness, while not directly associated with European colonization, can nonetheless lead to discrimination against people with darker skins in Southeast Asia and in Korea.

Some K-pop fans' critiques of Korean white-privileging colorism, however, often cloak the racism operating in the West by reproducing a post-racist fantasy of the West. For example, some self-identifying American allkpop users wrote that "we [Americans] have all sorts of shades, and anyone can be beautiful regardless of what shade they are" unlike "in Korea where they literally have ads for bleaching creams telling tan people they are ugly and better off pale." Despite the fact that, in the West, notions of skin color and colorism are closely related to race and racism, which were invented by (settler) colonialism (Dixon and Telles 2017), these users' equation of respect for "all sorts of shades" with respect for diversity simply reproduces a post-racist myth. This argument obscures the fact that people with darker shades face severe social oppression, as in the case of police brutality targeting Black people. Even when pale White people want to tan their skin, as L. Ayu Saraswati (2010) points out, this tanning practice is not described as "blackening" or "browning" but as having a "bronze color," which emphasizes the White subject's agency and self-control and does not threaten White supremacy. By using these Western post-racist ideologies and by flattening the complex, reconfigured relationship between Korean colorism and racism, these users' condemnation of Korean colorism leaves White supremacy intact. These Western audiences' denouncement of Korean colorism seems to maintain their position of superiority over Korean popular culture, which other K-pop fans on the allkpop website noted: "They're [White audiences] trying to use [Korean colorism] against Koreans here and trying to bury their own dirty laundry."

However, as discussed above, the K-pop fans who are critical of re-producing White supremacy and post-racist ideologies may be able to advance the intersectional critique regarding race, skin color, and gender. Some K-pop fans pointed out how the Korean preference for white skin establishes gendered social expectations for women to have clear skin and associates white skin with purity. Other fans thought that Sehoon's comment associating Ji-Yeon's white skin with "purity" and his relentless pursuit of her despite her nuanced rejection was a relevant example of such expectations and associations. In the *Single's Inferno* viewers' discussion, Sehoon's pursuit of Ji-Yeon was contrasted with his aggressive reaction to woman participant So-Yeon's advice for him to be open to other possi-bilities, including herself, as a romantic partner—So-Yeon was older than Sehoon and, with her tanned athletic body, was unpopular compared to Ji-Yeon and Ji-A. In making this contrast, some viewers suggested that Sehoon's preference for women with fair skin who seem "pure and inno-cent" can "be translated into [a preference for women who are] ignorant and easily manipulated." Some users made an analogy between Korean gendered colorism and the Western preference for "blonde hair and blue

Korean Romance

eyes" being "seen as 'angelic' or 'innocent'" while pointing to "the ongoing exclusion of people who are NATURALLY tan and brown and dark."

Some viewers further hoped their discussion of Korean colorism would affect Korean popular culture stakeholders, including pop culture industries and Korean and global fans. The colorism controversy led the vice president of Netflix Korea to "see this all as a learning opportunity to become even better and [we are] soaking it in with a humble attitude" (Adams 2022), even though Netflix's perspective is still limited to simplifying Korean colorism as an essentialized cultural difference. The controversy about Korean white skin preference that played out on the internet also flowed back into the Korean online public sphere. Although most Koreans on YouTube videos and in online communities shut down the critiques of Korean colorism as being a foreign intervention, self-reflexive Korean voices also emerged. For example, several Korean users in the online community Nate Pann agreed with the critique of gendered colorism, writing that "it is undeniable that Sehoon's obsession with women's innocence represents Korean men's general attitude." Another Korean viewer, referencing the lived experience of being made fun of for their darker skin tone during their childhood in Korea, suggested that "we rethink the controversy" and look at the social cultural context "rather than treating [white skin preference] as part of Korean culture and personal taste."

Conclusion

This study interrogates the questions of how hybrid audience positions are constructed vis-à-vis counter-media flows and local lived experience and how these hybrid positions are complicated when global audiences, using local lenses, negotiate with competing racial logics, heterosexual norms, and notions of authenticity. Addressing these questions, this chapter argues that Korean media counterflows are marked by racial translocalism constitutive of dialectic hybridity between East/West, East/East, masculinity/femininity, past/present, White/Asian, and real/unreal. This chapter makes two contributions to studies of global reception of popular culture. First, I used the relationship between media genre characteristics and audience response as a lens—between the ambivalence of the reality TV genre (being "real" and "unreal") and audiences' ambivalent positions of emotional engagement with and distancing from media—to clarify global audiences' complicated hybrid interpretation. This chapter is an attempt to move beyond focusing only on audiences' identification with Korean media, which has been examined in previous studies. I clarify how reality shows' ambivalence helps global audiences easily draw on local norms of heterosexuality and dominant racial logics to both invest themselves in and distance themselves from the reality show.

Second, this chapter articulates different local race and gender dynamics and contexts that ground the understanding of global popular culture for different audiences, since transcultural identifications are refracted by race and gender. While showing how global audiences forge transnationally shared affinities for Korean popular culture, the chapter also focuses on the locally specific American (post-)#MeToo movement that is inextricable from racism and the K-beauty industry's influence in Southeast Asia. Self-identifying American audiences oscillate between a desire for Korean nostalgic heterosexual dating culture and positioning that same culture as the unenlightened past. Some White American audiences employ post-racist logics to critique Korean white skin preference without challenging White supremacy, while Southeast Asian audiences point out how Korean skin-whitening cosmetics in their countries are entangled with the legacy of European colonization. By illuminating these hybrid audience positions between locality and global culture, I argue that hybridity can contribute to maintaining White supremacy and normative heterosexuality but can also offer the potential to challenge them.

Notes

1. Because Korean entertainment shows on Netflix had not become global hits beyond Asia in the same way that Korean dramas and films such as *Squid Game* and *Parasite* had, the producers did not expect *Single's Inferno*'s success. But South Korea, with 5.14 million Netflix subscribers (Frater 2021), is an important market for the global media platform.

2. Throughout the chapter, I distinguish White, a racial category (e.g., Caucasian White), and white, a skin tone, while noting the historical and colonial entanglement between White and white.

3. Netflix's translation, except for Sihun's last comment, "And I like people with that tone," which is my translation.

Korean Romance

References

Adams, Skylar. 2022. "Preference or Colorist? Netflix Korea Addresses 'Single's Inferno' Skin Color Controversy." *Koreaboo*, January 20, 2022. https://www.koreaboo.com/news/netflix-korea-skin-color-controversy-singles-inferno.

Ahn, Ji-Hyun. 2015. "Desiring Biracial Whites: Cultural Consumption of White Mixed-Race Celebrities in South Korean Popular Media." *Media, Culture and Society* 37 (6): 937–47. https://doi.org/10.1177/0163443715593050.

Ang, Ien. 2007. "Television Fictions around the World: Melodrama and Irony in Global Perspective." *Critical Studies in Television* 2 (2): 18–30. https://doi.org/10.7227/CST.2.2.4.

Ashikari, Mikiko. 2005. "Cultivating Japanese Whiteness: The 'Whitening' Cosmetics Boom and the Japanese Identity." *Journal of Material Culture* 10 (1): 73–91. https://doi.org/10.1177/1359183505050095.

Aslama, Minna, and Mervi Pantti. 2006. "Talking Alone: Reality TV, Emotions and Authenticity." *European Journal of Cultural Studies* 9 (2): 167–84. https://doi.org/10.1177/1367549406063162.

Bhabha, Homi K. 1994. *The Location of Culture*. London: Routledge.

Chin, Bertha, and Lori Morimoto. 2013. "Towards a Theory of Transcultural Fandom." *Participations* 10 (1): 92–108. https://doi.org/10.17613/M6RP98.

Cloud, Dana. 2010. "The Irony Bribe and Reality Television: Investment and Detachment in *The Bachelor*." *Critical Studies in Media Communication* 27 (5): 413–37. https://doi.org/10.1080/15295030903583572.

Dixon, Angela R., and Edward E. Telles. 2017. "Skin Color and Colorism: Global Research, Concepts, and Measurement." *Annual Review of Sociology* 43 (1): 405–24. https://doi.org/10.1146/annurev-soc-060116-053315.

Dubrofsky, Rachel E., and Antoine Hardy. 2008. "Performing Race in *Flavor of Love* and *The Bachelor*." *Critical Studies in Media Communication* 25 (4): 373–92. https://doi.org/10.1080/15295030802327774.

Dubrofsky, Rachel E., and Marina Levina. 2020. "The Labor of Consent: Affect, Agency and Whiteness in the Age of #metoo." *Critical Studies in Media Communication* 37 (5): 409–23. https://doi.org/10.1080/15295036.2020.1805481.

FlixPatrol. n.d.-a. "TOP 10 on Netflix in the United Kingdom on January 9, 2022." Accessed January 10, 2023. https://flixpatrol.com/top10/netflix/united-kingdom/2022-01-09/.

FlixPatrol. n.d.-b. "TOP 10 on Netflix in the United States on January 9, 2022." Accessed January 10, 2023. https://flixpatrol.com/top10/netflix/united-states/2022-01-09/.

Frater, Patrick. 2021. "Netflix under Pressure in Korea as 'Squid Game' Success Stirs Lawmakers and Internet Firms." *Variety*, November 3, 2021. https://

variety.com/2021/biz/asia/netflix-under-pressure-in-korea-1235104596/?sub
_action=logged_in.

Han, Benjamin. 2017. "K-Pop in Latin America: Transcultural Fandom and Digital Mediation." *International Journal of Communication* 11: 2250–69.

Han, Gil-Soo. 2015. "K-Pop Nationalism: Celebrities and Acting Blackface in the Korean Media." *Continuum* 29 (1): 2–16. https://doi.org/10.1080/10304312.2014.968522.

Holliday, Ruth, and Joanna Elfving-Hwang. 2012. "Gender, Globalization and Aesthetic Surgery in South Korea." *Body and Society* 18 (2): 58–81. https://doi.org/10.1177/1357034X12440828.

Iwabuchi, Koichi. 2007. "Contra-flows or the Cultural Logic of Uneven Globalization? Japanese Media in the Global Agora." In *Media on the Move: Global Flow and Contra-Flow*, edited by Daya Kishan Thussu, 67–83. London: Routledge.

Johnson, E. Patrick. 2003. *Appropriating Blackness: Performance and the Politics of Authenticity*. Durham, NC: Duke University Press.

Jung, Haein. 2022. "The Producers of 'Single's Inferno' Answer Our Burning Questions." *Tudum* by Netflix, February 14, 2022. https://www.netflix.com/tudum/articles/singles-inferno-season-1-reunion-location-questions.

Jung, Sun. 2011. *Korean Masculinities and Transcultural Consumption: Yonsama, Rain, Oldboy, K-Pop Idols*. Hong Kong: Hong Kong University Press.

Kim, Hyein Amber. 2020. "Understanding 'Koreanness': Racial Stratification and Colorism in Korea and Implications for Korean Multicultural Education." *International Journal of Multicultural Education* 22 (1): 76–97. https://doi.org/10.18251/ijme.v22i1.1834.

Korea Communications Standards Commission (KCSC). 2017. "방송심의에 관한 규정" [Regulation on broadcasting standards]. Seoul: Korea Communications Standards Commission, Korea Ministry of Government Legislation.

Kraidy, Marwan M. 2005. *Hybridity, or the Cultural Logic of Globalization*. Philadelphia: Temple University Press.

Lee, Hyunji. 2018. "A 'Real' Fantasy: Hybridity, Korean Drama, and Pop Cosmopolitans." *Media, Culture and Society* 40 (3): 365–80. https://doi.org/10.1177/0163443717718926.

Lee, Min Joo. 2020. "Intimacy beyond Sex: Korean Television Dramas, Nonsexual Masculinities, and Transnational Erotic Desires." *Feminist Formations* 32 (3): 100–120. https://doi.org/10.1353/ff.2020.0042.

Lee, Seungmi. 2021. "韓판 '투핫' 될까"… 넷플릭스, JTBC와 데이팅 리얼리티쇼 '솔로지옥' 제작" [A Korean version of *Too Hot to Handle*? Netflix and JTBC create a reality show *Single's Inferno*]. *Sports Chosun*, April 22, 2021. https://n.news.naver.com/entertain/article/076/0003719792.

Korean Romance

Maragh, Raven S. 2018. "Authenticity on 'Black Twitter': Reading Racial Performance and Social Networking." *Television and New Media* 19 (7): 591–609. https://doi.org/10.1177/1527476417738569.

Moss, Rachel. 2018. "Can You Be a 'Love Island' Fan and Still Support #MeToo?" HuffPost, March 10, 2018. https://www.huffingtonpost.co.uk/entry/can-you-be-a-love-island-fan-and-still-a-feminist-supporter-of-metoo_uk_5bb48161e4b01470d04cd4d3.

Muñoz, José Esteban. 1999. *Disidentifications: Queers of Color and the Performance of Politics*. Minneapolis, MN: University of Minnesota Press.

Netflix. n.d. "Global Top 10." Accessed January 10, 2023. https://top10.netflix.com/TV-non-english?week=2022-01-02; https://top10.netflix.com/TV-non-english?week=2022-01-09; https://top10.netflix.com/TV-non-english?week=2022-01-16.

Oh, David C. 2017. "K-Pop Fans React: Hybridity and the White Celebrity-Fan on YouTube." *International Journal of Communication* 11: 2270–87.

Oh, David C., and LeiLani Nishime. 2019. "Imag(in)ing the Post-national Television Fan: Counter-Flows and Hybrid Ambivalence in *Dramaworld*." *International Communication Gazette* 81 (2): 121–38. https://doi.org/10.1177/17480485188029813.

Park, Sojeong. 2020. "K-뷰티산업의 피부색주의" [Colorism of K-beauty industry]. *Korean Journal of Journalism and Communication Studies* 64 (6): 124–60.

Porter, Janette, and Kay Standing. 2018. "Love Island: Adam Shows Teenagers How Not to Treat Romantic Partners." *The Conversation*, June 25, 2018. https://theconversation.com/love-island-adam-shows-teenagers-how-not-to-treat-romantic-partners-98801.

Rondilla, Joanne L., and Paul Spickard. 2007. *Is Lighter Better? Skin-Tone Discrimination among Asian Americans*. Lanham, MD: Rowman and Littlefield.

Saraswati, L. Ayu. 2010. "*Cosmopolitan* Whiteness: The Effects and Affects of Skin-Whitening Advertisements in a Transnational Women's Magazine in Indonesia." *Meridians: Feminism, Race, Transnationalism* 10 (2): 15–41. https://doi.org/10.1215/15366936-8566045.

Sophie-Ha. 2021. "Korean Dating Reality Show '*Single's Inferno*' Triggers Heated Discussion about 'Pale Skin' between International Viewers and Korean Netizens." allkpop, December 28, 2021. https://www.allkpop.com/article/2021/12/korean-dating-reality-show-singles-inferno-triggers-heated-discussion-about-pale-skin-between-international-viewers-and-korean-netizens.

Strauss, Anselm L., and Juliet M. Corbin. 1990. *Basics of Qualitative Research: Grounded Theory Procedures and Techniques*. Newbury Park, CA: Sage Publications.

Taylor, Erin. 2020. "'Too Hot to Handle' Is a Conservative Nightmare of a

Reality Dating Show." *Bitch Media*, May 15, 2020. http://web.archive.org/web/20200524171700/https://www.bitchmedia.org/article/netflix-too-hot-too-handle-is-a-dating-show-that-hates-sex.

Thussu, Daya Kishan. 2007. "Mapping Global Media Flow and Contra-flow." In *Media on the Move: Global Flow and Contra-flow*, edited by Daya Kishan Thussu, 11–32. London: Routledge.

4

······

K-pop and the Racialization of Asian American Popular Musicians

······

DONNA LEE KWON

In season 1 of *The Masked Singer* (2019–present)—an American reality television show derived originally from a Korean program—panelist Ken Jeong was unable to correctly identify the singer behind the Poodle mask, despite having clues that the singer was a comedian with ties to San Francisco and the LGBT+ community. The Poodle was revealed to be a fellow Korean American friend and colleague Margaret Cho:

> MARGARET CHO: Ken, of all people I thought you would know!
> KEN JEONG: I know! She's my sister on *Dr. Ken*! I should know that. I had all the clues, and I knew nothing! I'm so dumb! This is a pioneer in Asian American comedy . . . you are the reason I'm a comedian. I love you so much, you have no idea. (*The Masked Singer* 2019)

My mind always returns to this moment whenever I think about the audibility of the Asian American voice. Despite having worked closely with Margaret Cho, Ken Jeong still struggled to recognize her voice. Judging from his subsequent shame and pointed recognition of their shared Asian American identity, I suspect that he was embarrassed to have fallen prey to a limited form of racialized listening that effectively sidelined Asian Americans as potential candidates for the competent Poodle performance of the well-known songs originally sung by Cyndi Lauper ("Time After Time") and Pat Benatar ("Heartbreaker").

In the context of this chapter, what do moments like this reveal about the audibility of Asian American artists and how does the disproportional success of K-pop artists in the United States today impact the continuing racialization of Asian Americans in the media? While the K-pop group BTS has sold-out multi-day stadium shows in 2021 (Los Angeles) and 2022 (Las Vegas), most Asian American artists would struggle to even book a single-day stadium show.[1] In other words, the overwhelming success of BTS and other K-pop groups in the United States has not necessarily translated into similar opportunities for Korean American or other Asian American popular musicians (Aran 2018). For example, while Asian American artists like Mitski have headlined festivals and toured extensively, they have not reached the multi-day stadium levels of BTS. In addition, Asian Americans are not getting signed with major labels in higher numbers. While the increased global popularity and presence of K-pop artists have certainly increased the visibility and representation of artists of Asian heritage, the same cannot necessarily be said of their audibility. Given this, I aim to explore audibility as a frame through which to understand the racialization of Asian and Asian American artists. In the absence of any visual markers of race or ethnicity that are obscured in *The Masked Singer*, the dominant racialized discourse imposed upon Asian Americans suggests that their audibility must somehow be marked by the perception of "foreignness" or some other kind of difference in order to be heard and recognized. Along these lines, I contend that K-pop is more coherent with a limited "racialized listening" of Asians and Asian Americans that is marked by difference and racial stereotypes (E.-Y. Jung 2014, 66). Given this, I argue that Asian Americans deserve a more expansive audibility that I define as starting with a reflexive awareness of the dynamics of racialized listening and moves toward a recognition of multivocality and multiple narrative selves (Meizel 2020).

I will explore these questions through a brief examination of how the success of K-pop in the United States is impacting the racialized reception of Asian American artists. Through online and personal interviews, as well as consideration of theories of Asian American racial abjection and triangulation, I will investigate the racialized musical terrain that Asians and Asian Americans face. I argue that K-pop can reinforce the problematic US-based notion that the only acceptable Asian is one who is perpetually "abject" (Shimakawa 2002) or "foreign" to the nation while also introducing

Racialization of Asian American Musicians

its own transnational discourses of race, ethnicity, colorism, and aesthetics of gendered beauty. In comparing the racialized reception of K-pop versus Asian American artists, I will focus primarily on Korean American artists because they are often compared with K-pop artists and are more directly impacted. In this endeavor, I build on my argument by examining three Korean American artists—St. Lenox (Andrew Choi), Eric Nam, and Audrey Nuna—who represent different generations, creative approaches, styles, gender identities, and sexualities.

Although I do gauge audience reception through performance tour ticket sales, festival programming, and digital streaming data, my approach to reception differs from others in this volume. For example, I focus on artists as important subjects of reception, who then process this information and use it to inform their work. My principal aim then is to better nuance how these artists perceive Asian and Asian American racial dynamics across a transnational popular music field and then go on to navigate this complex racialized terrain through their career choices, visual styling, artistry, marketing strategies, lyrics, and vocality. I argue that, together with their audiences, they are engaging in what Dorinne Kondo describes as the "unmaking" or "remaking" of race (2018, 11). By drawing on my training as an ethnomusicologist and integrating musical, sonic, and sociocultural analysis with artist-focused ethnography, I hope to provide an alternative perspective that demonstrates more directly how the reception of racial dynamics can directly impact artistic production. As alluded to in *The Masked Singer* example, I am especially sensitive to the ways in which difference is made audible in the voice and will examine how artists deploy their voices in multivocal ways to explore the boundaries of their artistic identities (Meizel 2020, 14). While there has been some coverage of the impact of K-pop on Asian American music (Aran 2018), this chapter explores new ground by emphasizing aurality, audibility, and multivocality, which has garnered much less attention in K-pop scholarship than visuality (H. W. Kim 2023, 74).

Defining the Racialized Popular Music Terrain

By the 1920s in the United States, the popular music industry segregated the sounds of a diverse field of musicians according to a "musical color line" where Black music was funneled into the "race" music category and White music into the "hillbilly" category (Miller 2010, 2). Although the genres have evolved, the legacy of this bifurcation persists until the present day. Missing from this picture, however, is a consideration of how Asian American musicians and other groups figure into this racialized terrain. In *Resounding Afro Asia: Interracial Music and the Politics of Collaboration*, T. Roberts draws on Claire Jean Kim's (1999) geometric model of racial triangulation to argue that Whiteness, Blackness, and Asianness are *co-constructed* "along axes of 'superior/inferior' and 'insider/foreigner'" (Roberts 2016, 4). I follow Roberts in arguing that the music industry in the United States is implicated in the co-construction of Asianness, both by limiting the representation of artists of Asian heritage through the logic of exclusion as well as by enabling only those artists who best "fit" along these dual axes. This explains why artists who embody both the "foreigner" and "model minority" stereotype (constructed as "inferior" to Whites but "superior" to Blacks) have often enjoyed the most success, from crossover cellist Yo-Yo Ma, to jazz legend Toshiko Akiyoshi, to the versatile Kim Sisters.[2] Although somewhat outside of the bounds of this chapter, Asians and Asian Americans have been remarkably successful in Western-style art music performance, in large part because being a "classical musician" fits so well with the model minority stereotype. In popular music, Asian Americans must work against this stereotype in order to be perceived as authentic in genres such as rock or hip hop where individuality, brashness, and rebellion are more highly valued.[3]

In the new millennium, the tides have shifted as both Asians and Asian Americans have wrestled with and contested these racializing and exclusionist tendencies. In K-pop, it took several generations of artists (such as BoA, Rain, Se7en, and Girls' Generation) to overcome limiting racial and gendered stereotypes as well as racist and exclusionary forces in the US market (E.-Y. Jung 2013). At first, K-pop was criticized for not sounding "different" enough from pop (especially within a "world music" paradigm), but eventually K-pop's markers of assimilated difference—such as its alternatively gendered visuals and intriguing mix of Korean and English—began to attract broad appeal.[4] Meanwhile, it helped that Psy came along in 2012 with his paradigm-busting, satirical hit "Gangnam Style." These cumulative efforts have paved the way for the unprecedented success of groups like BTS and Blackpink, and now many other groups such as TWICE, Tomorrow X Together (TXT), and Stray Kids are following suit.

Racialization of Asian American Musicians

Although Asian Americans have not duplicated this level of success, there has been some progress in representation at major US festivals. In 2017, the South by Southwest (sxsw) Music Festival curated its first Asian American showcase with an impressive forty-five acts, and other festivals followed suit by including more Asian American and Asian British artists. For example, in 2019, Coachella had one Asian British act, Lollapalooza featured five acts, and sxsw had six acts. By 2022, as festivals began to re-start in person after several years of cancellations due to the COVID-19 pandemic, Coachella had eight acts, Lollapalooza had four, and sxsw had approximately seventeen acts. Given this history, the first Asian American showcase in 2017 with forty-five acts proved to be an anomaly due to its status as the first of its kind. Except for Lollapalooza, Asian acts are generally programmed with much more frequency than their Asian American counterparts. This disparity is most stark at sxsw, where in 2019, there were forty-five Asian acts compared to six Asian American acts, and in 2022, there were fifty-one Asian acts compared to seventeen Asian American acts (table 4.1).

One of the artists who participated in the 2017 sxsw Asian American

TABLE 4.1. Festival Programming Data, 2019–22

Festival	2019	2020	2021	2022
COACHELLA	4 Asian 1 Asian-British (mixed race)	Canceled	Canceled	16 Asian 8 Asian American/Asian British
LOLLAPALOOZA	5 Asian American	Canceled	2 Asian American	2 Asian 4 Asian American
SXSW	45 Asian 6 Asian American	Canceled	Virtual 33 Asian 1 Asian American	51 Asian 17 Asian American

Kwon

showcase is singer-songwriter Andrew Choi, who goes by the name St. Lenox. In his website blog where he writes prolifically under the name Eponymous, he makes some additional cogent observations about the dynamics of diversity programming: "I think too often the sentiment—and it was even directly communicated to me by a music press industry person—is that if an outlet covers an act from Asia, that satisfies the diversity requirement, so that's okay. Of course, this is just expressly a statement that it's okay to define 'American' as 'white country.'... This awkward supremacy is what resulted in sxsw finally having an official showcase specifically for Asian-American acts" (Eponymous 2019). This is significant because it shows how Asian American artists are aware of how racial tokenization essentially conflates Asians and Asian Americans along the "foreign" axis and can lead to the replacement of Asian Americans by actual foreign acts. In Karen Shimakawa's (2002) theorization, Asian Americans are cast off as abject to the nation; they are seen as "symbolic foreigners" who then cannot compete with real foreigners in foreign cachet or exoticness. In my interview with Andrew Choi in 2018, he said that "things are changing, but I think with the illiteracy with the distinction between Asians and Asian Americans, that's definitely something people need to work on" (Choi 2018). Choi cleverly addresses this "illiteracy" in his 2018 song "Gold Star," when he sings:

> But you don't want to go "Gangnam style" with a shit-eating grin and bear it
> 'cause you've got a stupid sense of pride
> and you fall for it every damn time.

In referencing Psy's 2012 "Gangnam Style," Choi deftly conveys both his dismay with being conflated with K-pop but also his desire to push back against the pressure to follow in Psy's footsteps and adopt a more commercially exploitable persona. Even when competition with Asian acts is not an issue, Andrew Choi expressed his frustration with tokenization in convincing editors to include more Asian American content: "I'm sure a thought that is going through their head is that 'Oh, well, we've talked about Mitski this year, so we don't [need to cover anyone else]. She's doing great, so we gave them enough'" (Choi 2018).

Racialization of Asian American Musicians

The model minority stereotype that operates along the other "inferior/ superior" axis of Claire Jean Kim's (1999) model can also have complex effects. As a violin prodigy and Princeton undergraduate with a PhD in philosophy from the Ohio University and a JD from New York University, Andrew Choi can easily be touted as a so-called model minority and does gain attention for his unique background, but he also describes how it can work against Asian Americans: "I think there's definitely a significant mentality in the [music] industry that increasing diversity for Asian Americans is not required . . . they are so successful in some of these areas, we do not need to give them representation in entertainment and so we are going to withhold it. . . . It's across the board in entertainment . . . [it's the attitude that] because we are doing well enough, you are not going to distribute benefits because we have done enough in terms of diversity" (Choi 2018). In this way, the complex co-construction of Asianness (vis-à-vis Whiteness and Blackness) along the axes of "superiority/inferiority" and "insider/ foreigner" works as a double-edged sword impacting Asian Americans in a vicious circle of both inclusion in some areas and exclusion in others.

Approximately a decade younger than Andrew Choi, Eric Nam also has impressive credentials as a graduate of Boston College who had accepted a position at Deloitte Consulting but then deferred by exploring microfinance in India before detouring into music and entertainment in South Korea. With a major in international studies and a minor in Asian studies, Eric Nam is very aware of how racism impacts Asian Americans. In the aftermath of the 2021 Atlanta shootings of six Asian women, Nam wrote in a letter to *Time* magazine that as "'perpetual foreigners' and subjects of the model minority myth, Asians are invited but not fully integrated, or just largely ignored under the guise of being 'O.K.' in culture and politics" (Nam 2021a). He also speaks eloquently about how he grew up "believing we needed to be O.K. with racism in order to have a seat at the table. . . . To internalize racism at such a young age, in retrospect, warped my sense of normality" (Nam 2021a).

> I still remember the first time I saw an Asian comedian on TV . . . it was
> Margaret Cho . . . for people who aren't of the minority, you go like what's
> the big deal, but if you are not able to see yourself in a position of power
> . . . you are not allowed to dream or to imagine what you [can become]. If

Kwon

I could have started my career 10, 12 years earlier, just out of the States, in my mother language of English . . . but that was never a realistic option for me. (Partners In Health 2021)

As evidenced here, Nam's perception of the unequal racialization of Asian Americans can have very real consequences and caused him to preemptively leave the United States to pursue a career in Asia, which is reminiscent of the choices that many other prominent Asian American artists have made (such as Wang Leehom, Tablo of Epik High, and Jessi).

Eric Nam is a unique transnational figure because he has recently decided to promote himself more intentionally as an Asian American global pop artist with the release of the all-English albums *Before We Begin* (2019), *There and Back Again* (2022), and *House on a Hill* (2023). Although he is fine with fans associating him with either pop or K-pop, he recognizes the need to clear up any confusion that may arise from his transnational position. "There needs to be some delineation between K-pop artists and Asian American music artists. There is seemingly this idea that 'Oh, we have K-pop so we have diversity' but it completely neglects an Asian American experience which is so different from a K-pop experience. And so being a Korean American K-pop artist, I find myself in the middle being able to see both sides of it. . . . I want K-pop to keep going and killing it, but I also want this other underrepresented pocket of Asian American artists to really develop" (Nam 2021b). Like Andrew Choi, Nam understands how the popularity of K-pop can negatively impact Asian Americans and is not afraid to be vocal about these dynamics. In this way, he is helping to educate his audience and paving the way for younger artists such as Audrey Nuna. Furthermore, his experiences as a transnational artist resonate with ongoing debates in Asian American studies about the potential blurriness between the Asian and Asian American categories (Wong 1995, 5), and here he eloquently speaks to maintaining distinctions while giving voice to both K-pop and Asian American perspectives.

Audrey Nuna is approximately a decade younger than Eric Nam and was even a guest on his audiovisual podcast called the *Daebak Show w/ Eric Nam*. Unlike Andrew Choi and Eric Nam, Audrey Nuna is one of the few Asian American artists who have signed with a major label (Arista Records, under Sony Entertainment), and she performed a well-received set at Lollapalooza in August of 2022. As the youngest artist I focus on in this chapter, Nuna expresses wanting to move beyond a tokenizing discourse of multicultural diversity or "doll-ified" representation:

> There's no one way to be, there's no normal. Just be your goddamn self. I think the biggest thing is normalizing. . . . Seeing an Asian Barbie doll on the shelf, instead of it being like an Asian American Barbie doll, just girls growing up seeing it on the shelf and it not being a big deal . . . I think is huge. . . . It's not like this token thing, or you have to fill a certain role because you're Asian American. . . . People don't care as much anymore and we're getting closer to equality. (2021b)

In my interview with St. Lenox, Andrew Choi goes even further by making a point of rejecting diversity discourse. "Look, you are not presenting me as an Asian American artist. You are presenting me as St. Lenox. This is the music that I do. This is what I explained to them, 'Don't present me as somebody that will be a diversity component.' I told my publicist, maybe you do not understand my rationale but if you present me as a diversity pick, first of all, they may not take the music as seriously, but secondly, the editors will not think of Asian Americans as being a way of adding to diversity" (Choi 2018). In practice, this is challenging terrain for all three artists to navigate. Given her younger age, cutting edge appeal, and backing by a major label, however, Audrey Nuna may have the best chance of succeeding in a more race-neutral or normalized position as an Asian American artist.

Looking more closely at how the US music industry impacts K-pop artists, one could argue that it can be more welcoming to Korean artists than it is to Asian American artists. For example, both Andrew Choi and Eric Nam have observed that Korean acts can displace Asian American acts as tokens of diversity. While one can argue that K-pop merely has a leg up because of its high production values and trainee system, I posit that K-pop is more congruent with the racialized listening and co-construction of Asians and Asian Americans vis-à-vis Whites and Blacks as theorized in Claire Jean Kim's (1999) racial triangulation model. Along the "insider/foreign" axis, K-pop artists better fit the "foreigner" image through its dominant use of Korean in the lyrics, as well as through its robust experimentation with sonic and visual elements that draw not only from Korea but also from many countries around the world. By the same token, Asian American musicians who do not display obvious markers of "foreignness" struggle to gain the more expansive audibility that they deserve.

The position that K-pop hits along the "inferior/superior" axis is a little more complicated. Many influential figures such as Lee Soo-man of SM Entertainment and Park Jin-young of JYP Entertainment have been open about modeling K-pop on Black music, the legacy of which is evident in the primacy of R&B and hip hop–related styles in much of K-pop's music, vocal delivery, and style (Anderson 2020, 17–24; K. H. Kim 2021, 5–30). Although K-pop's aural alignment with Black music is given more attention, it also draws from other hybrid genres that are generally associated with White musicians, such as classic rock, heavy metal, European synth-pop, and light pop ballads. This potent mixture of influences in K-pop reflects an adherence to the "superior" position of *both* Black and White music in the United States and in global pop more generally.[5] Interestingly, the music of Korean American musicians reflects a similar position of adherence to Black and White norms in popular music.

By examining the sonic elements of K-pop, I would argue that both Blackness and Whiteness occupy a superior position to Asianness. However, if you consider the visual representation of the body in K-pop, a different picture emerges. South Korea has long been known for its high rate of cosmetic surgery, and many have taken note that some of the most common procedures align with Western facial ideals, such as the double-eyelid surgery and rhinoplasty procedures that elongate, elevate, or narrow-down the nose. In addition, Stephen Epstein and Rachael M. Joo have written about how changing gendered body ideals emerging in the first decade of the 2000s, including long, slender legs for women and muscled male torsos for men, reflect a desire to attract the international gaze and project a competitive national self through images of "confident women" and "powerful men" (2012, 15). Although Epstein and Joo focus their analysis of the dynamics of this phenomenon within the East Asian and Southeast region, it is obvious that these body ideals are based on images of Whiteness in Western media. Other body-related developments that normalize White bodies as ideals of beauty include slenderness (vs. curviness) for women, an obsession with height for both men and women, and extreme experimentation with hair and eye color (with blond hair and

Racialization of Asian American Musicians

blue eyes being common). Add to this the preference for maintaining pale, white skin (as opposed to tanning), and one might argue that South Korea goes beyond the United States in emphasizing Whiteness. Taking the sonic and visual elements together, then, K-pop occupies a complex but intermediary position that leans toward Whiteness but away from Blackness along the "superior/inferior" axis. In sum, K-pop visuals generally fit with the triangulated co-construction of Asianness, Whiteness, and Blackness, which may help to explain its immense appeal, especially in comparison to Asian American music.

Given K-pop's highly visual nature, it is necessary to look more closely at the racialized and gendered discourses that Korea brings to the United States and analyze its reception as well as how it is impacting Asian Americans. In this endeavor, I turn to sociologist Nadia Y. Kim (2008), who calls for the need for a transnational racial lens. Kim writes that South Koreans have been subject to US-based racial ideologies, primarily through their exposure to American mass media that began in earnest during the US military occupation during the Korean War (1950–53). As a result, they have come "to take American racial inequalities for granted, such as the 'normativity' of White America and the 'inferiority' of Black America" (N. Y. Kim 2008, 11). Kim also adds that these ideas were bolstered by "Koreans' longstanding valorization of the color white over that of black and the related agrarian hierarchy of light-skinned nobility over tanned or dark-skinned peasants" (2008, 12). According to Kim, Koreans have valued "white as representative of its people's purity and desire for peace since the Three Kingdoms Period of 57 B.C. to A.D. 668" (2008, 27). In addition, "lightness is further associated with the West and modernity while darkness is nonmodern third world Korea" (N. Y. Kim 2008, 27–28). At the same time, while South Koreans have embraced Black music, they have not been exposed to as much anti-racist or pro-Black discourse, so their unabashed emphasis on pale, white skin has not been subject to as much criticism inside of Korea (N. Y. Kim 2008, 37).

Outside of Korea, however, K-pop has been criticized for fostering colorist and racist comments and preferences, as Laura-Zoë Humphreys suggests in her contribution in this volume. In addition, K-pop has also been critiqued for not promoting body diversity, favoring uniformly slender and tall performers. Often, colorism and body-type preferences overlap

Kwon

with each other, as women who are considered darker and who have more curvaceous bodies, such as Jessi and Hwasa (from Mamamoo), attract undue attention as "sexy idols." These Korea-based racialized discourses can have a translocal impact on Asian American artists as they may feel some pressure to conform to K-pop ideals to succeed in the United States. For example, although there were several Asian American and Pacific Islander contestants on the 2022 *American Song Contest* (modeled on Eurovision), it was AleXa, a multiracial, light-skinned K-pop contestant (of Russian and Korean heritage), who ended up winning. Asian America is incredibly diverse, with many skin tones and body types, but there is some evidence that K-pop's popularity may be having undue influence in setting the expectations for what Asian American artists should look and sound like (Aran 2018).

Navigating the Racialized Musical Terrain through Multivocality

In writing loosely about competitive vocal shows such as *American Idol* (2002–present), ethnomusicologist Katherine Meizel writes that "failing consideration of voice as a value, the only voices allowed to matter are those embedded in the bodies allowed to matter, in the selves that are deemed acceptably narratable, and in the gazes that determine such acceptability" (2020, 4–5). Within this "neoliberal rationality" (Meizel's term), voices emanating from the most legible or acceptable bodies such as AleXa's are the ones that are "allowed to matter." Despite this, singers and communities disrupt this process, and Meizel argues that they do so by valuing the voice. Drawing on Adriana Cavarero, Meizel writes that "valuing voice recognizes every person as a 'narratable self'" (2020, 4; Cavarero 2000, 34) or multitude of selves. From the vocalist's perspective, "singing with 'many voices' may be seen as a practice *at once produced by and resistant to these neoliberal expectations*" (Meizel 2020, 5). Meizel connects this practice to the framework of multivocality and states that "multivocal singers are often those who must continuously identify and cross borders in their everyday lives—singers of color, singers who are immigrants, or singers navigating gender, ethnic, even religious boundaries" (2020, 15). This matters because "when singers habitually perform across stylistic, genre, cultural, and his-

Racialization of Asian American Musicians

torical borders, . . . they are performing multivocality—that is negotiating their narratable selves by singing with many voices" (2020, 7). This resonates with Lisa Lowe's earlier writing that urges us to consider "Asian American culture as nomadic, unsettled, taking place . . . in the multivocality of heterogeneous and conflicting positions" (1991, 39). Along these lines, I will further investigate how Andrew Choi, Eric Nam, and Audrey Nuna navigate the limiting racialized terrain of the music industry by engaging in multivocality and other strategies to (1) become more audible as Asian Americans and (2) assert multiple "narrative selves" that can potentially resonate with broader audiences.

If "foreignness" is one of the dominant filters of racial listening for Asians and Asian Americans, then it makes sense that K-pop has had an easier time being recognized through its mix of Korean language lyrics and accented English. Against this backdrop, the Korean American artists that I focus on in this chapter resist being marked as "foreign" and have had to work hard and take major risks to be heard through a mix of strategies and approaches to vocality. Andrew Choi (St. Lenox) told me in his interview that he has "aspirations to be considered one of the great American songwriters" but that Asian Americans are often "left out of the equation of Americana music" (Choi 2018). Part of his strategy, then, is to distance himself from the ocular-centric style of K-pop and not to dress up when performing. "A lot of times, I will just go in work clothes. I think it's important because I think that music needs more representation from people who aren't pursuing music as a full-time career because if you are going to try to write about the American experience, I think a part of that is working a 9-to-5 or 8-to-7 job on a regular basis. . . . There's Americana artists and sometimes they'll dress up in early nineteenth century stuff, and I get it. . . . Why just let me go in work clothes?" (Choi 2018). Another strategy that Choi employs is to simply work incredibly hard at his craft: "I have to try ten times as hard in order to get the same success. . . . I have some friends and they will write the first ten songs they will just release it. . . . I didn't start releasing anything until I had one hundred songs. I then picked the best ones and presented them from that" (Choi 2018). The strategy of creative surplus and going well beyond what is needed is something that Eric Nam also ascribes to as he spent much of 2022 touring more than fifty-two cities around the world promoting his *There and Back*

Again album. In addition, during the pandemic transition, he created and produced the *Daebak Show w/Eric Nam* podcast, which is now well over 150 episodes.

Coming back to St. Lenox and the issue of multivocality, Andrew Choi is an interesting case because instead of singing across genre or exploring different timbres or styles, he sings with a more singular, arresting vocal style but tells stories through "many voices." The source of the "many voices" in his songs is likely due to his position between several intersecting, but often opposing identities. When asked by Danny Hwang of *Korean Indie* "What has it been like to be you?" Choi responded, "Oooh, can I tell you it's pretty tough being me.... Everyone I know hates everyone else I know. The attorneys and the musicians. The New Yorkers and the Midwesterners. The Koreans and the gays. The Gen-Xers and the Millennials. White people and people of color. The academics and the attorneys. The social justice folks and the attorneys.... I'm just saying I get stuck in the middle of everything. Maybe that's why I have to make music" (St. Lenox 2018). Although Choi most often writes his lyrics in first person, his four-album discography explores the borders of his plural identities. For example, his 2016 "Thurgood Marshall" song is about searching for a hero figure to help get through the intense difficulties of law school. In contrast, songs such as "Fuel America" (2016) and "Gold Star" (2018) detail his life as a struggling songwriter. Many of his songs reference life as a midwesterner, such as "I Still Dream of the '90s" (2014), "Just Friends" (2014), and "First Date" (2018), while others plumb the details of living in New York, such as "Hashtag Brooklyn Karaoke Party" (2018) and "Don't Ever Change Me New York City" (2018). Several of Choi's songs also stem from his queer identity, with lyrics that refer to same-sex love interests or gay culture such as "Bitter Pill" (2014), "First Date," and "Hashtag Brooklyn Karaoke Party."

In my 2018 interview with Choi, he expressed that some of his most compelling work delves into the stories from his Korean immigrant background and includes the quartet of songs that conclude his 2016 album: "Korea," "People from Other Cultures," "What I Think About When You Say South Korea," and "When I Return." In Choi's words, "The Return Home is a kind of catch-all term I use for a concept or collection of concepts focused on the desire that a 1st or 2nd (or 3rd or 4th) generation-American might feel about returning to their country of ethnic origin" (Eponymous 2018).

Racialization of Asian American Musicians

In the songs "Korea" and "When I Return" in particular, the lyrics and videos put forward the possibility of multiple "Koreas": Koreatown as proxy for Korea, a distant and receding Korea portrayed in faded photographs, North Korea (where his parents originally had to flee from during the Korean War), South Korea as a proxy for home after the Division, and a fantastical Korean homeland that will somehow transform him and cure all of his problems.

And while the longing to visit one's "homeland" where one is no longer a minority is compelling for many Asian Americans, the point that Andrew Choi makes is that this theme is not necessarily an Asian American or even an immigrant-specific story. For Choi, the desire to connect with one's "home" or "place of origin" is a very quintessential story that many Americans and others can relate to that we often see in various guises in movies like *Superman* (1978) and *Guardians of the Galaxy Vol. 2* (2017). In this way, Choi intentionally draws the boundaries of his identity in broader, more porous strokes so that more people can see themselves within. Even so, Choi's purview is not limited to the immigrant experience, as he has also written about other imagined selves, such as the extreme survivalists and transgender gun enthusiasts of his "Conspiracy Theories" (2016) video and the mysterious pilgrims searching for the astrophysical secrets of the universe in "Superkamiokande" (2021).

Perhaps his most pronounced assertion of multiple narrative selves comes through his idiosyncratic use of extra-lyrical narrative and split-screen production in his music videos. I argue that he does this to express multiplicity by juxtaposing slightly varied perspectives and interpretations. As such, his videos encourage multiple views and resist easy consumption, challenging viewers to understand what it is like to experience split or double-consciousness (Du Bois [1903] 2018), where one is forced to become aware of both insider and outsider perspectives and modes of being. Choi explains, "I think if you grow up as a first or second generation American . . . there is a lot of putting things in boxes and keeping things separate and you do have multiple narratives that you have to keep running at the same time. And I would imagine for many people from immigrating communities, there's a kind of facility that you develop . . . it's a coping skill" (2018). He also expressed a desire to work against the "otherizing" of immigrant narratives by adding adjacent narratives in the videos, noting that the views of the protagonist of the videos sometimes differ subtly from the protagonist of the original songs and act as kind of an alternative voice that provides a more personal perspective that gestures toward interiority (Choi 2018).

For example, in the video titled "Korea" (2016), Choi reinforces the sense of double-consciousness and hyphenated identity by splitting the screen horizontally and calling attention to this intermediary space by placing extra-lyrical narrative text right at this central point of juncture. While the narrator of the song in the lyrics sings ambivalently about wanting to go to his "native home" of Korea, the narrator of the extra-lyrical text in the video muses more about the pros and cons of hyphenated identities, proposing that those who are hyphenated are the fortunate ones. Interestingly, one of the main melodic hooks of the song is modeled on the stereotypical "oriental riff" trope, which he then re-appropriates into the first line of the chorus "And have you ever been to my native home? It's a place they call Korea."[6] In both cases, St. Lenox conveys a feeling of double-ness and musically embeds a meta-awareness of the tropes that impact the reception of Asian Americans. While there are so many more examples of multivocality through his use of extra-lyrical narrative ("Thurgood Marshall," "Teenage Eyes," and "Superkamiokande" are but a few), I focus on "Korea" because of the way that it engages in the "remaking" of race by flipping some of the more negative aspects of the Asian American experience (orientalist tropes and hyphenated identities) into something more positive, not only through the lyrics but also through the music and video.

Finally, I would be remiss if I did not reflect on the power of St. Lenox's voice to convey these multiple narrative selves. Having heard him live in a more acoustic setting, I can attest that Choi possesses an explosive yet flexible voice that can stand on its own with few effects. Given his lyrical penchant for packing in a lot of words, he articulates his voice as if his life depends upon its audibility. Although many listeners notice the melismatic endings of his phrases, much of his singing is forcefully syllabic. He has mused that his combination of syllabic and melismatic singing may be his contribution to creating a distinctively Asian American vocal style (personal communication). And while his style is not directly modeled on Korean music, the idiosyncratic timing and rough thickness of his voice reminds me of the Korean storytelling bards of *p'ansori*, who were also masters of singing "many voices." Andrew Choi's engagement with K-pop has been

Racialization of Asian American Musicians

minimal, and if anything, he has resisted capitulating to K-pop by going "Gangnam Style" or by otherwise tailoring his artistry to the narrow racial expectations of Asian Americans. This is reminiscent of strategies employed by other Asian American artists, such as David Choi, who have chosen a more independent route to success on YouTube (Jung 2014, 63). While St. Lenox has generally received superb reviews from music critics, his multivocal efforts have reached a relatively small audience.

By contrast, Eric Nam chose to reach a larger audience through K-pop. His willingness to pivot away from his more native language of English and sing and converse more fully in Korean can be seen as part of an initial multivocal strategy to express an alternative narrative self as a performer of Korean heritage in an environment where he would be received in a more race-neutral fashion. Nam explains that "in Korea, minority issues were never an issue, it's just about the skill set" (Partners In Health 2021). His skill set took him quite far in South Korea, despite being older than most K-pop stars at debut. In addition to releasing music as a solo and collaborative artist, Nam also participated in various reality television shows, thereby gaining comprehensive skills as a performer and entertainer while also developing a recognizable brand, personal style, and dedicated global fan base. Even so, Nam confessed that this translingual, multivocal strategy did not come easy, saying that "while I was working in Korea, . . . I felt like I was forcing myself into singing in a language that I never understood completely the lyrics, or the nuances of what I was saying" (Nam 2021b). In an interview on the *Zach Sang Show*, Nam expressed that "I never felt I belonged to either place fully," but now that he is moving more into the United States and international market, he is trying to view it as a strength: "Now, we have a very unique perspective, in that we are third culture, we have a little bit of both sides, so what used to be a hindrance, feels like a superpower. It would be dumb not to take advantage to bridge the gap" (Nam 2022).[7] What is so fascinating about Eric Nam's case is the way he has been able to seamlessly transfer gains from working in K-pop to the American context.

In the context of his transition back to the United States, his choice to release his 2022 album *There and Back Again*, which literally references his transnational move to Korea and back, his choice to sing all in English is especially meaningful. This can even be seen as an exercise in multivocality, a way of increasing his audibility by expressing an alternative but more authentic self: "English is the best way for me to really, fully express myself. I also think I sound better in English. There's a difference in terms of vocal tone and how things are delivered. . . . I want to do things in English because right now I think Asian Americans and Asians are having a moment. . . . So to put it out in English and to do everything on my terms as a Korean American I think is incredibly important" (Nam 2021b). While it is difficult to measure whether Eric Nam "sounds better" in English, I did listen closely to "Love Die Young," a song that he recorded in both English (2019) and Korean (2020). From the first line of "What happens when it's over, when we've breathed our last breath" in the English version and "끝이라는 단어를 마주하게 된 우리" (*kkeutiraneun daneoreul majuhage dwen uri*) in the Korean rendition, it was apparent that he sounded much more relaxed in English, resulting in a warmer and more open tone. In general, Eric Nam has a brighter tone in Korean, resulting in a slightly younger sounding voice. In an interview with Audrey Nuna on Nam's *Daebak Show*, the first topic that they talked about was how their tone changes when they switch into Korean versus English (Nuna 2021a). While Audrey Nuna theorized that women often speak in higher tones while speaking Korean, Eric Nam responded that he did not know whether his tone goes lower or higher but that he did agree that his voice changes. In either language, though, Eric Nam possesses a natural warm breathiness to his voice with a beautiful falsetto range that has only gotten better with time. In sum, switching languages to Korean and now back to English has been a crucial pivot through which he has been able to make slight shifts in register that correlate with exploring different aspects of his identity. He has also had the opportunity to perform his various identities through his television appearances, podcasts, and touring performances. A natural storyteller and interactive entertainer, he is great at connecting with fans and extends this through his various social media and vlogging platforms. Taken together, the sheer magnitude of his multimedia, multivocal output is surely contributing to the normalization and audibility of transnational, multilingual Asian Americans such as Eric Nam.

Audrey Nuna is also working toward the normalization of Asian American artists, and since she was fortunate enough to be signed by a major US label relatively early in her career, she has not really had to go to Korea

Racialization of Asian American Musicians

first like so many other Korean American artists. As a result, she has had the freedom to be herself and pursue the strategy of crafting a unique multivocal sound and image. And while her career has been impacted by the COVID-19 pandemic, she is gaining a broader following as her successful set at Lollapalooza in 2022 attests. Veteran Asian American rapper Dumbfoundead remarked that Nuna does not look or sound like anyone else out there (Nuna 2020a). Visually, Nuna has her own unique style of layered, loose, and edgy sportswear that she describes as "futuristic dad," and she makes no attempt to style herself after the form-fitting and skin-baring looks of female K-pop stars (Nuna 2020b). She also plays a large role in co-directing her music videos (MVs), most of which are tailored to her own aesthetic palette of black and white, retro colors and moods, gritty backdrops, and the slightly unnerving inclusion of deconstructed or unnatural body close-ups, parts, and positions (Nuna 2020b).

In terms of vocal artistry, Audrey Nuna is the most experimental of the three artists featured here, and her multivocal efforts have already garnered critical notice. In an NME review of Nuna's *a liquid breakfast* (2021) album, Rhian Daly writes that "the 10-track project is characterised by its creative diversity: no two songs sound the same, ranging from ultra-cool anthems ('Comic Sans,' 'Damn Right') to mellower, softer songs that showcase their creator's beautiful singing voice ('Space,' 'Long Year'). On 'Cool Kids,' she lingers on the final syllable of each line in the chorus, drawing out words like '*us*' and '*dust*' like a hissing snake, while 'Get Luv' puts her voice through processors to transform it into something more digitised and sleek" (Daly 2021). Nuna also uses her voice to explore stylistic boundaries. Although she started out singing in an alternative R&B style, she has since applied her astonishingly agile rhythmic flow and love of words to rap. According to her interview with Dumbfoundead, "Comic Sans" was only her second rap song, but upon "cold-emailing" the track to Jack Harlow, it was already enticing enough for him to agree to collaborate on the track (Nuna 2020a). In her final verse, she interpolates her lyrics with playful vocal popping effects on a line already brimming with alliterative "p" sounds: "polymath, polyglot, Polly wants a cracker, but I just *pop* *pop* like a lipsmacker." Nuna also deploys enviable control over an arsenal of diverse vocal timbres, such as a low vocal fry on "yeah" in the chorus of "Comic Sans"; a cloudy, sweeping tone on the chorus of "Typical"; and a feathery light melody vocal

Kwon

on the chorus of "Damn Right." Some of these more intimate techniques do not translate well in live performance, but judging from her 2022 Lollapalooza performance, she has proven adept at adapting to the festival stage without compromising her multivocality. For example, instead of using vocal fry on "yeah" in her hit song with Jack Harlow "Comic Sans," she substituted it with a powerful "say yeah," thereby eliciting enthusiastic call-and-response "yeahs" from the audience. She also had the audience sounding "sexy" (Nuna's words) on longer call-and-response chorus lines on "Party." Finally, Nuna provided contrast to her belting stage voice by applying autotune-like effects on her voice on "Baby Blues" and "Molars." Whether in her recorded work or in live performance, interactive multivocal diversity is central to her artistic sound and identity.

While Nuna is not succumbing to any pressure to fit the K-pop mold, neither is she hiding her Korean heritage or trying to fit the mold of a "typical" R&B or hip hop star. Like Eric Nam, singing in Korean is an aspect of her multivocality, such as in her smoky torch number "That XX." She also includes snippets of her grandmother speaking in Korean on her song "Blossom" and is vocal about her Korean American background in interviews. She even told Eric Nam about how precious her grandmother's story of fleeing the Korean War is to her (Nuna 2021a). Although she does not dress like a female K-pop idol, Korean influences are evident in her penchant for all-white ensembles that are reminiscent of the white *minbok* used in a Korean folk genre such as *pungmul*. Her Lollapalooza outfit, with its white tapered *minbok*-style pants, sheer voluminous skirt, white top, and cropped puffy vest, could be interpreted as a deconstructed, sporty *hanbok*. In this way, Audrey Nuna is contesting expectations of what a popular performer should look like (Korean or otherwise), crossing stylistic, linguistic, and cultural borders and employing multivocality to expand the audible parameters of the Asian American voice.

Conclusion

In assessing impact and reception in music, one must always balance concerns about popularity and appeal versus artistic value and potential to incite change. In terms of inciting change, St. Lenox's power flows from his empathetic storytelling and social commentary, Eric Nam's impact lies in his smooth pop production and his willingness to speak out on issues such as anti-Asian hate, whereas Audrey Nuna's creative boundary-crossing energy is propelling the music industry forward. But how well are they navigating a racialized music terrain in which K-pop is the rampant elephant in the room? Although St. Lenox has gained sterling critical reception without compromising his musical vision or artistic integrity, this has not translated into high numbers of views, listens, or performances, which greatly limits his impact. In contrast, Eric Nam's ability to perform close to the standard set by K-pop has helped him greatly. On Spotify, Nam has over a million monthly listeners, and his 2022 world tour of medium-size venues was mostly sold out. His success is roughly comparable to other male K-pop soloists, which is remarkable given that he is an independent artist. Overall, Nam's successful efforts to re-brand himself as a global pop artist is encouraging news for other up-and-coming Asian American artists, such as Audrey Nuna or Keshi, who are largely forgoing the pressure to go to Asia. With this said, working hard to speak out about Asian American issues and representation while also connecting with fans seems to be making a difference for both Nam and Nuna. Although audiences seem to be more accepting of Asian American musicians through these efforts, Asian American artists must still live up to a "neoliberal rationality" of what a pop star should look like, a standard that is increasingly set by K-pop. Despite the numbers, it is important to recognize that all Asian American artists are working within varied niches, communities, and scales that are difficult to compare or quantify. The efforts of Choi, Nam, and Nuna prove that there is more than one way to increase the audibility of Asian American voices.

Notes

1. I am referring mainly to those artists who present as Asian American. While many artists with some Asian heritage have been exceptionally successful, such as Bruno Mars or Olivia Rodrigo, I exclude them here because they are generally perceived as more ethnically ambiguous.

2. For a more nuanced analysis of the reception of the Kim Sisters within the context of transpacific Cold War politics, see Benjamin Han (2018).

3. For more in-depth research about the prevalence and success of Asian Americans in classical music, see Grace Wang (2015).

Kwon

4. My concept of "assimilated difference" is related to Homi K. Bhabha's theorization of "ambivalent mimicry," in which the colonial subject is seen as a "recognizable Other, as a subject of a difference, that is almost the same, but not quite" (1994, 86; cited in Kim 2021, 10). Kyung Hyun Kim takes this further in his analysis of K-pop, theorizing it as the product of "hegemonic mimicry" and "racial opacity" (2021, 29, 93).

5. Although K-pop's creative hybridization includes many other influences (such as Korean, Pan-Asian, and Latin influences), I argue that it must *first* follow the conventions of global pop, which is dominated by White and Black music trends.

6. For more information on the "oriental riff" that is used as a stereotypical trope to represent Asians or Asian Americans, see "Oriental Riff," Wikimedia Foundation, last modified September 23, 2023, https://en.wikipedia.org/wiki/Oriental_riff.

7. Eric Nam's translingual ability can also be referred to as "code-switching," but I choose to frame this as multivocality because "code-switching" has received criticism for assuming the normativity of standard English as spoken by White Americans in public spaces and relegating minoritized languages and dialects to private, marginal spaces (Young 2009, 68–69; cited in Meizel 2020).

References

Anderson, Crystal S. 2020. *Soul in Seoul: African American Popular Music and K-pop.* Jackson: University Press of Mississippi.

Aran, Isha. 2018. "America Is in Love with Asian Music, but Asian American Artists Still Can't Catch a Break." *Splinter*, March 1, 2018. https://splinternews.com/america-is-in-love-with-asian-music-but-asian-american-1823038498.

Bhabha, Homi K. 1994. *The Location of Culture.* London: Routledge.

Cavarero, Adriana. 2000. *Relating Narratives: Storytelling and Selfhood.* Translated by Paul A. Kottman. London: Routledge.

Choi, Andrew. 2018. Interview by the author. September 28, 2018.

Daly, Rhian. 2021. "Audrey Nuna—'A Liquid Breakfast' Review: Rampant, Refreshing Creativity from R&B's Most Exciting New Voice." *NME*, May 20, 2021. https://www.nme.com/reviews/album/audrey-nuna-a-liquid-breakfast-review-radar-2944030.

Du Bois, W. E. B. (1903) 2018. *The Souls of Black Folk.* New York: Penguin Books.

Eponymous. 2018. "Year of Migration Lecture—The Return Home." St. Lenox, October 9, 2018. https://stlenox.com/2018/10/09/year-of-migration-lecture/.

———. 2019. "Anti-Asian-American Bias in Indie Music Journalism." St. Lenox, October 8, 2019. https://stlenox.com/2019/10/08/the-anti-asian-american-bias-in-indie-music-journalism/.

Epstein, Stephen, and Rachael M. Joo. 2012. "Multiple Exposures: Korean Bodies and the Transnational Imagination." *Asia-Pacific Journal: Japan Focus* 10/33 (1).

Han, Benjamin M. 2018. "Transpacific Talent: The Kim Sisters in Cold War America." *Pacific Historical Review* 87 (3): 473–98.

Jung, Eun-Young. 2013. "K-pop Female Idols in the West: Racial Imaginations and Erotic Fantasies." In *The Korean Wave: Korean Media Go Global*, edited by Youna Kim, 106–19. London: Routledge.

———. 2014. "Transnational Migrations and YouTube Sensations: Korean Americans, Popular Music, and Social Media." *Ethnomusicology* 58 (1): 54–82. https://doi.org/10.5406/ethnomusicology.58.1.0054.

Kim, Claire Jean. 1999. "The Racial Triangulation of Asian Americans." *Politics and Society* 27 (1): 105–38. https://doi.org/10.1177/0032329299027001005.

Kim, Hye Won. 2023. "Recording the Soundscape of K-Pop." In *The Cambridge Companion to K-Pop*, edited by Suk-Young Kim, 73–94. Cambridge: Cambridge University Press.

Kim, Kyung Hyun. 2021. *Hegemonic Mimicry: Korean Popular Culture of the Twenty-First Century*. Durham, NC: Duke University Press.

Kim, Nadia Y. 2008. *Imperial Citizens: Koreans and Race from Seoul to LA*. Stanford, CA: Stanford University Press.

Kondo, Dorinne. 2018. *Worldmaking: Race, Performance, and the Work of Creativity*. Durham, NC: Duke University Press.

Lowe, Lisa. 1991. "Heterogeneity, Hybridity, Multiplicity: Marking Asian American Differences." *Diaspora: A Journal of Transnational Studies* 1 (1): 24–44. https://doi.org/10.1353/dsp.1991.0014.

The Masked Singer. Season 1, episode 4, "Another Mask Bites the Dust." Directed by Alex Rudzinski and Brad Duns. Aired January 23, 2019, on Fox. https://www.fox.com/watch/83901f8388e3e22f4112e76b75faca87/.

Meizel, Katherine. 2020. *Multivocality: Singing on the Borders of Identity*. New York: Oxford University Press.

Miller, Karl Hagstrom. 2010. *Segregating Sound: Inventing Folk and Pop Music in the Age of Jim Crow*. Durham, NC: Duke University Press.

Nam, Eric. 2021a. "If You're Surprised by the Anti-Asian Violence in Atlanta, You Haven't Been Listening. It's Time to Hear Our Voices." *Time*, updated March 22, 2021. https://time.com/5948226/eric-nam-anti-asian-racism-atlanta/.

———. 2021b. "Rolling Stone Twitch 12102021 Live with Eric Nam (Part 1): Interview." Global Namnation. December 10, 2021. YouTube video, 42:32. https://youtu.be/kkTXqIWx6xc.

———. 2022. "Eric Nam Talks 'There And Back Again,' Kpop vs. Pop, Relationships & More." Produced by Sangasong, LLC. *Zach Sang Show*. June 4, 2022. Podcast, YouTube video, 38:55. https://youtu.be/amkcOPXt8vU.

Nuna, Audrey. 2020a. "Audrey Nuna - Fun With Dumb - Ep. 108." Hosted by Dumbfoundead. *Fun With Dumb*. November 4, 2020. Podcast, YouTube video, 55:00. https://youtu.be/uT3Cnno6M5A.

———. 2020b. "Baewatch: Audrey Nuna." By YeEun Kim. *Hypebae*, March 20, 2020. https://hypebae.com/2020/3/audrey-chu-nuna-korean-american-music-artist-hip-hop-singer-interview-comic-sans-jack-harlow.

———. 2021a. "Catching Up: Audrey Nuna." Produced by DIVE Studios. *Daebak Show w/ Eric Nam*. October 4, 2021. Podcast, YouTube video, 1:03:21. https://youtu.be/fvZ2oMaiQq8.

———. 2021b. "R&B Artist Audrey Nuna Wants to Normalize Diversity in Media." Character Media. June 3, 2021. YouTube video, 4:52. https://youtu.be/VD3_dU5iVOk.

Partners In Health. 2021. "Racism and Mental Health in the Time of COVID-19." May 20, 2021. YouTube video, 52:05. https://youtu.be/6c_EyGJZpA4.

Roberts, Tamara. 2016. *Resounding Afro Asia: Interracial Music and the Politics of Collaboration*. New York: Oxford University Press.

Shimakawa, Karen. 2002. *National Abjection: The Asian American Body Onstage*. Durham, NC: Duke University Press.

St. Lenox. 2018. "Interview with St. Lenox." By Danny Hwang. *Korean Indie*, September 24, 2018. https://www.koreanindie.com/2018/09/24/interview-with-st-lenox/.

Wang, Grace. 2015. *Soundtracks of Asian America: Navigating Race through Musical Performance*. Durham, NC: Duke University Press.

Wong, Sau-Ling C. 1995. "Denationalization Reconsidered: Asian American Cultural Criticism at a Theoretical Crossroads." *Amerasia Journal* 21 (1–2): 1–28. https://doi.org/10.17953/amer.21.1-2.wu3h237701655518.

Young, Vershawn Ashanti. 2009. "'Nah, We Straight': An Argument against Code Switching." *JAC: Journal of Rhetoric, Culture and Politics* 29 (1/2): 49–76.

5

······

"Soft" Koreans and "Sensual" Cubans

Race, Gender, and the Reception
of South Korean Popular Culture in Cuba

······

LAURA-ZOË HUMPHREYS

One early afternoon in February 2020, I found myself at a Havana movie theater for a concert with a young Korean Mexican pianist. As I waited with the small group of Cuban Hallyu fans gathered for the show, I struck up a conversation with the diplomat sent by the South Korean embassy in Mexico to help stage the event. When I asked why South Korea was interested in promoting such activities, he observed that Cuba held natural resources of interest, could serve as a potential market for South Korean products, and was a promising tourist destination. As one of the last remaining socialist countries in the world, however, Cuba had long been an ally of North Korea but, in 2020, was one of only three UN-member countries that did not have diplomatic relations with South Korea. South Koreans, the diplomat continued, feared that establishing an embassy in Cuba would not be possible until matters improved between South and North Korea. At the time, this seemed less hopeful after peace and denuclearization talks held in 2018 and 2019 between the two Koreas ended in failure.

In the meantime, South Korea hoped to lay the groundwork for future negotiations by exposing Cubans to Korean culture with the goal of communicating to fans, as the diplomat put it, "how we [Koreans] think." Such a venture, he explained, started with K-pop and K-dramas but must also include other aspects of South Korean culture. When he took the stage, the young pianist, who had migrated with his parents to Mexico as a child, echoed these sentiments. Hopefully BTS could come to Cuba to give a concert one day, he observed, eliciting enthusiastic cheers from the audience. For now, he was there to show them that there was more to Korea than BTS. Then he settled in for a classical piano concert performed before tourist-worthy videos of South Korea and Havana as well as images from a historical K-drama, pausing also to lead the audience in a singalong of the traditional Korean folk song "Arirang."

Scenes such as this were frequent occurrences during the five months of ethnographic fieldwork I carried out with Hallyu fans in Havana, Cuba, in 2018 and 2020.[1] They demonstrate the global popularity of the South Korean Wave and how it can elicit curiosity about South Korea on the part of fans in culturally and politically dissimilar parts of the globe, as well as the deliberate attempts by the South Korean government to harness that curiosity to their own ends. While the concept of soft power has been justly criticized for its lack of conceptual clarity, South Korean diplomats clearly see popular culture as an essential part of their diplomatic toolkit and a crucial means of improving the image of South Korea abroad. In Cuba in the late 2010s, such ventures went hand in hand with an increase in travel between the two nations and a rise in South Korean media representations of the archipelago. Nonetheless, the question remains as to what understanding foreign fans develop of South Korea and South Koreans as they engage with South Korean media, diplomats, entertainers, and tourists, as well as what understandings South Koreans glean from South Korean media representations of Global South nations such as Cuba.

This chapter takes up these questions by keeping the inextricability of modernity and coloniality in view. As decolonial theorists have demonstrated, ideals of modernity were part of a colonial project that cast White Euro-North America as superior to and more modern than its colonial and racial others. This paradigm plagued Latin American and Caribbean efforts to claim modernity and enforced racial hierarchies. Cuban and other Latin American and Caribbean elites founded myths of nationhood on practices of racial *mestizaje* or mixing while nonetheless elevating the region's White and lighter-skinned residents over its Indigenous, Black, Asian, and darker-skinned citizens (Cusicanqui 2012; Mignolo 2005; Rivero 2015). In the

"Soft" Koreans and "Sensual" Cubans

twentieth century, the treatment of White Euro-North America as the pinnacle of modernity was reinforced by US media's global dominance. The rise of competing culture industries from Latin American telenovelas through Hong Kong cinema, Bollywood, Nollywood, Japanese and South Korean popular cultures, and Turkish dizis is therefore significant. Early studies explained the popularity of non-US media cultures through the cultural proximity thesis, which holds that audiences prefer media with resemblances to their own life contexts (Straubhaar 1991). Brian Larkin (1997), for instance, compellingly demonstrates how the global circulation of non-US media challenges White Euro-North America as the unique reference point for modernity and contributes to the imagination of parallel modernities. Yet, as Marion Schulze contends (2013), the cultural proximity thesis cannot account for the appeal of global media across cultures experienced as acutely different. Even more problematically, as Schulze elaborates, some (most certainly not all) scholars working within the cultural proximity thesis treat cultures as though they are homogeneous and self-contained, ignoring diversity, global interconnections, and the structures of power that shape these dynamics.

This chapter intervenes in these debates by demonstrating the importance of a multi-scalar analysis to studies of global media circulation. Latin Americans have been barred full entry into Whiteness at the global level even as Whiteness is valorized within Latin American nations. Cuba has also both been essential to world socialism and is increasingly caught up in neoliberal world-making projects, such as that of the South Korean media industry. To understand how globally circulating media challenge and re/produce racial and geopolitical hierarchies in Cuba and elsewhere, we must therefore keep multiple global, regional, national, and local dynamics and their entanglements in view. In what follows, I show how, as elsewhere in Latin America (Han 2019; Min et al. 2018), Cuban fans turned to South Korean media to imagine a parallel modernity, one that challenged White Euro-North American dominance by prioritizing postcolonial nationhood in ways that updated socialist aims. Yet South Korean media representations of Cuba and Cuban experiences of Hallyu fandom also participated in creating a new racial and geopolitical hierarchy, one in which South Korea joined White Euro-North America at the apex while Cuba and Cubans were cast as exotic and backward. Finally, while Cuban fans demonstrated

Humphreys

genuine interest in learning more about Korea and challenged Cuban anti-Asian racism, the reception of South Korean media also converged uneasily with gendered racial stereotypes of Asian people and a politics of respectability that perpetuated anti-Blackness.

In Search of the "Real" Korea

As in other parts of the world, encounters with South Korean popular media sparked interest in Cuba in a country and culture about which Cubans had previously known very little. This curiosity was further complicated by Cuba's socialist allegiances. I begin, then, by recounting the history of Hallyu fandom in Cuba and how Cuban fans sought to satisfy their interest in South Korea amid official state suspicion.

Following the 1959 Cuban Revolution, the new socialist state nationalized all major media outlets. Infrastructural challenges further complicated media circulation. While significant improvements were made in internet services in the archipelago beginning in 2015, as of 2024, it remained prohibitively expensive for Cubans to directly download large media files. Hand-to-hand forms of digital media piracy stepped into this gap. As of approximately 2010, state control over media distribution was dislodged by what is known in Cuba as *el paquete*, or the packet: almost one terabyte of pirated digital media that, by 2024, was downloaded by entrepreneurial collectives on a daily basis and circulated across the archipelago using hard drives. The contents of the *paquete* were then sold as separate media files through what some Cubans referred to as *puntos de copia*, or copy places—physical locations, often attached to private homes, that were operated by vendors working with state licenses. The rise of the *paquete* is also tied to state efforts to decentralize the socialist economy. Copy places multiplied when the state opened small business licenses for the sale of DVDs and CDs in the early 2010s, thereby inadvertently authorizing piracy (Humphreys 2022). In 2017, the state stopped granting new licenses in this category. Those who already held this license, however, were allowed to continue operating, while new vendors sought legal status under licenses for computing and printing services. Finally, by the late 2010s, the sale of DVDs gave way to that of digital media files, which were copied directly onto clients' USB and hard drives.

"Soft" Koreans and "Sensual" Cubans

As I have described elsewhere (Humphreys 2021), this informal media ecosystem was essential to Hallyu fandom in Cuba. Several Cuban Hallyu fans with whom I worked downloading smaller files such as music videos, while a select few accessed South Korean dramas and movies through home or work Wi-Fi accounts or Telegram chat groups. Many more purchased K-dramas and other large files from favored copy places and shared files with friends. Media sharing also played a crucial role in the foundation of Cuba's first Hallyu fan club. Interest in South Korean popular culture took off in Cuba in 2012 when Cuban state television broadcast four K-dramas. Older women drawn to the shows began chatting through a Facebook fan page, then held an in-person meeting in Havana. This led to the creation of ARTCOR, or the Club Amistad de Arte Coreano (Korean Art Friendship Club), in 2015. In August 2016, the club was granted official status as a sociocultural project under a municipal branch of Cuba's Ministry of Culture. By 2016, in the absence of a South Korean embassy in Cuba, ARTCOR had begun collaborating with KOTRA, a state-funded South Korean organization that represents the nation's business interests abroad; with the South Korean embassy in Mexico; and with the Casa Cuba Corea (Cuba-Korean House), a museum and social center for the Korean diaspora in Cuba established in Havana in 2014. Membership in ARTCOR grew rapidly as first young women then young men joined, drawn by interests in K-pop. One of the first events the club held was a *festival de copia*, or copy festival, where members met to exchange media over laptops, smartphones, and USB and hard drives. Other activities—from *discoreas*, where youth gathered in the hundreds to dance to K-pop music videos, to *ajumma* (aunty) meetings for the club's older members—provided members with opportunities to meet like-minded people, spend time with friends, and share media.

ARTCOR events were also highly valued as opportunities to learn more about South Korea. For several fans, interest in Hallyu and South Korea built on passions for Japanese anime and manga. Even in these cases, however, fans insisted that their knowledge of South Korea had at first been limited, in part because of the Cuban state's political allegiances. Selena (age seventeen) for instance, noted that her mother often played anime for her when she was a child. This sparked a curiosity about East Asia, but what she knew of the region was restricted to Japan and the socialist nations of China and Vietnam, which, because they are Cuban allies, were featured in documentaries available on Cuban state television. Dayana (age twenty-four), another fan whose passion for South Korean popular culture got its start with anime and manga, also noted how her initial impressions of Korea were shaped by Cuban socialism. "From the time we are young," she told me, "they teach us that there are two Koreas, one that is socialist and the other that is capitalist. At first, this was all that I knew about Korea." Just as interest in Japanese popular culture had previously driven Dayana to learn more about Japan, investment in K-dramas and K-pop encouraged her to find out more about South Korea. While others were busy copying entertainment media at ARTCOR headquarters, she told me proudly, she read a graphic book that told the history of South Korea.

Others pointed out that South Korean entertainment media itself cultivated fans' interests in the nation's culture. Tamara (age seventeen) observed that South Korean popular culture was "like a virus, because I like Korean culture in general. It's not just K-pop, the music, doramas [K-dramas]. I like everything in general—how they dress, their traditions, their traditional clothing." Her friend Yolanda (age twenty-four) elaborated: "the telenovelas themselves teach you a lot of things [about South Korea.] Historical dramas teach you everything about their history, about when the Japanese were there, about the Mongolians, China." Others concurred. Celia (age twenty-seven) noted that "they sell their culture to you in the doramas and you end up wanting to try the same things." Watching culinary K-dramas, for instance, she explained, made her want to try chopsticks.

As comments about South Korean media as a virus or a means to "sell" South Korean culture suggest, however, fans were also aware of the market logics that propelled South Korean media and of the potential for a gap between representation and reality. One of the things that she disliked about South Korean media, observed Dayana (cited above), is that she "likes things that are sincere, and they hide the other side of the coin. I have a friend who lives in South Korea and she tells me, 'Dayana, things here aren't all *color de rosa* [not everything is as nice as it seems]. There are bad things as well and they try to hide all that.'" Critical depictions were also subject to doubt. As in Schulze's (2013) study of English-language online fan forums, when themes and tropes appeared across several shows, fans frequently reached for cultural explanations. But they also sought to verify these theories with those deemed "experts"—South Koreans, members of

"Soft" Koreans and "Sensual" Cubans

the diaspora, or people who had traveled to or lived in South Korea. Maritza (age seventy-five) was shocked by depictions of the mistreatment of children and employees in K-dramas. "When I see [these themes] repeated so many times I wonder if they are true," she noted. Nonetheless, she insisted, "I have no way of knowing. I would have to talk to someone from there to know." Just as Daniela consulted with her friend living in South Korea to question K-drama's gilded depictions of the nation, Maritza insisted that she would have to speak to a South Korean or resident in South Korea to check the veracity of these more negative K-drama representations.

One of the primary goals of ARTCOR was to provide fans with just such opportunities. ARTCOR organizers continuously cautioned fans against taking popular culture at face value and instead hosted a range of events designed to advance fans' understanding of South Korea or introduce them to South Koreans. Events included what organizers termed Jornadas Científicas (Scientific days), a conference in which fans gave research presentations on a variety of topics related to Korea; encounters with visiting South Korean or diasporic artists; and infrequent but much-sought opportunities to meet South Korean actors and K-pop stars. Such activities also played an essential role in ARTCOR organizers' efforts to establish the club's legitimacy. As organizers told me, one of the most significant obstacles they had to overcome was Cuban state suspicion of the group because of its affiliation with capitalist South Korea. To ward off such concerns, organizers insisted that "la cultura de Corea es una" (the culture of Korea is one) and had even (unsuccessfully) approached the North Korean embassy for support.

They also insisted on the educational and moral goals of the club. As one organizer put it, ARTCOR went to great efforts to ensure that the club would not be viewed as "una pila de chiquillas gritando por los coreanos" (a pile of little girls screaming for Koreans). ARTCOR's 2016 application for status as an official state sociocultural project, for instance, emphasized that the club drew on South Korean popular culture's "messages about education, respect for the elderly, for children, and for the family" to "foment values in youth that would strengthen their social and moral conduct and reduce social indiscipline." The club also aimed, the document continued, to communicate Korean cultural achievements to Cubans and to convey "the cultural milestones of our country" to Koreans. Yet efforts at cross-cultural communication, as we shall see, were often mired in racial and geopolitical inequalities.

Not-So-Parallel Modernities

On a June afternoon in 2018, a group of women ARTCOR members, ranging in age from early twenties through fifties, sat in the hot sun of Casa Cuba Corea's outdoor courtyard, waiting for the arrival of a middle-aged South Korean poet. As we waited, the women gossiped about the poet's work, which they had read in translation in English, and mused excitedly about its erotic explicitness, which, they noted, was a stark contrast to K-dramas' sexual restraint. To the disappointment of at least one attendee, however, when the poet finally did arrive, instead of addressing his poetry, he turned to a topic that he had been told would interest them—K-dramas. Via a translator, he apologized for his looks and reassured the women that, although he was less attractive than the actors and idols to whom they were accustomed, his face was acceptable in Korea. Then he summarized the plot of a recent K-drama in which a man is laid off by his company when it goes bankrupt. What would happen to employees if a company went bankrupt in Cuba? he asked the women. They explained that the worker would be transferred to another place of employment. The poet nodded approvingly. As the conversation continued, one attendee described a K-drama that focused on child abuse and asked how prevalent this problem was in South Korea. The poet assured the audience that the drama exaggerated the scope of the issue, albeit to draw attention to an existing social problem. The session concluded with the poet inviting the women to spend time with him during his stay. When the then president of ARTCOR questioned how this would work given the poet's poor English and non-existent Spanish, he reassured them that one can communicate through the gaze. This solution was met with some skepticism mixed with efforts at hospitality and all departed.

This exchange is suggestive of several of the themes I have discussed thus far and on which I will expand in this section. First, the encounter shows how visiting South Koreans and Cuban Hallyu fans sought to expand their knowledge of one another's nations, even as—both in the poet's choice of topics and in the question about child abuse posed by the audience

"Soft" Koreans and "Sensual" Cubans

member—popular culture remained their primary avenue for doing so. Second, the poet's decision to emphasize a TV show that discusses the vicissitudes of the South Korean economy and his curiosity about labor in Cuba suggest the central role that comparisons of neoliberal capitalism to socialism played in such exchanges. Finally, the women's excited gossip about the eroticism of the poetry and the poet's suggestive offer to communicate through the gaze speak to how gender and sexuality intersected with race and culture in encounters between Cubans and Koreans, as they speculated on each other's physical attractiveness and erotic potential. I will delve further into this latter topic in the final section of this chapter. For now, I want to elaborate on how comparisons of South Korean neoliberal capitalism with Cuban socialism both enabled Cubans to imagine a parallel modernity and reinforced racial and geopolitical hierarchies.

As noted in the introduction, scholars have argued that global circulations of non-US media are fueled by audiences' desires to view media that more closely resemble their own life contexts. This in turn enables social groups to negotiate tensions between tradition and social change in ways that provide an alternative to White Euro-North American modernity. The reception of South Korean media in Cuba cannot easily be explained through arguments of cultural proximity. Indeed, fans often emphasized the differences between Cubans and South Koreans. It is perhaps all the more surprising, then, that Cuban fans found in South Korea a model for modernity that resonated with their own experience. The 1959 Cuban Revolution is celebrated in Cuba for finally achieving national autonomy, after the United States intervened in national governance following drawn-out wars for independence from Spain. Following the collapse of the Soviet Union in 1989, however, capitalist globalization took new hold on Cuba as the state opened the nation to foreign investment and travel in an effort to mitigate economic disaster.

Reflecting this history, Cuban fans frequently admired South Korea's ability to emerge from colonization by Japan and a neocolonial relationship to the United States to become an economically and technologically developed nation. What she most respected about South Korea, observed Maritza (cited above), was "its development. It's a country that has survived many things—the Japanese intervention, the wars with North Korea—and nonetheless it has advanced a lot. After the thirteen colonies, nothing happened to the United States. They call themselves the most developed country in the world, but they haven't suffered anything. It's not like countries like Korea or Vietnam." Others saw in South Korea a model for how to merge technology and openness to global flows with the preservation of tradition. What she liked about K-pop, noted Claudia (age eighteen), was that "what they do is unique, even though they draw on a mix of other cultures. They bring that together and make it their own." Marina (age fifty-eight) admired "the household appliances and the excellent conditions of the homes in films and novelas" as well as how South Koreans "respect their tradition." "Roots are important," she observed. "A person without roots is like a mutilated tree. I can love Korean culture, but my roots are Cuban." Statements like these provide an interesting complement to the discussions of transracial fantasy by Irina Lyan and Min Joo Lee in this volume. As it did for the fans and influencers discussed by Lyan and Lee, interest in Hallyu inspired many Cubans to adopt Korean customs, from eating with chopsticks to bowing as a greeting, suggesting cross-cultural and transracial play and experimentation. But fans' insistence that South Korean popular culture provided a model for the preservation of *cubanidad* in a globalized world demonstrates how, especially for citizens of a postcolonial nation long threatened by US imperialism, Hallyu can also reinforce desires to forge their own culturally distinctive parallel modernity.

Efforts to merge interest in South Korea with the promotion of Cuban national culture also sometimes lead to celebrating histories that are often erased in the archipelago. At an event hosted by ARTCOR in 2016 in the Rampa movie theater in Havana, displays of traditional Korean dance and slideshows of South Korean idols and actors were punctuated by a performance in which a man sang a song from Cuba's Lucumí religion. Lucumí centers on orishas, deities who were brought to Cuba by enslaved and free West Africans. The performance at first appeared to perturb the two teenage girls seated next to me, Ana (age fifteen) and Elena (age sixteen), who had previously been joining in rapturous screaming over projected images of their favorite Korean stars. When the man finished singing, an ARTCOR organizer came on stage and explained that the performer was of Korean descent and had chosen his song to show that "we are all Cuban." Elena, who is Black, nodded emphatically in response. She enjoyed Korean culture, but she had also received her saint, she explained to me, referencing

"Soft" Koreans and "Sensual" Cubans

131

an important rite within Lucumí. Such displays of Cuban tradition may well be a defensive tactic designed to ward off the suspicion of authorities. ARTCOR was subsequently denied the use of the Rampa movie theater for their events because, as one organizer told me, "they say we are promoting the culture of another country." Nonetheless, moments such as these also suggest how fans worked their interest in South Korean popular culture into a parallel modernity. As Martin Tsang (2017) demonstrates, Asian indentured laborers, migrants, and their descendants have contributed significantly to Afro-Cuban religious traditions, yet such intersectional and diasporic experiences are not often acknowledged. Hallyu fandom thus gave rare visibility to these experiences.

At the same time, Cuban fans were also critical of certain aspects of South Korean modernity. As the encounter with the South Korean poet with which I opened this section suggests, South Korean popular culture itself provided fans with tools for criticizing the worst exigencies of that nation's capitalism. South Korean films and television series often touch on the challenges of capitalism through the depiction of villainous chaebols or workers down on their luck while K-pop groups such as BTS sing about the economic precarity confronting youth. For their part, Cuban fans took such representations as signs of shocking inequality within South Korean society. Fans acknowledged the existence of growing class differences in Cuba, but they insisted that these were minor compared to class dispari-ties in South Korea. Cuban fans were also critical of the exploitative work conditions of the K-pop industry itself. Far from causing them to reject K-pop, however, they responded by insisting that they must love and sup-port the idols even more (Humphreys 2021). Such arguments, in turn, also enabled Cuban fans to cast themselves as superior to South Koreans. My interlocutors frequently argued that South Korean fans were excessively cruel to and critical of idols compared to Cuban or Latin American fans.

Even as fans questioned South Korean capitalism and asserted regional and national pride, however, they were also incorporated into global Hal-lyu fandom in ways that denied their own capacity to be modern. Fans lamented that Cuba was off the regular routes for South Korean idols and actors, making attending a live concert an impossible dream. Many were therefore immensely excited when South Korean media began to pay more attention to the archipelago. In 2013, actor Yoon Sang-hyun visited

Cuba to act as representative for Korea in a KOTRA stand in the Havana International Fair. In 2018, the Korean Broadcasting System's (KBS) *2 Days & 1 Night*, a reality-variety show that typically films cast members and guests traveling to different locations in South Korea, featured ten-year anniversary episodes in which the cast divided into two teams and traveled to Havana, Cuba, and Almaty, Kazakhstan, in search of their fans abroad. In response to this show, BTS created a video greeting for their Cuban fans. In 2018 to 2019, TVN aired the K-drama *Encounter*, in which an older and successful divorcée meets a younger man in Havana and they become smitten with one another, only to encounter social disapproval in Korea. Also in 2018 to 2019, relatively unknown actors Ryu Jun-yeol and Lee Je-hoon took a backpacking trip across Cuba in the JTBC ten-episode reality TV travel documentary *Traveler*.

Several fans told me that such shows were a welcome sign of South Korea's growing recognition of Cuba. At a copy festival, a group of teenage fans complained to me that Cuba was never included in the concert tours of K-pop stars. In the midst of this conversation, one young woman (age eighteen) recalled meeting the *2 Days & 1 Night* cast when they visited the Casa Cuba Corea. The Cuban Hallyu fans gathered for this event had been told to arrive for a KBS news report, she recalled. When they realized what show it was and saw the cast members, she was overcome by tears. "People who had been so distant were suddenly in front of me," she observed. Other fans reported being similarly moved by the BTS video greeting. Amalia (age fourteen) noted, "We always said that BTS didn't know anything about Cuba—that for them Cuba doesn't exist." When she first saw the video greeting that BTS had sent their Cuban fans, she recalled, "I started crying and screaming, because it didn't seem possible that they knew about Cuba." Finally, several fans shared with excitement their experiences of being extras on the set of *Encounter*. Aida (age twenty-six) and Mayda (age twenty-three) recalled following the leads of *Encounter* through the city until they secured their autographs and commented happily how, following the show, internet searches for Cuba had reportedly risen in Korea.

Yet these same South Korean media representations of Cuba also traded in well-worn stereotypes. Whether in newspaper editorials urging foreigners to visit Cuba "before it changes" or in musical projects that nostalgically recover aging musicians such as the Buena Vista Social Club, foreign media

"Soft" Koreans and "Sensual" Cubans

has consistently depicted Cuba as magically stuck in time, while repeat references to romance and passion play into stereotypes of Caribbeans and especially Afro-Caribbeans as hypersexual. Such depictions are backed by a predictable repertoire of images, including classic US and Russian Lada cars, ruined buildings, socialist billboards, rum, cigars, aging musicians, dance, seductive inhabitants, and picturesque shots of old Havana and the Malecón, the wall that separates Havana from the ocean. *2 Days & 1 Night* parted to some extent from such representations. The TV show depicts encounters with Korean descendants in Cuba and with Cuban Hallyu fans, thereby delving into a history that is little known even to Cubans. Yet even *2 Days & 1 Night* devotes copious amounts of time to Havana's typical tourist sites. In one scene, the show's hosts participate in a contest on the Malecón to see who can learn to salsa best. In another, they play a guessing game about which Cuban chauffeur is driving a classic US car; the award for winning is a city tour in a 1950s convertible.

Encounter and *Traveler*, for their part, treat Cuba as an exotic time capsule. In *Encounter*, the couple's mutual interest despite age and class differences is enabled by the romance of Havana, while the younger man's obsession with photographing the city through an antique camera relegates Cuba to relic. In the opening sequence of *Traveler*, a backpacker lists Che Guevara, Ernest Hemingway, cigars, mojitos, and Buena Vista Social Club as highlights of Cuba, then describes the archipelago in sonorous tones as a country that has "grown old and worn out." Other scenes depict the hosts' struggle to navigate Cuba's limited internet access or its aging technology, reinforcing what Benjamin Han (2022) refers to as an "infrastructural imaginary" in which only Korea emerges as modern. Significantly, numerous scenes depict the backpackers in the company of White Euro-North American tourists. Through such tactics, all three shows assert the rights of South Koreans to join White Euro-North Americans in consuming the pleasures of Global South nations such as Cuba. As Moisés Park shows in this volume, this tactic also comes to the fore in South Korean representations of other Latin American nations.

Geopolitical and racial hierarchies also emerged in the personal experiences of the few Cuban fans who were fortunate enough to travel to South Korea. After winning the Cuban national competition of the K-pop World Festival, the cover dance group Limitless traveled to South Korea to participate in a week-long training and live filming of a competition between winning groups from around the world. While the young women reported enthusiastically about their experience and their interaction with other competing groups at the festival, their experience was marked by obvious power differences. Limitless won the Cuban national competition performing the choreography for a lesser-known song, "Lilili Yabbay," by K-pop boy group Seventeen's performance team. They chose this choreography with care, they told me, because it "had a level of complexity that not everyone can master" and an unusual mix of "contemporary dance with hip-hop," then began practicing it in March for the July national competition. The group also went to great lengths to secure costumes that would emulate the look of the dancers in the music video, a task that was not easy given Cuba's widespread material shortages. A cousin of one dancer was entrusted with purchasing white shorts for the group in Panama, a riff on the white pants worn by the Seventeen performance team in the original music video (MV). The mother of another dancer designed and sewed white shirts for the group, working with fabric that the group was able to secure for an affordable price only at the last moment.

Despite these efforts, however, Limitless was asked by KBS to change their choreography to a cover dance of Blackpink's "Ddu-Du Ddu-Du" and to secure new costumes to fit the new performance only a week and a half before their trip to Changwon. As the group explained to me, this song by Blackpink was high in the charts at the time, and the KBS representative felt that its greater recognizability made it a better choice. It was also a more conventional match for the "Girl Crush" category in which Limitless was assigned to compete, suggesting that gender norms may have informed the KBS decision. Limitless refused the request that they secure new costumes, a demand that would have been impossible to meet in the time remaining and that revealed the organizers' ignorance of Cuban material and financial circumstances. But they reluctantly agreed to the request that they change their choreography. While Limitless members liked the Blackpink song, they told me, because of its simplicity, it was not a choreography they would have chosen. Nonetheless, they ceded out of fear that KBS would rescind their opportunity to compete. This made it all the more bitter for the group when they lost to a cover group from Ukraine, a group of all women who performed their originally chosen choreography, which, like Limitless's ini-

"Soft" Koreans and "Sensual" Cubans

tial choice, was by a K-pop boy group ("District 9" by Stray Kids). Further compounding geopolitical and racial inequalities, the televised competition prefaced each performance with a short video introduction to the competing group's nation of provenance. Echoing the stereotypes reproduced by other South Korean media representations of Cuba, Limitless's introduction begins with a close-up of a Cuban flag, salsa music, and an intertitle describing Cuba as "a country of romance and passion."

Race, Gender, and Respectability Politics

In early 2020, exoticizing stereotypes of Cubans also seemed set to manifest themselves in interpersonal relationships. Just before the COVID-19 pandemic put a temporary halt to my in-person fieldwork, I spoke with two young women in their late teens who had met South Korean boyfriends over internet dating applications. They described the romantic gestures and politeness of their South Korean boyfriends, who were themselves in their mid-thirties, and talked of their eventual plans to marry and migrate to South Korea. At least prior to the pandemic, South Korean interest in Cuba was thus beginning to resemble that of dynamics between the nation and many other countries, in which age- and power-gapped sex tourism and romance shape relationships between foreigners and Cubans dreaming of futures elsewhere.

The young women's characterizations of their foreign beaux, however, also suggested how gendered racial stereotypes shaped Cuban views of South Koreans. As noted earlier, Cuban and other Latin American and Caribbean nations have long been denied Whiteness on the global level even as elites valorized Whiteness within nations at the expense of Black, Indigenous, Asian, and darker-skinned peoples in the region. Similar to patterns throughout the Americas, Asian migration to Cuba commenced in the mid-nineteenth century. Amid growing threats to slave routes and a global demand for sugar, plantation owners turned to indentured Asian labor to supplement that of enslaved African peoples. The majority of indentured laborers in Cuba were Chinese, with approximately 125,000 arriving between 1857 and 1874. Beginning in the 1860s, a smaller influx of Chinese migrants with capital arrived (Hu-DeHart 2010; López 2010). The early twentieth century saw renewed efforts to contract Asian workers in Cuban agriculture. In 1905, following misleading recruitment advertisements, 1,033 Koreans left for Mexico to work in the henequen plantations in the Yucatán as indentured laborers. Their work contracts expired in 1909, but when Korea was colonized by Japan in 1910, their road home was blocked. In 1921, 288 Koreans from the Yucatán migrated to Cuba after hearing promises of a sugar boom and improved conditions of labor (Lim and Ruiz 2000).

Asian migrants to Cuba and the Americas encountered exploitative, dangerous, and often fatal work conditions as well as other forms of racism and xenophobia. Like other Cubans, they also faced family separation and further emigration following the 1959 Cuban Revolution and the nationalization of small businesses under the socialist government in 1968. The Korean-Cuban population also faced an additional burden of invisibility and a lack of institutional representation. In Cuba as elsewhere throughout Latin America, people with Asian phenotypical characteristics are referred to as *chino* with no regard for ethnicity. And while the Cuban state invested in the revitalization of Havana's Chinatown in 2006 as economic and political relations with China grew in importance, Korean Cubans were left out of official Cuban state support. They instead relied on South Korea's Overseas Korean Foundation to establish the Casa Cuba Corea in 2014, the first museum and cultural center dedicated to the Korean diaspora in Cuba.

In this context, Hallyu fandom has played an important role in intervening in anti-Asian racism and Korean-Cuban invisibility. Several non-Asian Cuban Hallyu fans reported being ostracized by friends and family for their interest in *esos chinos* ("those Chinese") and noted proudly how they corrected such statements by asserting Hallyu's Korean origins. Cuban Hallyu fans were also actively involved in the Casa Cuba Corea. The Casa Cuba Corea pursued its goal of maintaining and celebrating Korean culture and customs through a variety of cultural activities, including providing Korean language, cooking, and tae kwon do lessons; hosting encounters with visiting South Korean artists, such as the visit with the poet described earlier in this chapter; and preparing simple meals complete with kimchi. These activities were open to all, and, indeed, non-Asian Hallyu fans were in the majority at the events I attended.

Non-Asian Hallyu fans also contributed to the museum and its displays. An older woman hand-sewed traditional *hanbok* that were proudly displayed. Drawing only on a tourist pamphlet that didn't specify dimensions,

"Soft" Koreans and "Sensual" Cubans

a group of five younger women with training in architecture and design created an elaborate model of Seoul's Joseon Dynasty Gyeongbokgung Palace. This model, too, was a central attraction in the Casa Cuba Corea's exhibit. Several non-Asian Cuban Hallyu fans also used the Casa Cuba Corea as a recreational center. On one visit, I was ushered into a back room plastered with posters of K-pop and K-drama stars where three high school–aged girls were busy practicing K-pop choreographies. Their parents, they noted, had come to visit the Casa Cuba Corea and, once they reassured themselves that all involved were *gente decente* (good people), allowed the girls to spend their after-school time at the museum.

Hallyu fans in Cuba also often confronted gendered racial stereotypes of Asian people, without entirely escaping these stereotypes themselves. Hollywood and US media have long depicted Asian men as nerdy, asexual, and effeminate. The counter to such depictions, as Vincent Pham and Kent Ono (2009) rightly point out, should not be to assert normative or toxic masculinity. The soft masculinity promoted by South Korean popular culture thus suggests a possible solution, engendering a new valorization of Asian masculinity among fans while also licensing experimentation with alternate and queer masculinities (Kim 2021). As Kam Louie (2012) describes it, this pan–East Asian soft masculinity challenges ideals of competition and dominance, instead emphasizing urban stylishness, sensitivity, and treating women as friends rather than sex objects. As others have observed (Lee, Lee, and Park 2020), however, when fans naturalize soft masculinity and equate it with all Koreans or Asians, it can reinforce orientalizing stereotypes of Asian men as feminized and asexual.

A similarly ambivalent reception of South Korean soft masculinity can be seen among Cuban fans. Anticipating the descriptions of their real-life South Korean boyfriends by the fans noted above and akin to the reactions by Euro-North American fans discussed by Rebecca Chiyoko King-O'Riain in this volume, numerous women with whom I spoke praised the care and gentleness of Korean men protagonists in K-dramas. They were bemused by how it takes protagonists several episodes to kiss and contrasted this gentleness with both Latin American telenovelas and the real-life behavior of Latin American men. "In Brazilian novelas there are a lot of unhealthy scenes. People are having sex or kissing one another in ways that are too intense," observed Adela (age seventeen). "But in the Korean novelas you don't see this. For the protagonists to give each other a kiss it takes 7 or 8 episodes!" Tamara (cited above) explained that "Korean men aren't the typical Latino who is more forward and will tell you directly 'let's go to this place.' Korean men aren't like that, they take their time. They're the type of guy who is romantic. It's like the *principe azul* (Prince Charming). They dedicate time to you, words, and they show you every day that they care." Celia (cited above) concurred with this assessment, adding that the care Korean protagonists showed women contrasted drastically with Cuban men who, "if they buy you a beer, think you have to give them a kiss. It's like they're trading 2.50 CUC for a kiss."[2] Cuban fans often acknowledged the gap between K-dramas' rose-tinted romances and reality, while their assessments of Korean men protagonists resonate with depictions of romantic heroes as strong and nurturing that cross genres and national media. Indeed, such comments arguably served more as a criticism of enduring machismo or sexism within Cuba than as an assessment of South Korean men. Yet the ease with which fans slipped from discussions of fiction to reality and comparisons of Korean with Latin American men demonstrates how media reception fueled racial and cultural generalizations.

Discussions of the fashion sense and physical attributes of K-drama actors and K-pop idols similarly countered without overturning stereotypes of Asian men. Women fans of all ages gushed over the physical attractions of actors and idols, while young men found fashion inspiration in their favorite idols. Yet this admiration was also tinged with uneasiness over perceived effeminacy. Enrique (age twenty-one) noted that when his cousin first showed him a video of BTS, he liked the music but not the visuals "because they're always wearing makeup and they look like women." After a while, however, he began to see this as normal and adopted brightly colored hair and earrings after styles worn by BTS's Suga. Marcos (age twenty-four) was also inspired by the fashion sense of K-pop idols. "Korea and Japan are the cradle of fashion in Asia. Before fashions arrive in Latin America they are already there," he noted. In the K-pop scene in Cuba, he observed, he had found a space where he was accepted as a gay man while also avoiding what he viewed as the promiscuity of the circuits of gay men in Cuba.

Like Enrique, however, he found the makeup used by men K-pop idols excessive, albeit for reasons that seemed largely to reflect his fears about the perceptions of others. "When you want other guys to like K-pop and you show them a picture of one of the idols wearing makeup, the first thing they'll say to you is—is it a boy or a girl and then they call them gay," he lamented. Indeed, numerous fans reported being criticized by friends and family for liking "those effeminate gay *chinos*." One woman recounted how her nephew told her that Korean stars were all *pajaros* (birds, a slang term for gay). She responded, "it doesn't matter. If they're *pajaros*, then I'll make them a nest." In the best of cases, in sum, Cuban Hallyu fandom worked against stereotypes of Asian men and provided crucial space for young straight and queer Cuban men to experiment with an alternative masculinity. Yet in spite of their willingness to confront the homophobia and anti-Asian racism of friends and family, fans themselves manifested discomfort with what they, too, sometimes perceived as the excess femininity of male stars.

Cuban Hallyu fans also struggled with stereotypes of Asian women as docile and subservient. Similarly to what Min Suk Kim (2021, 177–213) observed in her study of Mexican and Peruvian K-pop fans, at the time of my research, the K-pop groups Blackpink and 2NE1 were among the most popular of girl groups, precisely because they were viewed as modeling a strong femininity that steered clear of what fans saw as the little girl image of Girls' Generation or the excessive sexualization of Hyuna. At the same time, as Limitless's original choice in choreography suggests, time and time again Cuban K-poppers insisted that they preferred the dance routines of K-pop boy groups because the movements were *fuerte* (strong), whereas the movements of K-pop girl groups were too *nanita* (little girl). Sometimes this led to criticism of the K-pop industry or to further research. One fan presented a comparative study of the history and rights of women in Korea versus Cuba as part of ARTCOR's Jornadas Científicas in 2020, suggesting how fans might work toward an inclusive global feminism. More often, however, the versions of femininity advanced by K-drama narratives and girl groups prompted fans to conclude that Korea and Asia lagged behind the West, including Cuba, in advancing the rights of women, a position that also foreclosed further critical analysis of gender in Cuba.

Finally, even as interests in South Korean popular culture opened possibilities for fans to challenge anti-Asian racism in Cuba, they also risked perpetuating classism and anti-Blackness. These tendencies were fueled by the respectability politics that underlay Cuban Hallyu fandom. Fans

Humphreys

repeatedly told me that part of the draw of K-pop was that it was *sano* (healthy) and inculcated values such as respect for the elderly, commitment to hard work, and avoidance of alcohol and other vices. One ARTCOR organizer insisted that the club restored values that had been lost in "this globalized world" and that it provided young people and elderly alike with a safe and healthy space for recreation. As elsewhere in Latin America, claims to respectability also figured in repeated contrasts between K-pop and reggaeton. Some fans insisted that reggaeton was good to dance to and distinguished between different genres. Many others, however, compared what they viewed as the genre's misogynistic, consumerist, and vulgar lyrics to K-pop. Elena (cited above) noted, "there are reggaetoneros whose music is good, but the ones people know sing profanities and talk poorly about women. There's a meme I like a lot in which there's a picture of a reggaetonero and it says: 'he was in prison, didn't finish his studies, and talks poorly about women.' And then it says, 'the rapper I like.' And there's an image of BTS that says, 'he was one of the three top students in his school and speaks several languages. So why do people criticize me for listening to healthy music that feeds my soul?'"

Misogyny and consumerism can indeed characterize reggaeton. Scholars, however, note that these issues are often just as prevalent in other genres while the moral panic that reggaeton elicits reflects efforts to enforce middle-class White standards of morality against music that has been historically associated with Black, urban, and working-class communities (Gámez Torres 2012; Rivera-Rideau 2015). K-poppers' defense of their taste in music and ARTCOR organizers' insistence on the social contributions of the fandom reflected their efforts to justify their activities in the context of homophobia, anti-Asian racism, and Cuban state suspicion of a foreign capitalist nation. At the same time, the repeated contrast of K-pop to reggaeton played into a respectability politics that perpetuated classism and an anti-Blackness that has long plagued the archipelago, despite state claims that racism was eradicated with the 1959 Cuban Revolution.

Conclusion

As this chapter has made clear, intersecting dynamics of race, gender, and sexuality were central to Cuban reception of South Korean media and

"Soft" Koreans and "Sensual" Cubans

South Korean media representation of Cuba. It is therefore significant that over sixty years after diplomatic relations between South Korea and Cuba were severed they were restored on February 14, Valentine's Day, 2024. South Korean state officials directly credited ARTCOR and the Cuban reception of South Korean popular culture alongside years of quiet diplomatic work for the historic event and celebrated it as a win in the battle to isolate North Korea (Ji 2024; Lee 2024). For its part, Cuba's cession was viewed by many commentators as a desperate bid to alleviate a devastating economic crisis sparked by the pandemic, spiraling inflation, an authoritarian crackdown on nationwide protests in July 2021, mass migration, and escalating US sanctions. Indeed, by 2024, ARTCOR itself had lost significant momentum as the result of the tragic death during the pandemic of the group's most popular president, Magalys Domínguez Santos, as well as migration and internal conflicts. And while commentators speculated about the potential of Cuba to serve as a new market for South Korean goods or as a destination for South Korean tourism, all acknowledged that US sanctions rendered such possibilities tenuous.

The outcomes of the normalization of diplomatic relations between Cuba and South Korea, therefore, remain to be seen. What this chapter has demonstrated is that while the global circulation of media can participate in transforming racial and geopolitical dynamics, it can also introduce new inequalities. Cuban and other Latin American nations have long been denied entry into Whiteness at the global and international level. South Korean media representations of Cuba and interactions between South Koreans and Cubans transformed this dynamic, but it did so by virtue of producing a new racial hierarchy in which South Koreans joined White Euro–North Americans at the apex, while Cubans, like other Global South nations, were treated as exotic but primitive. At the intranational level, the reception of South Korean media in Cuba combated anti-Asian racism but also sometimes participated in gendered racial stereotypes and anti-Blackness. It is only by bringing the inter- and the intranational levels together that we can see how the global circulation of South Korean media can at once displace White Euro-North American dominance and re/produce new racial hierarchies in which only some are incorporated into the privileges of Whiteness.

Notes

1. This fieldwork built on over a decade of ethnographic research on media in Cuba and entailed participant observation and semi-structured interviews with fifty-three Cuban Hallyu fans as well as South Koreans in Cuba. Quotations are taken from interviews conducted in Spanish by the author. Pseudonyms have been used to protect the identity of interlocutors. Because of the history of *mestizaje* or racial mixing and the existence of multiple and shifting racial categories in everyday use in Cuba, as in many other Latin American nations, racial identifications can have complex relationships to an individual's lived experience and personal biography. For this reason, I identify individuals' race only when this was clearly known and is immediately relevant to the argument, while nevertheless playing close attention to how race played out in broader, structural terms. This research was made possible by generous grants from the Wenner-Gren Foundation and Tulane University's COR Research Fellowship, the Carol Lavin Bernick Faculty Grant, the Stone Center for Latin American Studies, and Newcomb College Institute. Special thanks to David Oh for his astute feedback.

2. Cuban convertible pesos or CUC was a second official Cuban currency, roughly equivalent to the US dollar.

References

Cusicanqui, Silvia Rivera. 2012. "Ch'ixinakax utxiwa: A Reflection on the Practices and Discourses of Decolonization." *South Atlantic Quarterly* 111 (1): 95–109. https://doi.org/10.1215/00382876-1472612.

Gámez Torres, Nora. 2012. "Hearing the Change: Reggaeton and Emergent Values in Contemporary Cuba." *Latin American Music Review* 33 (2): 227–60.

Han, Benjamin M. 2019. "Fantasies of Modernity: Korean TV Dramas in Latin America." *Journal of Popular Film and Television* 47 (1): 39–47. https://doi.org/10.1080/01956051.2019.1562823.

———. 2022. "Reckoning with the World: Infrastructural Imaginaries of Cuba in Contemporary Korean Television." *Seoul Journal of Korean Studies* 35 (1): 51–73. https://doi.org/10.1353/seo.2022.0004.

Hu-DeHart, Evelyn. 2010. "Indispensable Enemy or Convenient Scapegoat? A Critical Examination of Sinophobia in Latin America and the Caribbean, 1870s to 1930s." In *The Chinese in Latin America and the Caribbean*, edited by Walton Look Lai and Tan Chee-Beng, 65–102. Leiden, Netherlands: Brill.

Humphreys, Laura-Zoë. 2021. "Loving Idols: K-pop and the Limits of Neoliberal

Solidarity in Cuba." *International Journal of Cultural Studies* 24 (6): 1009–26. https://doi.org/10.1177/13678779211024665.

———. 2022. "Utopia in a Package? Digital Media Piracy and the Politics of Entertainment in Cuba." *boundary 2: An International Journal of Literature and Culture* 49 (1): 231–62. https://doi.org/10.1215/01903659-9615473.

Ji, Da-gyum. 2024. "Seoul Side-Eyes N. Korea while Forging Ties with Cuba." *Korea Herald*, February 15, 2024. https://www.koreaherald.com/view.php?ud=20240215050592.

Kim, Min Suk. 2021. "Hallyu Fandom in Mexico City and Lima: Soft Power, Gender, and New Media Self-Fashioning of Transcultural Youth." PhD diss., University of Texas at Austin.

Larkin, Brian. 1997. "Indian Films and Nigerian Lovers: Media and the Creation of Parallel Modernities." *Africa: Journal of the International African Institute* 67 (3): 406–40. https://doi.org/10.2307/1161182.

Lee, Jaeeun. 2024. "Seoul Touts Economic Potential of S. Korea-Cuba Ties." *Korea Herald*, February 18, 2024. https://www.koreaherald.com/view.php?ud=20240218050102&ACE_SEARCH=1.

Lee, Jeehyun Jenny, Rachel Kar Yee Lee, and Ji Hoon Park. 2020. "Unpacking K-pop in America: The Subversive Potential of Male K-pop Idols' Soft Masculinity." *International Journal of Communication* 14: 5900–5919.

Lim Kim, Martha, and Raúl Ruiz. 2000. *Coreanos en Cuba*. Havana: Fundación Fernando Ortiz.

López, Kathleen. 2010. "The Revitalization of Havana's Chinatown: Invoking Chinese Cuban History." In *The Chinese in Latin America and the Caribbean*, edited by Walton Look Lai and Tan Chee-Beng, 211–36. Leiden, Netherlands: Brill.

Louie, Kam. 2012. "Popular Culture and Masculinity Ideals in East Asia, with Special Reference to China." *Journal of Asian Studies* 71 (4): 929–43.

Mignolo, Walter D. 2005. *The Idea of Latin America*. Malden, MA: Blackwell Publishing.

Min, Wonjung, Dal Yong Jin, and Benjamin Han. 2018. "Transcultural Fandom of the Korean Wave in Latin America: Through the Lens of Cultural Intimacy and Affinity Space." *Media, Culture and Society* 41 (5): 604–19. https://doi.org/10.1177/0163443718799403.

Ono, Kent A., and Vincent Pham. 2009. *Asian Americans and the Media*. Cambridge: Polity Press.

Rivera-Rideau, Petra R. 2015. *Remixing Reggaetón: The Cultural Politics of Race in Puerto Rico*. Durham, NC: Duke University Press.

Rivero, Yeidy M. 2015. *Broadcasting Modernity: Cuban Commercial Television, 1950–1960*. Durham, NC: Duke University Press.

Schulze, Marion. 2013. "Korea vs. K-Dramaland: The Culturalization of K-Dramas by International Fans." *Acta Koreana* 16 (2): 367–97. https://doi.org/10.18399/acta.2013.16.2.004.

Straubhaar, Joseph D. 1991. "Beyond Media Imperialism: Asymmetrical Interdependence and Cultural Proximity." *Critical Studies in Mass Communication* 8 (1): 39–59. https://doi.org/10.1080/15295039109366779.

Tsang, Martin A. 2017. "The Power of Containing and the Containing of Power: Creating, Collecting, and Documenting an Afro-Cuban Lukumí Beaded Vessel." *Journal of Museum Ethnography* (30): 125–147.

PART II

......

Intersectional Connection and Imaginaries

6

······

Latin Orientalism and Anglo Hegemony in Korean Rock

Seo Taiji's "Moai" (2009)

······

MOISÉS PARK

South Korean cultural products often reproduce Anglo-hegemonic tendencies that inherit and inadvertently perpetuate racial hierarchies (Anderson 2020; Kim 2021). In turn, the audience internalizes "Latin Orientalism," in which cultural products represent Latin America with encoded ethno-racial hierarchies contributing to Asians and also Latin Americans as alien and exotic. The audience negotiates its own positionality as well as the represented racialized subjects within the larger scheme of hegemonic structures. Commercial musical cultural products from South Korea reiterate countercultural aspects from Anglo hegemony addressing social issues that could be universal calls for solidarity and social justice (Anderson 2020; Jenkins 1992). This chapter examines the reception of Korean Anglo hegemony through a messianic representation in "Moai" (2009), a music video by one of Korea's most influential rock star, Seo Taiji (b. 1972). The music video was partially filmed in Rapa Nui (Easter Island), where nearly one thousand enigmatic moai statues reside and are central to the song and music video. The music video exemplifies racialized views of Latin America (and Polynesia) filtered through mystic orientalism and racial subalternity. In turn, the reception of mystic orientalism in "Moai" is that of internalized racialization that Chileans and Polynesians are otherized, neglected, or ignored in the imaginary of K-pop audiovisual narratives.

The chapter will combine reception and textual analysis in order to examine how the audience negotiates racialized meanings encoded in the video. The visual aspect of the form, music video, will be emphasized rather than the lyrics or any other live performances or covers, as the visual narratives of the media reveal interpretations that are undetected in an exclusive close reading of the lyrics. Since most of the lyrics are in Korean, unless the audience knows or recognizes Hangul or revisits the lyrics, much of the reception highly relies on the visuals. In other words, a close reading of "Moai" is of less interest for this study. Though apologetic readings of the music video are plentiful, the interpretations offered here are critical. Enough is said about Seo Taiji's seminal role in fighting censorship laws, his explicit rebellious songs and music videos that resist the so-called K-pop idol aesthetic and ideology, and his contributions to less market-driven structures (Jung 2017, 144–45). Yet ultimately, highly influential aspects of Anglo hegemony in Korean (pop/alt) rock can still be traced in his evolving and versatile projects.

This chapter dialogues with established and developing studies of reception of Korean music and fandom studies. Two other chapters in this volume are relevant works for comparison as they both also intersect studies of race and ethnicity as part of the subjective globalization of Korean popular culture. Crystal S. Anderson's chapter in this volume analyzes reaction content creators who do not identify as fans and react positively to popular Korean music, challenging stereotypes of Black K-pop fans as "culture police" who recognize cultural appropriation in K-pop. Similarly, this chapter will also draw some insights from fan and non-fan comments and how race and ethnicity intersect with racialized hierarchies derived in the music video. YouTube engagement often overrepresents fans; thus, user-generated comments might provide some evidence of internalized normative structures of Anglo hegemony. These comments reveal aspects of users' identity politics and geopolitics that confirm some previous studies regarding K-pop reception. Laura-Zoë Humphreys's chapter in this volume includes ethnographic work with Cuban fans, which is instrumental in addressing how fans' reception of Korean popular culture shapes their imaginary of Cuba and Korea. Although my chapter focuses on representation and reception of Easter Island in a music video, Humphreys supplements reception studies through analysis of social media platforms. She theorizes that anti-Blackness and middle-class civility explain Cuban fans' com-

Park

parison of Korean popular culture with reggaeton. Likewise, my chapter extrapolates comments from YouTube confirming the normativity of Seo's hegemonic mimicking of Anglo rock music, compared to idol aesthetics.

Methodology

For this chapter, YouTube comments were collected using the open-source tool for text mining Textable, which helps extrapolate significant information in a less subjective manner, in order to detect patterns, trends, language recognition, and so on. Language recognition software was used to determine the languages represented in the online comments of the music video. Since racial and ethnic identities of comments were not knowable, only the content that revealed geographic or linguistic self-identification was used to determine demographic categorizations. In other words, text mining software was used to establish if comments were representative of national origin/residence, which can further determine some racial/ethnic standpoint. Needless to say, the data is incomplete and insufficient as it mostly relies on subjects who choose to leave comments, which in the case of this music video tends to be overwhelmingly favorable. The demographic data of the commentors is not public information, but enough evidence determines that the vast majority of commentators are Korean-speaking fans or are familiar with Korean pop music and have positive reception of this act. Text mining attempted to focus on the fewer comments from English and Spanish speakers that might reveal some perspectives on their reception and how those non-Korean viewers negotiated meaning from the music video.

In addition, a survey of twenty Chilean subjects between the ages thirty and fifty was conducted to examine the reception of "Moai." All twenty Chileans interviewed did not consider themselves K-pop fans, in order to avoid the apologetic defensive attitudes that might be contrasted to YouTube comments, which are likely younger and frequent listeners of Korean popular music. None of the subjects interviewed are aware of Seo Taiji's fame or musical trajectory. Five of the interviewees identified as Rapa Nui, so their answers included some reflections of racial and ethnic representation or lack thereof. Interviewees were surveyed in Spanish and in person, by phone conversation, and through social media platform messaging systems or distance communication between October 5, 2022, and January 5, 2023. Chilean and Rapa Nui comments responded in Spanish to the following questions: (1) How are Rapa Nui culture and Rapa Nui people represented in the music video "Moai"? (2) Please share any comments on this Korean performer writing and singing about moais in Rapa Nui and then performing and filming a music video in Rapa Nui, featuring the island. I acknowledge that my positionality as a middle-aged academic Korean Latino cisgender male might have impacted the responses, even if most of these interviews were conducted through social media platforms with chat features and in the interviewees' native language.

Easter(n) Island: Alienizing Rapa Nui Culture

With about 1.3 million views in Seo Taiji's official YouTube channel, the "Moai" music video has no "reaction videos," which are common for many idol groups and other K-pop acts. The vast majority of the 1,310 comments (more than 85 percent) are by Korean speakers, which confirms that Seo Taiji's reception and fame is limited mostly among Koreans and Korean speakers, compared to idol groups that are part of global K-pop or Hallyu. Those remarks in Korean barely mention Chile and focus on the song and the celebration of the artist's comeback. English speakers and Spanish speakers also tend to provide succinct positive reactions. For instance, among the more noticeable comments in Spanish, a 2021 user writes, "125 losers did not like it (10 YEARS SINCE THIS MASTERPIECE!)."[1] The response reveals prejudice against idol group fanatism: "K-pop fans surely do not like this." This interaction might distinguish a Spanish speaker's differentiation of pop rock that happens to be in Korean and what the user pejoratively refers to as "kpop moda" ("k-pop trend"), as if (alt) rock is not a trend and the idol fanatism is merely a fleeting devotion, of lesser quality and longevity. It is not surprising that rock is often elevated over K-pop, as K-pop fandom has a younger following, mostly women, and fans who are not always public about their fandom, whereas rock fans do not experience the same stigma. Another comment in Spanish recognizes Seo's fame, and it can be assumed that the commentator is Chilean: "It's 2021 and I still cannot believe that Seo Taiji has come to the island to shoot this song. . . . A great singer."

Overall, the word "Chile" appears seventeen times in English and Span-

Park

ish comments to the video, but in Hangul it appears only twice. Most of those comments thank Seo Taiji for being in Chile or visiting the island. The words "Easter Island" appear only twice (omitting users who posted the lyrics of the song), while "Isla de Pascua" and "Rapa Nui" appear five times and once, respectively. In other words, the country is mentioned more than the island. Outside Chile, the island is seldom referred to with the original Indigenous name "Rapa Nui," which explains why it is only mentioned once, most likely by a Chilean netizen. On the contrary, the word "moai" or in Hangul appears twice as much (omitting references to the title), agreeing with Seo Taiji's fascination with the up to thirty-three-feet statues and the natural beauty of the isle.

The reception of the music video by Korean-speaking netizens is almost exclusively and positively centered on the singer. The othering of the statues and the complete omission of the residents, in turn, highlight his presence. Rapa Nui culture is minimized as moais become a backdrop to his crooning, implicitly suggesting the cliché of "the savages" that blend into nature and hide. The ending, moreover, literally alienizes the inhabitants of the isle by showing the only residents as extraterrestrials. The word for extraterrestrial (or alien) in Korean, *Wae Gae In* (외계인), appears ten times, in the context of the ones responsible for the moais or that the singer himself is "out of this world." No obvious comments criticize the singer or the music video, predictably confirming that music video engagement tends to highlight fandom rather than criticism.

Among comments in English, a few make comparisons to other orientalized cultural products: "Seo Taiji sounds like an anime, sorry i know he makes me feel a japanese aura, I dont know. Im crazy i know, but anywhere he is the best in the world" (2019). The panethnicism of "anime" or "japanese aura" is not surprising, as Seo Taiji's musical trajectory acknowledges what is generally popular without going back to the 1990s idol aesthetics that he once championed but opts for heavier rock and more electronic sounds, which were popular early in the twenty-first century. It is ironic that one comment in English exclaims, "Come to chile seo taiji! <3" in a comment for a video shot in Chile. Perhaps, the invitation is for future visits (i.e., coming again), but it could also be interpreted as inviting him to come to "mainland Chile" or the much more populated capital Santiago, since the images from Chile are limited to Rapa Nui and the northern region.

Latin Orientalism and Anglo Hegemony

Additionally, most Rapa Nui and Chilean subjects interviewed find the musical project "interesting" and with "uplifting lyrics" if they read the translation. They also shared that they did not expect this to be Korean. "If you close your eyes this is just a pop rock song from the US." Their understanding of Korean music was reduced to boy bands and girl bands, or Psy's viral "Gangnam Style" (2012). In other words, the vocalization and sonic experience was difficult for the audience to distinguish between Seo Taiji's Korean lyrics and other pop rock songs in English. "Korean music" can be as familiar as "Anglo music" even if the interviewee was semi-fluent in English. Singing vocal articulation often distorts the language to the point that even fluent English speakers have trouble deciphering the lyrics. Some remarks were less about the lyrical and musical content than the visual content of the video. For instance, one of the Rapa Nui interviewees was noticeably bothered that the band was "touching ... [and were] too close" to the statues, which are now protected from tourists who used to be able to touch and even climb them. More recent policies created barriers and limited spaces for visitors with noticeable distance from moais. Four non-islander Chileans mentioned that the alien connection was predictable but not offensive, although my Korean last name, phenotype, and academic positionality might have derailed possible talks of cultural appropriation and excessive use of exoticism to portray (or omit) Rapa Nui. When further discussing my own reception of the music video, there were some more candid comments regarding disapproval: "It all sounds the same: K-pop, Anglo music.... Better than the kid groups ["los grupos con cabros"], but still not what I prefer." Most interviewees immediately recognized that some of the images are not from the island but from the Northern Chilean desert (Atacama) and North America, specifically Niagara Falls. In fact, the climax of the music video was not filmed in Easter Island at all but in Northern Chile using visual effects.

Korean netizens overwhelmingly reacted with praise with minimal mentions of Chile and the statues. In other words, the otherizing of Rapa Nui was so normalized that it resulted in no mentions of the people or of the proven fact that these giants were built and transported throughout the isle by local Indigenous peoples. Although most documentaries of Rapa Nui include the people and re-enactments of their ancestors' lives, the music video opted to present an island completely uninhabited, recalling archetypes of White archaeologists who discover abandoned ruins and theorize about the source of the ancient civilization's demise. The results are not surprising as the audience negotiates differing meanings for evolving projects by the star. During much of his last two albums with Seo Taiji and Boys (1991–96), songs such as "Classroom Idea" (1994) echoed Rage Against the Machine, becoming social commentaries of South Korea's cultural conservatism, prison-like educational system, and authoritarian censorship. But in his solo career, most of his songs can be eclectic enough that no political and social commentary is as explicit as his trio's final two albums. "Moai" exemplifies that departure from controversy, and the user-generated comments reflect that lack of explicit social commentary that made him the relevant censorship challenger he became in the 1990s.

Coincidentally, Rapa Nui received its Westernized name Easter Island (Isla de Pascua, meaning Easter, in Spanish) on Easter Sunday, April 5, 1722, when Dutch explorer Jacob Roggeveen "found" the island while looking for Terra Australis or Davis Land, which he called Paaseiland ("named Paasch Island or Paasch Land after Paasch meaning Easter Day") (Roggeveen 1970). In other words, the more globally known name of the island is from the Western perspective, whether it is in Dutch, English, or Spanish. By positioning Rapa Nui in a subaltern imagined community, mediated by English, the island is reformulated as Latin Orientalism by not challenging normative Eurocentric White masculinity and, in turn, whitewashing modern pop music Koreanness as an extension of Anglo-hegemonic soft power. In other words, the original East/West binary that Edward Said ([1978] 1979) problematized, in which the Orient is represented as bizarre, has evolved to renewed ways to reformulate the East/West dichotomy, in which South Koreans model Western and Anglo White Savior archetypes. Other approaches that are delimited by reductionist binaries (e.g., North vs. Global South) are insufficient to address the reality that Anglo hegemony still dominates in Korean popular music, even in genres that are not as market driven as idol groups, such as acts in (alt) rock, namely Seo Taiji's solo projects. The musical genre might be linked to youth rebellion and angst but was and still is highly influenced by music in English. In turn, this music video ascribes to messianic discourses of contemporary multinational neoliberal triumphalism, in spite of efforts to distance themselves as

Latin Orientalism and Anglo Hegemony

alternative to formulaic idol production. The fandom of the rock star seems overshadowed by the more successful idol projects, which does not surprise, as solo acts since Seo Taiji and Boys tend to fall behind in commercial success compared to idol groups or former members of groups, with few exceptions in the earlier stages of the "second wave" of Hallyu (BoA, Rain, and Seven) or more recently in the "third wave" (IU and Chungha). The view count and the comment engagement confirm that fandom is much more active with idol groups, but the engagement is also generational and gender specific. Demographics for idol group fandom is largely younger and female, although some studies demonstrate that fandom has become less homogeneous. The reception, nonetheless, welcomes and normalizes the view that Koreans are part of the neoliberal gaze in which South Korea is positioned as part of the Anglo hegemony. However, examining reception through rhetorical analysis and reader-response methods is still lacking, and this chapter hopes to dialogue with other chapters in this volume and other publications that focus on audience reception and responses.

Rock and Hip Hop before K-pop: Seo Taiji

Seo Taiji is often recognized as the pioneer of what is now called K-pop. He was relatively prominent in the 1980s rock scene as a bass guitar player for Sinawi, a legendary act on its own. Seo Taiji then evolved over the following decades to explore other subgenres, including rock ballad, folk fusion rock, rap metal, heavy metal, nu metal, punk rock, and alt rock. He is known for introducing subgenres of rock to Korean mainstream but most importantly for becoming an icon of youth rebellion. Since the 1990s, he has reinvented himself in ways that have led some to refer to Korean popular music marked by initial social insurrection in the 1990s as an aftermath of the "Seo Taiji Syndrome" (Jung 2017, 143–45). Currently, though less radical, he has regained popularity and recognition due to acknowledgment from idol groups (most notably BTS on the twenty-fifth anniversary of Seo Taiji's solo debut) and other cultural events that recognize him as a major turning point in Korea's development of contemporary music.

"Moai" was the first single of a three-part project that was also known as a "mystery project" trilogy. According to the singer himself, he was fascinated by moais since he was young (Hong 2013a). It is a fascination

Park

often shared not only by mainland Chileans but also by many outsiders, exacerbated by media that mention the isle as an enigmatic place with giant stones. South Korean mass cultural products have very limited mentions of Chile, and they can be reduced to Salvador Allende's rise to power (1970–73), Augusto Pinochet's military government (1974–90), tourism, winery, and fishery, or in literary circles, mentions of Nobel Laureates Pablo Neruda and, to a much lesser degree, Gabriela Mistral. In 2019 to 2020, however, Chile's most massive social unrest in history, known as the *Estallido Social*, was linked to K-pop, as a local newspaper leaked that the Chilean Ministry of Interior named "K-pop fans" as responsible for some of the protests. The scandal was part of a big data analysis of social media activity, which became highly ridiculed as K-pop is often viewed as escapist and apolitical (Park 2019). South Korea does not have a major historical and cultural link with Chile, compared to other Latin American countries such as Argentina, Brazil, and Paraguay, which have a much larger Korean diaspora. Chileans' perception of Korea and Koreans is changing and evolving due to an increased visibility of K-pop and K-drama, Korean electronic and car brands, and a growing workforce due to large Korean companies such as Samsung, LG, and POSCO opening branches and offices in Chile.

When it comes to Easter Island, however, the territory is seldom linked to Chile but rather is disconnected to the geopolitical Chilean territory and Latin America. Similarly, in mainland Chile, self-orientalization of Rapa Nui is common, as the island's cultural trajectory is recognized. Although it has been politically associated to the mainland since 1888, it preserves its Polynesian roots, practices, and identity. Rapa Nui have strived to preserve autonomy and, with failed attempts, to keep mainlanders from exploiting the isle. Moreover, moais are presented as the esoteric side of Chile, seldom considered Latin America but rather a Polynesian liminal place, which happens to be geopolitically Chilean. Outsiders looking into the dances, clothing, and phenotype predictably position the island in Polynesia rather than "the Americas."

In the 2011 mini documentary *Seotaiji Moai: The Film*, Seo Taiji explains: "Easter Island: Rapa Nui is known for being the most mysterious island in the world. The many legendary Moais are a mystic presence. . . . I have been waiting for this moment and I finally have met them" (Hong 2013b). He kneels and bows down to moais while smiling and laughing.

Latin Orientalism and Anglo Hegemony

The dialectic attitude of worship-mockery culminates as he says that the stones resemble an alien or Ultraman. For the Korean musician, moais are extraterrestrial or resemble a fictional character. Ultraman is a *tokusatsu* superhero from Japan; *tokusatsu* is a Japanese term to refer to characters in a sci-fi realm that are created with a type of special effect very popular in Japanese films and TV shows, which employ a combination of puppetry, heavy costumes, rudimentary visual techniques, and mechanical tricks that seem theatrical. In the early 1990s, *tokusatsu* aesthetics and narratives were successfully readapted for US audiences with the *Mighty Morphin Power Rangers* (1993–96). Fans will quickly notice the self-referential fascination with the Japanese character Ultraman from his hit song on his second solo album, *Ultramania* (2000), which also introduced nu metal to Koreans. This genre was highly popular globally in the late nineties. Although the genre was particularly consumed by suburban, White men, Seo Taiji had already amassed a fandom among Korean Gen Xers and millennials who welcomed his versatility appropriating sounds that were flooding American radio and MTV. In that sense, not only did Seo Taiji effectively mimic Black music in the 1990s, he reinvented his sound and look to mimic nu metal and pop punk aesthetics from the United States as well. He is sonically but more importantly transracially and transculturally performative in order to adapt or appropriate Anglo aesthetics into Korean bodies, featuring red dreadlocks during his nu metal phase but eventually evolving into a clean-cut, professionally dressed look in the past decade.

The nu metal audience in the American scene overrepresented White and male, reinstating rock's often homosocial creation and reception, countering the fandom that was created by White boy bands in the 1990s, which was mostly White and female. Seo Taiji's fandom has at times been male dominated, although he has had a large female fandom since 1992, during his height as the original "king of K-pop" and "boy band" model with the trio act, which also danced and sang romantic ballads. However, this particular music video was part of his solo project that distanced itself from boy band aesthetics and predictably resembled rock that was more successfully consumed globally in the first decade of the twenty-first century, such as Arctic Monkeys, Blink-182, Creed, Evanescence, Green Day, Limp Bizkit, and Linkin Park. Part I (2008) and Part II (2009) of Seo Taiji's albums echo what was highly successful in the previous few years globally.

"Moai" ends with retro visual aesthetics, a noticeable 16mm grainy filter as if he were in an early century excursion led by groups of European men in exotic places à la *Indiana Jones*. It also reminds us of images in *Tierra sola* (*Solitary Land*, 2017), a documentary by Tiziana Panizza and Macarena Fernández, which compiles and edits thirty-two documentaries from 1935 to 1970 in an attempt to create a visual narrative that features more natives and their testimonies in postcolonial context, rather than the moais. Panizza writes that after surveying those thirty-two old reels, "there are more moais." She carefully "counted more images of moais than people," confirming that historically, the statues eclipse local residents and towns, highlighting the interest of the stones by previous filmmakers who had visited Rapa Nui in the early and mid-century: "As if people disappeared. As if escape was possible."

The documentary argues that Rapa Nui people had been colonized and oppressed to the point that their own land and island had become a prison. In Seo Taiji's video, filtered clips in 1:1 ratio images of the statues are edited along with "reels" from their visit to Niagara Falls to recreate the early century travel film cliché of a tropical exotic space with an emblematic waterfall, cinematically a motif that signifies the beauty-danger dialectic of foreign places. These mysterious statues, desertic canyons (San Pedro Atacama in Northern Chile), and waterfalls are part of iconic exotic spaces in the global imaginary, which are often deserted or inhabited by mysterious "savages," or in the case of this music video, aliens responsible for giant statues. This moment recalls Hye Jean Chung's (2017) reformulation of Foucault's heterotopia (1971, 1984), as she asserts that multiple editing and filmmaking tools create a digital reality so convincing that the labor is erased in the eyes of the audiences. The climax of the video consists of an earthquake followed by the rise of three massive flying saucers leaving Nazca Line–like symbols on the land before disappearing into the sky: the mystery of the statues is thus resolved by alien entities hid underneath the island whose civilizations are responsible for the statues. Steven Spielberg's 2008 film *Indiana Jones and the Kingdom of the Crystal Skull* (a year prior to the "Moai" music video) culminates in alien spaceships as responsible for the mythical underground city of Akator. The 2009 music video removes any evidence of human involvement and also opts for the more commercially appealing suggestion that mysterious aliens are responsible for the

Latin Orientalism and Anglo Hegemony

giant statues. Nevertheless, since the 1990s, groundbreaking research and experiments that later were proven by several archaeologists and engineers have replicated the manufacturing and ingenious methods to transport the giants (Lipo and Hunt 2005; Lipo, Hunt, and Haoa 2013). Yet the fascination of aliens or extraterrestrials has not ceased, as confirmed by a 2023 US congressional hearing about unidentified flying objects (UFOs) or unidentified anomalous phenomena (UAPs) that have once again normalized Westerners' "discovery" of mysteries in the Orientalized East/Global South/Third World.

At the very end of the music video, including Egyptian hieroglyphics insists on the mystery of the moais as evocative of the "secret" origin and construction of the pyramids: namely, that aliens and not local Indigenous civilizations have built those monuments. Rapa Nui, Ancient Egypt, and the Inca Empire are all commonly otherized spaces that popular pseudo-archaeologists have exploited as alien-manufactured constructions. The theories that moais and pyramids were built by extraterrestrials rather than humans are legacies of hegemonic supremacist revisionisms, still perpetuated today by popular media such as the History Channel (Burns 2009) and *National Geographic* (Drake 2017) and debunked by several other platforms, including PBS (Nova/PBS Online Adventures 1998) and the BBC (Broome 2000). A postcolonial reading unveils an ideological hierarchy in which Indigenous cultures, civilizations from the Global South, are not capable of sophisticated architecture or art. Rapa Nui is not considered part of the civilized Western world, though it is politically a Chilean territory, part of Latin American geopolitics, but located in the southeasternmost point of the Polynesian Triangle in Oceania, bordering Oceanian (or Australian) and American continents. It is by far the closest Chilean territory to Korea. Nevertheless, Rapa Nui is often considered less Chilean or Latin American and more of an isolated mysterious island, a "special territory," and it happens to be colonized by and annexed to Chile. The statues have become a metonymy and the semiotic of mystery to the world: evidence, like many other ruins, that large civilizations become extinct and an oral history no longer exists to trace the origins of some buildings and artifacts.

Seo refers to the stones as a source of inspiration: muses that are anthropomorphic but uncanny enough to suggest that they do not have a real link to the isle's inhabitants or even humanity. It is not the only time

Korean singers use the image of moais. Four years after "Moai" was re-leased, during a cover of "Gracias a la vida" by ballad singer duo Davichi in 2014, the background image onstage was a brightly saturated red sunset in Easter Island and easily distinguishable silhouettes of enigmatic moai statues (Park 2019, 35). A multi-band tour organized by Music Bank, a Korean music show and K-pop promoter, planned to orchestrate a show that would honor Chile's most iconographic images while covering the most popular and recognizable Chilean tune. The reference to the island was exclusively limited to the moais, and though the duo sang a Chilean song in Spanish, Rapa Nui people and Chilean people in general were not featured anywhere in the staging or the visual narratives in the background or the act. In other words, Koreans were the featured protagonists in these acts, and local fans were fully relegated to the role of observers and listeners. Likewise, weeks after the release of "Moai," Seo Taiji replicated giant moais as part of a live performance in 2010; surrounded by the statues, Seo Taiji re-enacted the performance in the music video, again without evidence of the isle's inhabitants. Ethnographic studies show that audience members in 2014 recall the euphoria of seeing Korean singers acknowledging the racial and ethnic diversity in the act by recognizing how the Korean music industry catered to local audiences (Park 2019, 32–34). In other words, by using images of moais and singing an iconic popular Chilean song, the Chilean audience felt the visitors seemed to acknowledge what imagery was considered "local" or "Chilean."

Paradoxically, Easter Island is less alien and arguably more Eastern (Asian), which problematizes the illusory binary racialization of local Rapa Nui. According to several and a growing number of anthropologists and geneticists, there is abundant evidence that Rapa Nui has genetically more Asian (possibly Taiwanese and Southeast Asian) than "Latin American" or Euro-American ancestry (Bellwood and Dizon 2008; Oppenheimer 2004). In other words, there is an anthropological case that argues that ancestral Rapa Nui are genetically more Asian than Indigenous South American or Euro-American (the vast racial and genetic composition of mainland Chileans) (Hagelberg, Cox, and Schiefenhövel 2008). Chileans, however, do recognize that, racially, Rapa Nui are significantly different from mainland Chileans who claim a majority mestizo discourse, mentioning the larger Indigenous Mapuche ancestry as well as the Peninsular Spanish heritage.

Latin Orientalism and Anglo Hegemony

Nicolás Palacios's *Raza chilena* (1904) theorizes that Chileans can mostly be identified with the figure of the *roto*—that is, the mestizo race that came from the militarily minded and two "superior" races from two continents: the Visigoths of Spain and the Mapuche Indigenous peoples of Chile. In a later edition (1918), Palacios mentions the islanders but not as part of the Chilean racial composition but rather as victims of abuses even if they are fellow countrymen ("compatriotas") and live in a "fertile land" that could be military strategic and more populated by Chileans from the "mainland" (1918). In fact, he is disappointed that the island is not populated enough and that the federal government is not doing enough to manage the "vacated" island. The book seldom addresses the people on the island, as if their minority status does not implicate anything to his insights about the "Chilean race" or "Chilean people." Understanding Rapa Nui culture through the lens of Chilean mestizo foundational mythology exoticizes that Polynesian side of Chilean demographics. It glamorizes the hybridity and to a certain extent the harmony of two "master races" in Chileans mestizos, who happen to be in the "mainland."

Modern Korean music certainly gained in popularity as musicians appropriated several aspects of Anglo/Western aesthetics. For instance, Seo Taiji rose to fame in 1992 with "Nan Arayo" ("I Know"), which blended new jack swing rhythm, rap, and rock, and as many critics increasingly point out, much of the aesthetics, both musically and visually, come from Black culture. "Nan Arayo" has obvious similarities with Milli Vanilli's 1989 "Girl You Know It's True." Additionally, "Come Back Home" (1995) has been criticized for sounding like "Insane in the Membrane" (1993) by Cypress Hill. Needless to say, K-pop has been borrowing and sampling much of African American culture and art with limited acknowledgment of this practice since the 1980s and '90s (Anderson 2020). In the twenty-first century, the genre has evolved away from the initial importation and sampling of African American music but with an ongoing musical importation from Anglo hegemony (although Seo's solo projects still include highly harmonized songs that recall 1980s and '90s R&B).

Kyung Hyun Kim's concept of hegemonic mimicry is helpful to address Seo's evolution. Hegemonic mimicry addresses "that the Korean popular culture that blossomed during the twenty-first century was incubated from a contested field of negotiation between two national identities—the hegemonic American culture and the local culture—and between . . . two racialized subjectivities, off-white and blackish" (Kim 2021). Seo's solo projects since 1998 have what Kim would consider noticeable "adaptation of American sensibilities and genres" that homogenize global racial subjectivities contemplating "off-white and blackish" as models (Kim 2021). All of Seo Taiji's albums and songs now have English titles or at least provide a translation from Korean, something that was less common in his trio project with the "boys." In his nu metal and pop punk phases (1998–2004) as a solo artist, Seo followed the dominant trends in rock in the United States in the late 1990s and into the next decade, no longer coming back to the new jack swing rhythms that were once more danceable and that the idol market formula inherited as a part of their schemes to expand globally. "Moai" belongs to the more recent blend of pop rock and alt rock (perhaps emo subgenre) that might not garner as many fans as idol groups do, but as an icon, Seo endures the passing of time and his cult following is generationally more diverse, including Korean Gen Xers, millennials, and Gen Z. His music has retained American influence, to the point that trends in the United States could be predictably featured in his records two years later.

Although perhaps not Seo's or the Korean music industry's intention, the "Moai" video alienizes Easter Island given the influence of successful conspiracy theorists. Several narratives have garnered attention and mass popularity since the UFO sighting craze prevalent in the United States was heightened by the possibility of nuclear missiles due to remnants of Cold War panic. Most notably, Swiss Erich von Däniken's *Chariots of the Gods? Unsolved Mysteries of the Past* (1968) helped propel the idea of extraterrestrial intelligence involved in several "world mysteries." The book became a commercial success worldwide, followed by an increase of ratings in several programs that featured "scholarly" or "expert" commentaries, leading more to suggest that Egyptians could not have built the pyramids or that Olmecs, Mayas, Aztecs, or Amerindians were not responsible for and capable of building the pyramids and large structures in the Yucatán peninsula, Central America, or South America. Von Däniken's book also claims that the Nazca Line drawings were not drawn by local peoples but were orchestrated from space and likely used as landing signs for alien vessels. Von Däniken has been featured in multiple popular documentaries,

Latin Orientalism and Anglo Hegemony

normalizing the explanation that advanced civilizations in the Americas and Africa were more likely the result of extraterrestrial authorship than human ingenuity, labor, and/or exploitation. In conclusion, Von Däniken's thoughts on Rapa Nui in his writings and interviews are reflected and perpetuated in the music video "Moai."

The music video reflects orientalist perceptions of disappeared or absent Indigenous American cultures as perceived by hegemonic voices that only consider that past Euro-hegemonies, Asian dynasties, or extraterrestrials were capable of creating sophisticated structures and art such as the volcanic stone giants, complex architectural structures, or mathematically perfected designs. According to this co-cultural theory, ancient peoples from the Americas and Africa were not cultured or were never present to labor for these ruins and structures that seem abandoned and left with no documentation of their engineering. Korea's orientalization and othering of Latin America is connected to appropriation of Black music and culture (Anderson 2020). This hegemonic mimicry inherits the superiority complex while self-assessing its product as an improvement unto global marketability (Kim 2021). In other words, while Afro-Latin American cultural products have had their own trajectory in hybridizing and interacting with Indigenous and other diverse influences, the main source of orientalization and othering by this music video is through Anglo-hegemonic off-white lenses rather than the postcolonial power structures.

Jeju Island should be mentioned as a mirror heterotopic Korean parallel of Rapa Nui, as the island also contains several statues whose origins are not clear. *Dol hareubangs* (stone grandpas), as they have been more recently called, are phallic yet anthropomorphic statues that are abundant on the Korean island. Popularly known as ancient statues from the eighteenth century, they allegedly guarded strategic entrances of Jeju. Although they are far fewer (over forty compared to nearly one thousand moais) and much smaller (up to ten feet high compared to moais that average thirteen feet but are as high as thirty-three feet), the similar volcanic material and mysterious origins function as comparable heterotopic artifacts: objects that seem to retain time and become part of the otherizing process of capitalistic tourism that exploits these objects as non-consumable fetish through visual and experiential documentation. In other words, these artifacts become visual exploits to remind the observer of the passing of

Park

time and, perhaps, the triumph of the eternal market that no longer needs these guards, but they are still preserved as a means to extract capital in the form of fetish tourism. However, since Seo Taiji is Korean and Jeju Island is a few miles off the Korean mainland, *Dol hareubangs* are not as exoticized and exploited as moais. Jeju is visited regularly by Koreans, and the statues are not as dominant in the island's identity as the moais are in Rapa Nui's identity. There are no serious claims that these phallic objects were built by aliens. The phallic imagery in the Jeju statues has evolved such that these artifacts are considered humorous and anecdotally as sources of fertility. Coincidentally, Jeju has become the most common destination for Korean honeymooners. Rapa Nui, on the contrary, draws much or all of its tourism exclusively from the presence of the giant moais and seldom as a honeymoon destination. Moreover, Rapa Nui has a legacy of cultural colonization by mainland Chile and independent aspirations, while Jeju has also had independent movements from Japan and Korea.

Conclusion: Korean Off-White Anglo Hegemony

Although Hallyu is triumphally glamorized as an effective soft power battling US/UK Anglo hegemonies, superseding Japanese and Chinese cultural global influence, I argue that South Korean "neo-hegemony" perpetuates and inherits from Western hegemony "K-Anglo hegemony" conceits of discourses of messianic neoliberalism and Anglo-hegemonic exceptionalisms. In short, South Korean popular music industry is part of the musical Anglo hegemon, in spite of geopolitical distances and ideological differences. An increasing number of Korean music creators are native or near-native English speakers, including members of the diaspora (Yoon 2022). "Moai," however, is not written by native English speakers but mainly by Seo, who often includes English phrases in his songs, which he has commonly done since the 1980s. The reception of this video is formulaically Westernized, not despite but because of how they are filmed in non-English-speaking spaces, embodying the European colonizer's persona and otherizing emblematic postcolonial spaces that exemplify caricatures of the Third World, Global South, and post-communist spaces. Perhaps it relates to Mel Stanfill's (2018) thoughts in "The Unbearable Whiteness of Fandom and Fan Studies," in which she suggests that the default audience

Latin Orientalism and Anglo Hegemony

and fandom culture at large is thought of as White. Laura Mulvey (1975) theorized that the "male gaze" normalized female body objectification; thus, the audience was accustomed to and expected the female body as an object of desire by diegetic characters but also by the audience, a heterosexualized male. A parallel phenomenon could be observed with the "Moai" video as it expects the audience to be White, or at least English speaking, and to hear music closely inheriting from Westernized musical genres. K-rock has distinct aesthetics, but the reception and expectations are challenged, as the binary of East/West is illusory and deficient in addressing more important issues regarding the construction and politization of racialized hierarchies.

Although the rise of Korean popular music is significant in Latin America, the dominant languages on radios and other mainstream platforms are still Spanish and English, with a more noticeable massive rise of Korean popular music in streaming services, "as a subculture that transforms into transcultural fandom via digital mediation" (Han 2017, 2250). As more Korean popular songs are heard and rise through charts, more portions of the lyrics seem to include English, with noteworthy cases of acts that released singles entirely in English (e.g., BTS's latest songs before military services, "Ice Cream" by Blackpink ft. Selena Gomez, "I Can't Stop Me" by TWICE) despite fans (both Korean and non-Korean) preferring more Korean lyrics (Yoon 2022, 122–23). Moreover, Korean rock and hip hop are also known for borrowing phrases and at times entire verses and choruses (hooks) in English. The fandom is no longer surprised by the saturation of English in the albums, but at the same time, it allows the reception of Seo's songs to be more palatable for the Westernized audience and, by default, the global audience who consumes mass popular music with the seldom challenged de facto English dominance. In fact, there are virtually no K-pop artists (as well as in hip hop and rock) who are marketed using their Korean names.

The preference to refer to the island in English reiterates the hegemonic impetus that governs modern Korean language. Unlike most K-pop artists, Seo Taiji retained his Korean name rather than use an English or anglicized name, a predictable marketing move in idol groups. Although the video was set in a non-English-speaking space, lyrics include English, a practice that is common in all major pop "new" music genres in Korea: rock, pop, ballad (including R&B), and hip hop, with heightened frequency in songs

Park

by idol groups. The awkward ending of the lyrics of "Moai" include the determiner "the" for the phrase "In *the* Easter Island," revealing a lack of fluency and forced way to include "all I need" as the only other moment in the song that English is used.

Although the music video is not explicit propaganda favoring Anglo-hegemonic neoliberal capitalism, the ideological subalternity of pre-Columbian mysticisms in Rapa Nui by esoteric representations of alien moais is noticeable. On the one hand, the racial reference in "Moai" is extraterrestrial, and the absent inhabitants of Rapa Nui emphasize the orientalization of the island, reproducing orientalization of East Asian and Middle Eastern peoples. The heterotopic placement of moais highlights the messianic racial superiority of Koreans or the whitening of South Koreans—namely, as visitors and explorers in search for truth and answers that they "already" knew (i.e., the idea that ancient Black and Brown cultures are not capable of "civilized" structures). Rapa Nui is shown as empty, a civilization that has succumbed to its own ecocide due to deforestation and rats (as some anthropologists claim) or an alien invasion (Lipo, Hunt, and Haoa 2005, 2013). In turn, South Koreans are reformulated as neoliberal "neocolonizers" underscoring the postcolonial logic of "Westerners" by "discovering" an unfamiliar, remote, and exotic space. With this new logic, these images perpetuate the Western or off-white representation of colonial othering mediated by South Korean cultural products.

Rapa Nui is thus reformulated as a subaltern imagined space, compared to the First World South Korean neo-hegemonic visitors. Since race is socially constructed, the colonizers in this case are reformulated as South Koreans. In turn, these representations ascribe to messianic discourses of multinational neoliberalism as the solution to underdeveloped and exploitable lands. Neo-colonizing South Korea(n) becomes part of the "Old Orient" that no longer belongs to the postcolonial Global South, or the orientalized East, but is recognized and received as an off-white extension of the neoliberal Anglo hegemony.

Note

1. All comments in Korean and Spanish are translated by the author.

Latin Orientalism and Anglo Hegemony

References

Anderson, Crystal S. 2020. *Soul in Seoul: African American Popular Music and K-pop.* Jackson: University Press of Mississippi.

Bellwood, Peter, and Eusebio Dizon. 2008. "Austronesian Cultural Origins: Out of Taiwan, via the Batanes Islands, and Onwards to Western Polynesia." In *Past Human Migrations in East Asia: Matching Archaeology, Linguistics, and Genetics*, edited by Alicia Sanchez-Mazas, Roger Blench, Malcolm D. Ross, Ilia Peiros, and Marie Lin, 23–39. London: Routledge.

Broome, Kate, dir. 2000. *The Lost Gods of Easter Island.* Written and presented by David Attenborough. BBC.

Burns, Kevin, dir. *Ancient Aliens.* 2009. Season 1, pilot, "Chariots, Gods & Beyond." Aired March 8, 2009, on History Channel. https://www.hulu.com/series/ancient-aliens.

Chung, Hye Jean. 2017. *Media Heterotopias: Digital Effects and Material Labor in Global Film Production.* Durham, NC: Duke University Press.

Drake, Nadia. 2017. "7 Ancient Sites Some People Think Were Built by Aliens." *National Geographic,* October 26, 2017. https://www.nationalgeographic.com/premium/article/ancient-sites-built-by-aliens.

Foucault, Michel. 1971. *The Order of Things: An Archaeology of the Human Sciences.* New York: Vintage Books.

———. 1984. "Des Espace Autres." *Architecture, Mouvement, Continuité* 5: 46–49. Published in 1986 as "Of Other Spaces, Heterotopias," trans. Jay Miskowiec, *Diacritics* 16 (1): 22–27.

Hagelberg, Erika, Murray Cox, Wulf Schiefenhövel, and Ian Frame. 2008. "A Genetic Perspective on the Origins and Dispersal of the Austronesians: Mitochondrial DNA Variation from Madagascar to Easter Island." In *Past Human Migrations in East Asia: Matching Archaeology, Linguistics, and Genetics*, edited by Alicia Sanchez-Mazas, Roger Blench, Malcolm D. Ross, Ilia Peiros, and Marie Lin, 388–407. London: Routledge.

Hall, Stuart. (1973) 2007. "Encoding and Decoding in the Television Discourse." In *CCCS Selected Working Papers*, edited by Ann Gray, Jan Campbell, Mark Erickson, Stuart Hanson, and Helen Wood, 386–98. London: Routledge.

———. 1990. "Cultural Identity and Diaspora." In *Identity: Community, Culture, Difference*, edited by Jonathan Rutherford, 222–37. London: Lawrence and Wishart.

Han, Benjamin. 2017. "K-Pop in Latin America: Transcultural Fandom and Digital Mediation." *International Journal of Communication* 11: 2250–69.

Hong, Won Ki, dir. 2013a. "SEOTAIJI MOAI: THE FILM #1 Chile." seotaiji, November 12, 2013. YouTube video, 8:34. https://youtu.be/pdOGcCiRoZQ.

———, dir. 2013b. "SEOTAIJI MOAI: THE FILM #2 Easter Island." seotaiji, November 12, 2013. YouTube video, 13:56. https://youtu.be/LMrFPDOFUwM.

Jang, Hyunsuk. 2022. "Pandemic to 'Fandomic': The Revival of Fandom Publics in the Digital Space of Latin American K-Pop Fandom." *Seoul Journal of Korean Studies* 35 (1): 29–50. https://doi.org10.1353/seo.2022.0003.

Jenkins, Henry. 1992. *Textual Poachers: Television Fans and Participatory Culture.* New York: Routledge.

Jung, Eun-Young. 2017. "Seo Taiji Syndrome: Rise of Korean Youth and Cultural Transformation through Global Pop Music Styles in the Early 1990s." In *Made in Korea: Studies in Popular Music*, edited by Hyunjoon Shin and Seung-Ah Lee, 143–54. New York: Routledge.

Kim, Kyung Hyun. 2021. *Hegemonic Mimicry: Korean Popular Culture of the Twenty-First Century.* Durham, NC: Duke University Press.

Lipo, Carl P., and Terry L. Hunt. 2005. "Mapping Prehistoric Statue Roads on Easter Island." *Antiquity* 79 (303): 158–68. https://doi.org/10.1017/S0003598 X00113778.

Lipo, Carl P., Terry L. Hunt, and Sergio Rapu Haoa. 2013. "The 'Walking' Megalithic Statues (*Moai*) of Easter Island." *Journal of Archaeological Science* 40 (6): 2859–66. https://doi.org/10.1016/j.jas.2012.09.029.

Mulvey, Laura. 1975. "Visual Pleasure and Narrative Cinema." *Screen* 16 (3): 6–18. https://doi.org/10.1093/screen/16.3.6.

Nova/PBS Online Adventures. 1998. "Secrets of Easter Island." Public Broadcasting Service. Accessed February 28, 2023. https://www.pbs.org/wgbh/nova /easter/.

Ono, Kent A., and Jungmin Kwon. 2013. "Re-worlding Culture? YouTube as a K-pop Interlocutor." In *The Korean Wave: Korean Media Go Global*, edited by Youna Kim, 215–30. London: Routledge.

Oppenheimer, Stephen. 2004. "The 'Express Train from Taiwan to Polynesia': On the Congruence of Proxy Lines of Evidence." *World Archaeology* 36 (4): 591–600.

Palacios, Nicolás. 1918. *Raza Chilena.* 2nd ed. Santiago, Chile: Editorial Chilena.

Panizza, Tiziana, and Macarena Fernández, dirs. 2017. *Tierra Sola* [*Solitary Land*]. Chile: Domestic Films and ICEI.

Park, Moisés. 2019. "'Gracias a la vida': Violeta Went to Heaven and Came Back Wearing a K-Pop Mini Skirt." *Studies in Latin American Popular Culture* 37: 25–50. https://doi.org/10.7560/SLAPC3702.

Roggeveen, Jacob. 1970. *The Journal of Jacob Roggeveen.* Edited by Andrew Sharp. Oxford: Clarendon Press.

Said, Edward W. (1978) 1979. *Orientalism.* New York: Vintage Books.

Seo, Taiji. 2008. "Moai." Track 1 on *8th Atomos Part MOAI.* Seotaiji Company.

Latin Orientalism and Anglo Hegemony

———. 2009. "서태지(SEOTAIJI) - 모아이(MOAI)." seotaiji, June 29, 2010. YouTube video, 4:58. https://youtu.be/yUor2pLDleY.

Soares, Pedro, Teresa Rito, Jean Trejaut, Maru Mormina, Catherine Hill, Emma Tinkler-Hundal, Michelle Braid, Douglas J. Clarke, Jun-Hun Loo, Noel Thomson, Tim Denham, Mark Donohue, Vincent Macaulay, Marie Lin, Stephen Oppenheimer, and Martin B. Richards. 2011. "Ancient Voyaging and Polynesian Origins." *American Journal of Human Genetics* 88 (2): 239–47. https://doi.org/10.1016/j.ajhg.2011.01.009.

Spielberg, Steven, dir. 2008. *Indiana Jones and the Kingdom of the Crystal Skull.* Lucasfilm Ltd.

Stanfill, Mel. 2018. "The Unbearable Whiteness of Fandom and Fan Studies." In *A Companion to Media Fandom and Fan Studies*, edited by Paul Booth, 305–18. Hoboken, NJ: Wiley.

Tanter, Marcy, and Moisés Park, eds. 2022. *Here Comes the Flood: Perspectives of Gender, Sexuality, and Stereotype in the Korean Wave.* Lanham, MD: Lexington Books.

Urban Zakapa. 2017. "Moai." Music video. Stone Music Entertainment, July 11, 2017. YouTube video, 5:41. https://youtu.be/CuFtHgjdCII.

Von Däniken, Erich. 1968. *Chariots of the Gods?* New York: Putnam.

Yoon, Kyong. 2022. *Diasporic Hallyu: The Korean Wave in Korean Canadian Youth Culture.* Cham, Switzerland: Palgrave Macmillan.

7

......

"I Was Probably Korean in a Previous Life"

Transracial Jokes and Fantasies of Hallyu Fans

......

IRINA LYAN

"I was probably Korean in a previous life," giggles Neta, a White-looking Israeli woman, at the very beginning of her public talk at the Korean Embassy in Israel in 2019 on how to prepare one's tourism route to South Korea (hereafter Korea). The audience of about fifty Israelis politely giggles back, and she continues her lecture. What Neta does not know is that there is nothing original in her joke. Transracial jokes and fantasies like hers, with only slight variations in their level of seriousness, sincerity, or similarity—such as "I'm half Korean" or "I feel part Korean"—are common among non-Korean fans of Korean popular culture (Yoon 2019; Lee, Lee, and Park 2020), foreign employers of Korean firms (Lyan 2021), and ethnic diasporic Koreans and adoptees (Docan-Morgan 2010; Yoon 2022).

What does surprise us here and calls for academic attention is the commonality of these jokes and fantasies, which span heretofore unbridgeable racial, ethnic, and national categories—an act often considered a social taboo or negatively associated with cultural appropriation. Moreover, as a diasporic half-Korean myself, I was puzzled as to why someone would wish, even under the mask of a joke or fantasy, to identify with such a troubled identity, which is often perceived as an imposter-like mask. Somehow being or becoming White-like is widely considered to be a "normal" wish and behavior, even encouraged, while being or becoming non-White is stigmatized. To understand the latter wish, the goal of the current chapter is to examine the role of transracial humor and fantasy among non-Korean fans of Korean popular culture in creating racial translocalism on being self-identified with more than one race.

With the rise in popularity since the late 1990s of Korean cinema, TV drama, and K-pop abroad, known as the Korean Wave or Hallyu, the interest in Korea and Koreans has expanded in different and sometimes unexpected directions. While the fans' strong identification with Hallyu fandom through involvement in Korean studies and language (e.g., Saeji 2018; Lyan 2019), entrepreneurship (e.g., Otmazgin and Lyan 2018), tourism (e.g., Lee 2020), the plastic surgery industry based on Hallyu-inspired beauty standards (e.g., Elfving-Hwang 2018), and more are widely addressed in the academic literature, the theme of fannish transracial humor and fantasies still awaits academic attention.

The closest theme to the fantasy of being or becoming Korean by non-Korean fans is connected to the contested topic of *Koreaboo*, a term used to describe Hallyu fans who "are singled out for their fetish of liking, buying, and promoting all things Korean" (Yoon 2019, 184; 2022). These fans, who often fantasize about being or becoming Koreans or even mimic what they consider to be Korean looks and behaviors, are usually laughed at while being criticized for appropriating cultural Others and breaking monoracial taboos. Similar to and probably derived from *weeaboo*—extreme White fandom of Japanese anime and manga—among the majority of Hallyu fans, the term *Koreaboo* is pushed to the margins of Hallyu fandom, aiming especially to criticize White fans whose racial difference and distance from Koreans is highly visible.

To fill this gap theoretically, I first address the previous studies on ethnic and racial humor and fantasy. More specifically, I argue that ethnic and racial humor and fantasy provide resources or tools for symbolic boundary work "in creating, maintaining, contesting, or even dissolving institutionalized social differences" such as class, race, and gender to create "alternative systems and principles of classifications" (Lamont and Molnár 2002, 168; Gieryn 1983). Such work is often used to normalize and rationalize social boundaries, yet it also has the potential to contest and replace them through raciolinguistics—that is, the ability of language to construct and reconstruct race and vice versa (Rosa and Flores 2017).

Lyan

To engage with this theme empirically, I offer my findings from a case study of the Israeli community of Hallyu fans, which I have followed for more than ten years both online and offline. This includes online ethnography of the virtual communities of Israeli fans, surveys, interviews, and informal talks with the most active fans; participant observations in Korea-related events; and continuous interaction with students of the Korean Studies Program at the Hebrew University, most of whom define themselves as Hallyu fans. For the purposes of the current study, I selected transracial jokes and fantasies from previously collected data and complemented them with open discussions with my students in my course Popular Culture in South Korea in 2021 to 2022. Unlike a Koreaboo, who directly and openly violates monoracial taboos, Hallyu fans, under the guise of transracial humor and fantasy, attract less attention, allowing the impossible desire to be or to become Korean-like while avoiding social sanctions.

The Israeli case study provides fertile ground, since the significant racial distance between Koreans and Israelis makes any joke or even the slightest hint at any physical similarity immediately sound an alarm and raise an eyebrow.[1] Even though Israeli or Jewish membership in the racial category of Whiteness might be disputed (given its geographical location and Sephardi origins in the Middle East), because of its Western (meaning American and European) geopolitical proximity and Ashkenazi ancestry, especially among elites, most Israelis identify themselves as "White" and "Western." Israelis define themselves in this way especially when compared to Koreans, whose claim to Whiteness or Westernness is often perceived as partial, fragmented, or even false (Lyan 2021). Such high racial distance—be it actual, perceived, or relative—foregrounds the role of transracial jokes and fantasies in bridging the supposedly unbridgeable racial categories through the work of imagination.

The findings demonstrate the importance of what I call *minority capital* on symbolic wearing of the mask of non-White identity to gain legitimacy, attributes, and rights associated with minorities. It allows fans to identify with the subject of marginalized fandom, which comes with a price tag due to the stigma attached to Koreaboo and non-White fandom in general. To achieve both minority capital and social legitimacy, fans employ transracial humor and fantasy as a carnivalesque performance that in turn deals with the social anxieties, uncertainties, and uneasiness involved in

"I Was Probably Korean in a Previous Life"

fans' nonnormative choice of non-White fandom. Thus, the perceived transracial similarity, intimacy, and even unity bring fans closer to the subject of their fandom within their imagined community while maintaining a safe racial distance through the ongoing negotiation of supposedly closed monoracial social boundaries.

Rather than declaring their transracial dreams directly, I found that fans employ three imaginative temporal routes to keep a safe racial distance under the mask of transracial joke and fantasy. The *past category* deals with both humorous and spiritual beliefs in reincarnation from a prior life; the *present category* examines the achieving of Koreanness through the momentous "mergers and acquisitions" of national sound, such as language and music; and the *future category* explores romantic and sexual fantasies of possible transracial encounters. Such a temporal framework echoes the broader imagination of the Orient as premodern, modern, or postmodern imitation or alternative to the Occidental, recreating a hierarchy between the two, well addressed in the seminal work of Edward Said (1978) on Orientalism.

By focusing on transracial humor and fantasy, this chapter aims to address the volume's main question, "how racial difference matters in the uses and reception of Korean popular culture," in order to advance the growing body of critical studies on Hallyu acceptance through the theoretical concepts of race, core-periphery, and Otherness (i.e., Lee, Lee, and Park 2020; Lyan 2023; Oh 2017; Oh and Oh 2017; Park 2015).[2] These and other studies have already sounded an alert regarding optimism and celebration behind the global acceptance of the non-Western Other and the possibility of alternative cultural globalization. This in turn might further privilege racial Whiteness and Westernness and its dominant position while tacitly disciplining and stigmatizing fans of Korean popular culture and Korea at large.

Theoretical Background

ETHNIC AND RACIAL HUMOR AS SYMBOLIC BOUNDARY

The existing research on humor, defined as the ability to amuse or to make one laugh, generally reveals its three major functions: superiority while laughing at the misfortunes of others, relief in releasing emotional or psychic tension, and highlighting of the incongruity between two subjects (Watson 2014). Confirming previous research, ethnic and racial humor works to (re)create hierarchies, to overcome uneasiness in interethnic and interracial encounters, and to safely bridge unbridgeable identities and distances between them. For instance, studies of ethnic and racial humor reveal tension and ambivalence in the process of immigrant assimilation that "corrected" the "wrong" identity but also emphasized a pride in its origins (Shifman and Katz 2005); address the duality of potentially racist jokes that symbolically create in-group solidarity by both underlining and erasing racial distance (Wolfers, File, and Schnurr 2017); and examine the dual role of humor in escaping racist accusations while maintaining and "softening" color-blind national ideologies (Sue and Golash-Boza 2013).

In the Korean context, a similar incongruity and ambivalence is found in the ethnic and racial humor studies of uneasy encounters such as migration, adoption, and intermarriage. For example, Elaine Chun's (2004) analysis of a Korean American comedian who uses "Mock Asian" (a stereotyped Asian speech) suggests that such humorous re-voicing both empowers and disempowers the American Asian community vis-à-vis hegemonic Whiteness. Similarly, Adrienne Lo and Jenna Chi Kim's (2012) work on linguistic mockery examines the ridiculing of Korean Americans' lack of Korean-language competence while challenging their authenticity and reversing their supposedly elite position of a transnational South Korean returnee. Finally, according to Sara Docan-Morgan's (2010) study, humor has been an effective coping strategy in managing sensitive social boundaries, both inside and out, in the case of White American adoptive families and Korean adoptees to accept their racial differences and to create in-family closeness.[3] These and other examples demonstrate the role of creating alternative symbolic boundaries for in-group identification while also acknowledging and replacing rigid social categories between non-White minorities and White majorities.

ETHNIC AND RACIAL HUMOR AS HIERARCHY BUILDING

Besides simultaneous (dis)identification with ethnic and racial norms, "being or becoming something one is not" involves an immediate hierarchy

"I Was Probably Korean in a Previous Life"

building between the "original" and "authentic" model and its imitation. Known as *mimicry*, a postcolonial concept advanced by Homi K. Bhabha (1984, 1994), it reveals how perceived similarities overlap and enhance differences, as seen in grammatical structures such as "we are similar, but different" or "almost the same, but different," in which colonizer and colonized both recognize and erase differences to (re)produce power asymmetries.

In the Korean context, the mocking of Korean people and culture by the White Canadian hosts of a popular YouTube channel, Eat Your Kimchi, also demonstrates postcolonial racial asymmetries that otherize and exoticize Koreans (Oh and Oh 2017). Such troubled coexistence of humor and hierarchy building is well presented in Kyong Yoon's recent book, *Diasporic Hallyu*, which shows diasporic identity in failed attempts at "negotiating racialization" (2022, 36). My own research on Israeli-Korean business collaborations also underlines the ambivalence of imagined cultural (dis)similarities by tacitly recreating an East/West binary between "Western" Israelis and "Western-like" Koreans in which the suffix "like" both connects and separates the latter from the hegemonial West (Lyan 2021). Even though the equation "Koreans are the Israelis of the East" is often said to amuse or surprise, rather than to laugh or mock, its humorous effect and hierarchy building are undeniable.

To sum, the role of humor and fantasy to amuse or to laugh at/with aims, sometimes simultaneously, in two opposite directions: (1) to acknowledge and strengthen the existing social boundaries and hierarchies of race and ethnicity and (2) to resist and replace them with alternative categories to create alternative in-group similarity. To examine this paradox in depth, I suggest turning to the transracial humor and fantasy in fandom studies of Korean popular culture. More specifically, I look at the *direct* mocking and ridiculing of Koreaboo fans who wish to identify with the Korean race and nation and at the *indirect* mocking of Hallyu fans and Koreans at large by associating them with the Koreaboo category.

Mocking Koreaboo

The existing academic discussion on the extreme and stigmatized label of Koreaboo is rather episodic, anecdotal, or even judgmental, since an overt wish of being or becoming even partially Korean is negatively associated with breaking monoracial taboos and doing cultural appropriation. For instance, Jeehyun Jenny Lee, Rachel Kar Yee Lee, and Ji Hoon Park's recent study on the US reception of K-pop in relation to race and masculinity echoes Asian women K-pop fans' harsh criticism, as one respondent notes: "The biggest thing is fetishizing Asian men and Asian women. They just think Asian men are specifically Korean men. I have also seen so many people on Twitter just pretend to be Asian [laughter] just trying to get away with it. They are like 'I am part Korean.' But they are just full White. I don't know why you have to pretend to be Asian" (quoted in 2020, 5909). Mostly perceived as an offensive joke, Koreaboos are ridiculed and mocked for the seriousness of their transracial fantasies. The stigma attached to Koreaboo reveals the social construction of race as a natural and unchangeable state to be born with rather than acquired or appropriated. This might explain, for example, the criticism and mockery of mimicking Korean-like looks, including a fannish practice of K-pop-inspired plastic surgeries as challenging monoracial norms (Elfving-Hwang and Park 2016; Elfving-Hwang 2018).

The most famous such case is that of Oli London, a White British man in his thirties who underwent multiple plastic surgeries to become a look-alike for the Korean mega-popular band BTS's singer Jimin and even released a song and a YouTube video titled "Koreaboo" (London 2021a). Despite its humorous message, the video mostly enraged both K-pop fans and the non-fan community alike. London's (2021b) declaration of himself as "transracial" and his call for racial freedom of choice on Twitter further challenged the social construction of race as a biological, and therefore unchangeable, condition: "TRANSRACIAL is a thing! I invented it! If you can be transgender you can be TRANSRACIAL. Live your life to the fullest, be who you want to be and spread love." Similar to other jokes and fantasies that employ symbolic resources and tools, such as the adoption of a pun-like raciolinguistic category of "transracial," London creates here an alternative category to the monoracial one to identify with while achieving minority capital of both the transgender and Hallyu communities. This might explain the mixed reaction from mocking to relating to Koreaboo-like transracial jokes and fantasies as emancipating.

The link between transgender and transracial categories was already established in another troubled transracial identity case: that of Rachel

"I Was Probably Korean in a Previous Life"

Dolezal, a White American woman who self-identified as Black and performed Blackness while hiding her European origins. Amid controversy over her racial identity in 2015, Dolezal's story has brought to the academic debate a range of opinions, from harsh criticism of cultural appropriation to acceptance of self-chosen (trans)racial identities. For example, in 2017, the philosopher Rebecca Tuvel used Dolezal's case in her article titled "In Defense of Transracialism," questioning the celebration of transgenderism while being critical of transracialism. Cited more than 190 times on Google Scholar, Tuvel's article has divided the academic community over whether to accept emergent transracial identities and to support one's choice of one's own race or to reject them as unethical, false, and inappropriate.

What is surprising in the overall negative reaction of concern and anxiety at challenging monoracial norms by adopting non-White identities is that a lack of local cultural (or, in this case, racial) "odor" might actually encourage odorless, non-Western pop cultures to spread globally, as argued by Koichi Iwabuchi (2002) in the successful case of Japanese anime and manga. In the case of K-pop, its "hypermodernity," "hybridity," or "post-nationality"—that is, "a lack of national flavor, in which the essentialized national signifier of 'K' in K-pop has been diluted" (Jin, Yoon, and Min 2021, 89)—might actually contribute to its global appeal and success.

Moreover, following Henry Jenkins's definition of the transcultural fan as a pop cosmopolitan—"someone whose embrace of global popular media represents an escape route out of the parochialism of her local community" (2004, 114)—what about fandom power in imagining post-racialism, hyper-racialism, poly-racialism, de-racialization, transracialism, or araciality? Fan-fueled cosmopolitan globalization (Yoon 2018), poly-cultural Black-Korean encounters beyond the category of Whiteness (Oh 2017), trans-culturalism (Han 2017), or fan-nationalism (Lyan 2019) can become such symbolic escape routes from socially bounded partitions.

Mocking Hallyu Fans and Koreans

Another paradox embedded in mocking Koreaboo is that it tacitly mocks the rest of Hallyu fans and even Koreans and Korea at large, building hierarchy by reinforcing and perpetuating hegemonic Whiteness and Westernness. For instance, Sara Rosenau's (2022) raciolinguistic study of mocking Koreaboo's language style as racist—including extensive visual use and misuse of Korean words, spelling mistakes in both Korean and English, cap locks, emoji, textual irrational emotions, childish fantasies, and the misunderstanding of Korean culture—demonstrates an indirect and tacit mocking of the rest of Hallyu fans, as well as the Korean language and Koreans themselves.

Yong-Jin Won, Huikyong Pang, Jun-hyung Lee, and Marisa Luckie's study (2020) on BTS fandom reached a similar conclusion by arguing that the word *Koreaboo* was coined to degrade American K-pop fandom as a whole. A binary between "normal" fans vis-à-vis Koreaboo-like fans (1) racially discriminates against all fans for their "strange" cultural taste and (2) indirectly discriminates against Koreans and Korean popular culture as peripheral. Paradoxically, by dissociating themselves from Koreaboo, Hallyu fans tacitly reinforce Western-dominant racial logics. According to both studies, even though those engaging in the mockery strive to define themselves as anti-racist cosmopolitans and "normal" fans, their protection of Korean "authentic" culture strikes back in the opposite direction as a double-edged sword.

To conclude, the dual role of ethnic and racial humor and fantasy plays out in (1) mocking Koreaboo to punish transracial fantasies as nonnormative and thus ridiculous and (2) countering monoracial norms by replacing them with alternative categories to create an imagined community of transracial fans. Rather than reducing Koreaboo's controversial desire to be or become transracial to mere racism, cultural appropriation, or White privilege claims, I suggest to understand the nature of socially forbidden transracial dreams and their role in Hallyu fandom. With various shades and layers of meanings, such jokes and fantasies might thrust fans into alternative realities to fantasize about possible past, current, or future lives.

Findings

PAST: "I WAS PROBABLY KOREAN IN A PREVIOUS LIFE"

My interest in the theme of transracial humor and fantasy dates back to my study of Israeli fans of Korean TV dramas conducted back in 2012 (Lyan and Levkowitz 2015a, 2015b). After collecting and analyzing more than three hundred online surveys, I was surprised to find the following message left at the open comments part of the survey, by a forty-five-year-old female Israeli fan of Korean TV drama: "Until today, in my mind the Far East was the most far-away place, the end of the world. In the first [Korean] drama that I watched, I didn't like the language and I had my hand on the remote control to switch the channel. But I got used to it and today [watching Korean drama] is like going home.... I was probably Korean in a previous life" (Lyan and Levkowitz 2015b, 8). As this was a written message, I could not tell whether it was a whimsical joke or a serious belief in reincarnation. Back then, we theorized it as a symbolic pilgrimage between a real home and a fannish one—"Hallyuland." Based on religious associations, scholars discuss actual and symbolic pilgrimages of fans who are ready to invest a great deal of effort in reaching their imaginative fandom land (e.g., Hills 2002; Bickerdike 2015; McCloud 2003). Due to significant geographical and cultural distance, Hallyu fandom has become an imaginary journey between the known and the unknown, resembling the religious practice of pilgrimage—that is, an emotional exploration of new places accompanied by a deep sense of fulfillment.

When I raised the theme of this chapter during my Popular Culture in South Korea course back in 2021, I was quite surprised by the students' reaction. One of them mentioned that her mother always laughs at the suggestion that her daughter was probably Korean in a previous life to explain her unexplainable attraction to Korea. In contrast, another student rejected the humorous part and confessed her belief in actual reincarnation as the only possible explanation for her own attraction to Korea. Even though both students' remarks differed in their degree of humor and seriousness, as well as the directness of the message (self or other's definition), they shared the difficulty—or lack of a logical explanation—for being so involved in a distant and foreign culture. In other words, transracial jokes and fantasies functioned here as legitimacy tools for students' nonmainstream choice of non-Western fandom and academic degree. While one can easily challenge transracial logic, how can one argue with humor or a spiritual feeling?

Such an uneasy coexistence of serious and humorous reincarnation beliefs can also be seen in Neta's joke (if it was indeed a joke) that begins this chapter. Besides public lectures, in 2019 she created a Facebook page titled "The Korean" (הקוריאנית in Hebrew) to offer her expertise on Korea-

Lyan

related issues. The page, which at the time of writing has more than one thousand followers, states her spiritual connection in her introductory post from April 18, 2022, this time in poetic form:

Who am I?
[. . .]
I found Korea
a few years ago
the first Korean TV drama was broadcast
and I was wondering what did I see
the internet was weak
the smartphone was too new
I found myself waiting for the weekly episode
trapped by time and broadcasting schedule
from episode to episode something inside me
got on fire
my interest has grown
I was thirsty for information
it was like a cosmic attraction that it's difficult to explain
a connection
some would say spiritual
some would say ancient
some would argue that maybe in the previous life
I was Korean[4]

Unlike the icebreaker joke in the public lecture's example, here Neta employs a spiritual language to suggest the possibility of an actual re-incarnation supported by her own photo in front of the ancient Korean palace in *hanbok*, a Korean traditional dress. Softened by a lengthy poetic explanation and indirect message (a double repetition of "some would say/ argue" and "maybe"), she builds a spiritual connection to Korea as a part of her own identity building and Korean expert status by asking at the beginning, "Who am I?" Elevated by the poetic form and romantic belief in the supernatural, this and other examples demonstrate the possibility of transracial fantasy as a symbolic bridge between the socially unbridge-able categories as legitimacy-building tools to address the always-asked judgmental and stigmatized question guided by monoracial norms and standards: Why would a White woman be interested in non-White Korea?

To address this frequent question, another admirer of Korean culture and a Korea expert posted on Facebook the following transracial identity joke: "One Korean told me that I was for sure a Korean in the previous life, because otherwise how can it be possible that I love Korea so much? Another Korean overheard our conversation and said, 'No chance she was a Korean in a previous life. If it was true, no chance she would love Korea!'" (post from May 17, 2022).

In this case, the indirectness of comparison ("one Korean told me") softens the message and adds to it a credibility, as it was a "real" Korean who told it. Moreover, the humorous twist at the end serves to further soften the seriousness of the uneasy transracial equation. Such spiritual connections allow for the symbolic possibility of alternative lives, deaths, and rebirths parallel to fans' social realities, while humor and fantasy make them ambivalent, thus avoiding criticism and keeping the racial boundaries safe.

To address the importance of temporality, I would like to underline why the reincarnation joke or fantasy has become so commonplace a pattern. First, as I mentioned above, the popular belief in spiritual and supernatural cannot be proved to be true or false. This is what makes these comparisons attractive to use as an ambivalent possibility one cannot totally agree with or deny. Second, Neta's use of the word *ancient*, as well as the visualization of the past through the images of the Korean palace and *hanbok*, is reminiscent of romantic imagination and even nostalgia toward "Asia" as a premodern Other, exotic space and time and an alternative past in which such Orientalist fantasies are possible.

By identifying with "ancient" Asia, fans acquire the minority capital by symbolically gaining attributes associated with minorities as well as Korea-expert status. The transracial joke and fantasy provide both a symbolic escape and a homecoming, into the distant past, away from being stigmatized as a "White" fan of Korean popular culture while acknowledging the limitations of the transracial identity as an imaginative one. In addition to stretching the racial boundaries, the transracial joke and fantasy also function here as an indirect and tacit hierarchy-building mechanism between alternative Koreanness (past) and hegemonic Whiteness (present).

Lyan

PRESENT: KOREAN SOUND ACROSS BORDERS

Besides the reincarnation theme, the transracial jokes or fantasies can occur in situ and in vivo.[5] Oli London's Koreaboo example can be categorized as the most extreme one, but it has endless shades of gray manifested in various fannish practices, such as achieving *racial similarity* by mimicking Korean-like looks and beauty standards through cosmetics and plastic surgeries, and *national similarity* by mimicking certain behaviors such as learning the Korean language, especially pop culture vocabulary and slang, traveling to Korea, wearing a *hanbok*, going to a *norebang*, making a cover dance, and more.[6] Despite their closeness, unlike transracialism, which is usually criticized and mocked, transnationalism is often encouraged, welcomed, and even promoted, especially by the Korean government as a part of its public diplomacy strategies. Admiration for Korea, manifested in being or becoming Korean-like in the latter case, declares Korea's superior position as a model for non-Koreans around the world to aspire to and imitate.

In the Israeli case study, while some fans have tried adopting Korean looks, they mostly have achieved Koreanness by acquiring national similarity. In our previous research, for example, we studied fans among our university's students of the Korean Studies Program who often identify as cultural missionaries, ambassadors, or even patriots of Korean culture (Otmazgin and Lyan 2014). Even though the connection between fandom and nationalism is far from obvious, as is the connection between Hallyu and Korea, fan-nationalism has allowed such fans to manage the stigma associated with their choice of non-Western fandom and "strange" degree by their national pride in Korea, at least temporarily during the annual Korea Day event they organized (Lyan 2019).

The acquisition of a foreign language is another example of the naturalization process of cultural "merger and acquisition" through national sound. As Benedict Anderson (1983) taught us, imagined communities of nations are simultaneously open and closed, and through the process of naturalization, one might join the community from outside. Even though the slightest accent or mistake will immediately signal the difference between natives and foreigners, the door remains quite open. For instance,

"I Was Probably Korean in a Previous Life"

during the 2022 Korean-language meeting at the Hebrew University, the Korean-language teacher humorously complimented, on at least three occasions, students' Korean as so good that *for a moment* he was confused and thought that they were real Koreans. In reaction, the audience (which consisted of about thirty-five Israeli women, both Jews and Arabs, religious and secular) laughed and enthusiastically applauded the successful joke. For the Korean-language students, it is the highest compliment they can receive and celebrate, especially when given by the "real" Korean. At the end of the meeting, the students' singing of "Arirang," an unofficial Korean hymn, brought to the temporal national unity, or "unisonance" in Anderson's language (1983, 145), a physical manifestation of performing imagined community by reconnecting to the national sound, history, and tradition.

In another telling example of the "merger and acquisition" of Korean national sound, I met a musician who, since becoming interested in Korean TV dramas, has also become an active promoter and unofficial cultural ambassador of Korean culture, including the playing and teaching of Korean traditional instruments to ethnic Koreans. In the course of one of our informal talks, she proudly told me that she had met a Korean person who heard her speaking the Korean language before actually seeing her. When he realized she was an Israeli, he was surprised, as he was sure that she was Korean. Here again, an indirect equation by a "real" Korean and ability of national sound to be(come) Korean, even for just a passing moment of confusion, overcome and transverse the racial distance, eventually achieving momentary and partial (trans)racialism.

To address once again the importance of in situ and in vivo, momentous being or becoming Korean-like for the duration of a Korea-related event or when fans talk or sing in Korean, reconfigures existing social boundaries to create symbolic unity for a short period of time of such transracial carnival. Here as well, fans gain the minority capital by being or becoming Korea experts and Korean-like: both similar but different from the minority group. The recognition's shortness, like a temporal seizure and confusion, followed by a quick reinstatement of both national and racial borders, makes it harmless to the existing social order and therefore attractive to use. At first glance, it also reverses the common hierarchy by underlining the non-Koreans' desire to become Korean-like. Yet the temporal and humorous side of the reversal makes it ambivalent at best, questioning its

Lyan

possibility. Similar to the premodern alternative, Korea as a modern role model remains an imagined one, or a model minority, and thus inferior to the Western hegemony.

FUTURE: KOREA WITH LOVE

Besides spiritual and national connections, some Hallyu fans expressed their transracial fantasies by way of another powerful feeling—love. This ranged from falling in love with Korean culture to actual intermarriage. Before the introduction of Korean popular culture, international couples consisted mostly of Israeli husbands and Korean wives who met randomly in a third country. In contrast, since the Hallyu introduction to the Israeli public after the 2010s, the number of Israeli wives among Hallyu fans and Korean husbands has undergone a reversal and growth. Such a gender reversal might indicate changes in beauty standards and masculinity ideals as well as the influence of future-oriented transracial fantasies and sexual attraction.[7]

In a similar vein, the emergence of transracial romantic fantasies might explain, from a different angle, why Western—and especially White— women would consume Korean popular culture and travel to Korea in search of a potential love object (Lee 2020). We found similar fantasies and even hopes for romance across racial and national borders in the study of Israeli Hallyu fans by way of the survey question "Why do women in particular watch Korean TV dramas?" One of the respondents brought up the true love thesis:

> I think that women like me have found a connection [to Korean TV dramas] because they struggle to find true love. . . . I personally found myself withdrawing further and further away from Israeli men. . . . Korea gave me a hope of [finding] a different type of man. Women are more sensitive to small differences that are the most important in cultures. Korean culture, which is all about manners, tenderness, honor, and care at all costs for the family and spouse, certainly enchants women that suffer from cynicism, rudeness and almost complete ignorance of beauty, [and] pure and real feelings in our culture. (quoted in Lyan and Levkowitz 2015b, 15)

Similar to the spiritual or religious-like premodern feeling of homecoming, romantic attraction is difficult to argue with, thus challenging monoracial

"I Was Probably Korean in a Previous Life"

taboos. Moreover, the transracial fantasy of a true romance, akin to a touristic attraction to a distant—and even exotic—place, might empower female fans by escaping everyday patriarchal formations in search of a romantic alternative elsewhere. By imagining their aspired-to future with a Korean "Prince Charming," they build a utopian world in which racial norms are powerless or irrelevant, whereas racial differences might be attractive.

Similar to other transracial fantasies, future-oriented ones may vary in their degree of humor and seriousness. For instance, when one of the students of my Popular Culture in South Korea class, who had self-defined as a Hallyu fan since age twelve, said during her presentation that in the past she sincerely believed that she was going to marry a Hallyu star, the class laughed in response. The humorous part was enhanced as she defined it as a childhood fantasy while showing a photo of herself as a teenager opposite three different pictures of the mega-popular Korean actor Lee Min-Ho. The student's textual and visual messages and the audience reaction demonstrate the importance of humor in such future-oriented fantasy to avoid social criticism.

The story of an actual intermarriage between Daria and Adam provides a revelatory illustration of a humorless fantasy that became a reality. Daria's Jewish-Israeli family had begun to be interested in Korean TV dramas in the late 2010s, resulting in her marriage to a Korean man and herself becoming a Korean expert. The decision of Adam (a former Korean Christian) to become Jewish was met with racial resistance, despite the supposed openness of Judaism to conversion. For instance, his wife recalled such resistance in a recent media interview on her husband's "inappropriate" looks: "You look Korean, . . . [your eyes] are slanted, it's unthinkable. You don't look like a Jew." Yet after the conversion, Adam himself expressed a feeling of religious unity: "Thank goodness, after the conversion I finally feel [like] a person. A whole person" (quoted in Choukroun 2022). Such racial incongruity and ambiguity, along with religious unity and wholeness, once again demonstrate the interplay between social categories of race and ethnicity and alternative escape routes through religion and love.

Similar to past and present transracial humor and fantasy, the future-oriented ones, which are based on romantic attraction, have a symbolic power to escape from existing monoracial norms and realities. This correlates with a common view of Asia as a postmodern utopia (or dystopia) in which racial

Lyan

norms disappear or dissolve into something new in a truly global world that transcends racial barriers. Fantasizing about romantic relations with a Korean person provides another way to gain the minority capital through the future-oriented alternative for transracial unity. Such an alternative challenges a monoracial hegemonic model but also moves it toward an undefinable and distant—both in time and space—future, questioning its possibility. Akin to other cases of temporal racial translocalism, future-oriented fantasies challenge monoracial categories while keeping them safe.

Conclusion

In line with previous studies, I found that transracial jokes and fantasies are ambivalent in their ability to both strengthen and resist the existing social boundaries and hierarchies of race and ethnicity. While their content might have a transracial potential, the amusing, surprising, whimsical, humorous, and spiritual context in which they are placed weakens them. Besides embedded text vis-à-vis context incongruity, I found that such ambivalence is achieved by their temporality, expressed in nostalgia for a near-religious past spirituality, momentary national "merger and acquisitions," and future-oriented romantic fantasies. On the one hand, by turning to the ancient past, momentous present, or utopian future, fans symbolically challenge race as a natural and unchangeable social construct. On the other hand, the temporality of racial translocalism that exists in the imagined time and space weakens this challenge. Moreover, the allusion to the common imagination of Asia as a premodern, modern, or postmodern Other echoes the East/West hierarchy, according to which Asia forever remains an alternative only to Western hegemony.

Other ambivalence-building mechanisms include a sometimes intentional confusion between a humorous joke and a serious belief or feeling that sends a contradictory message regarding the possibility of transracialism, especially when expressed in public. The message might be humorous or sincere, while its audience might laugh with or at the messenger, since besides visual or (con)textual hints, one can only guess the degree of humor and seriousness. The common indirectness of such jokes and fantasies—someone else, rather than oneself, defines one as Korean-like—also makes their potential for disruption weaker and stronger at the same time.

"I Was Probably Korean in a Previous Life"

Unlike Koreaboo's direct addressing transracialism and attracting social criticism, transracial jokes and fantasies, both humorous and serious, direct and indirect, act as "softeners," "brokers," or "bumpers" in the symbolic negotiation of monoracial norms and standards. They evasively function as legitimacy-building recourses and tools in response to hegemonic monoracial logics, according to which White fans are questioned and even criticized for their not-White-enough fandom. Equipped with transracial jokes and fantasies, fans thus carefully engage in stigma management by symbolically redrawing social boundaries. These might explain the commonality and popularity of transracial humor and fantasy, which allow fans to avoid direct criticism of Koreaboo while achieving minority capital and Korea-expert status.

By addressing "how racial difference matters in the uses and reception of Korean popular culture," this chapter demonstrates the symbolic potential of transracial humor and fantasies in facing monoracial norms by creating imaginative realities within real ones. Spiritual connection, merger and acquisitions of the national sound, and romantic fantasies co-create alternative pasts, presents, and futures, generating a space and metamorphosis, even if partial or temporal, to be(come) Korean-like. As symbolic boundary work that touches on monoracial taboos, transracial jokes and fantasies both resist and facilitate the ongoing reproduction of social order. Such simultaneous (dis)identification between a usually White fan and a non-White fandom subject both challenges and naturalizes the asymmetric power relations between them. Even though studies of humor, as well as of fantasy, fiction, and fans, are often criticized as not serious enough, I hope that the current study sheds light on the critical discussion of negotiating (trans)racial (dis)similarity in the fannish reception of Korean popular culture.

Notes

1. Still, some parallels and similarities between Jews or Israelis and Koreans do exist. In the nineteenth century, Pyongyang was referred to as the "Jerusalem of the East" due to the growth of the local Protestant community (Hwang 2010), and some even believe that the mythological founding father of the Korean nation, Dangun, had his origins in the lost Jewish Dan tribe (Choi 2009, 3–5).

Lyan

Moreover, today some call Koreans "the Israelis of the East," given the national similarities between the two countries, such as being smaller nations surrounded by hostile neighbors and relying on human resources and American support (Lyan 2021).

2. See David C. Oh and Benjamin M. Han's introduction to this volume.

3. Docan-Morgan provides an excellent illustration of transracial humor and adoption: "And then, my mom never had a problem telling people like, our story, and she would just be like 'Yeah, we adopted them and they're our family and that's my daughter' and she would just make funny jokes like 'Why can't you tell it's my daughter? We have the same nose'" (2010, 151).

4. See https://www.facebook.com/TheKoreanit. These and the following translations from Hebrew are my own; the original poetic form and lack of punctuation have been deliberately retained.

5. One striking example of perceived racial similarity appeared in my previous study on Israeli-Korean business collaborations, in which Korean colleagues of an Israeli manager revealed in the sauna that he has a Mongolian spot, a blue birthmark believed to be a racial sign of Korean people. Amused by the finding, they immediately declared him a Korean being born by mistake as an Israeli (Lyan 2021).

6. On cosmetics and plastic surgeries, see Min Joo Lee's contribution to the current volume on race transition cosmetics tutorials tagged as #Korean and #wannabeKorean, non-Asian actors' portrayals of Asians, and Oli London's declaration about penis reduction surgery to become more Korean-like. Ji-Hyun Ahn's article (2023) on racial imagination and controversy surrounding non-Korean and non-Asian K-pop band members also provides a good illustration.

7. The possibility and size of this change should be addressed carefully. For instance, in a study on perceptions of Asian masculinity by American K-pop fans of boy bands, researchers reached the conclusion that, in general, Asian masculinity is not seen as surpassing or disrupting notions of mainstream masculinity but instead expresses a different (less masculine) desirable form (Lee, Lee, and Park 2020). Such alternative masculinity once again questions the potential of transracial humor and fantasies to challenge hegemonic White masculinity.

References

Ahn, Ji-Hyun. 2023. "K-pop without Koreans: Racial Imagination and Boundary Making in K-Pop." *International Journal of Communication* 17: 92–111.

Anderson, Benedict. 1983. *Imagined Communities: Reflections on the Origins and Spread of Nationalism.* London: Verso.

Bhabha, Homi. 1984. "Of Mimicry and Man: The Ambivalence of Colonial Discourse." *Discipleship: A Special Issue on Psychoanalysis* 28: 125–33. https://doi.org/10.2307/778467.

———. 1994. *The Location of Culture*. London: Routledge.

Bickerdike, Jennifer Otter. 2015. *The Secular Religion of Fandom: Pop Culture Pilgrim*. London: Sage Publications.

Choi, Chongko. 2009. "History of the Korean-Jewish Relationships." Unpublished paper.

Choukroun, Liat. 2022. "צעיר קוריאני השתוקק להיות יהודי. זה נגמר בחתונה עם דתיה מרמת הגולן" [Young Korean longed to be a Jew. It ended in the wedding with a religious woman from Ramat HaGolan]. *Shabaton*, June 29, 2022. https://shabaton1.co.il/?p=26020.

Chun, Elaine W. 2004. "Ideologies of Legitimate Mockery: Margaret Cho's Revoicings of Mock Asian." *Pragmatics* 14 (2/3): 263–89. https://doi.org/10.1075/prag.14.2-3.10chu.

Docan-Morgan, Sara. 2010. "Korean Adoptees' Retrospective Reports of Intrusive Interactions: Exploring Boundary Management in Adoptive Families." *Journal of Family Communication* 10 (3): 137–57. https://doi.org/10.1080/15267431003699603.

Elfving-Hwang, Joanna. 2018. "K-pop Idols, Artificial Beauty and Affective Fan Relationships in South Korea." In *Routledge Handbook of Celebrity Studies*, edited by Anthony Elliott, 190–201. London: Routledge.

Elfving-Hwang, Joanna, and Jane Park. 2016. "Deracializing Asian Australia? Cosmetic Surgery and the Question of Race in Australian Television." *Continuum* 30 (4): 397–407. https://doi.org/10.1080/10304312.2016.1141864.

Gieryn, Thomas F. 1983. "Boundary-Work and the Demarcation of Science from Non-science: Strains and Interests in Professional Ideologies of Scientists." *American Sociological Review* 48 (6): 781–95. https://doi.org/10.2307/2095325.

Han, Benjamin. 2017. "K-pop in Latin America: Transcultural Fandom and Digital Mediation." *International Journal of Communication* 11: 2250–69.

Hills, Matt. 2002. *Fan Cultures*. London: Routledge.

Hwang, Kyung Moon. 2010. *A History of Korea: An Episodic Narrative*. New York: Palgrave Macmillan.

Iwabuchi, Koichi. 2002. *Recentering Globalization: Popular Culture and Japanese Transnationalism*. Durham, NC: Duke University Press.

Jenkins, Henry. 2004. "Pop Cosmopolitanism: Mapping Cultural Flows in an Age of Media Convergence." In *Globalization: Culture and Education in the New Millennium*, edited by Marcelo M. Suárez-Orozco and Desirée Baolian Qin-Halliard, 114–40. Berkeley: University of California Press.

Jin, Dal Yong, Kyong Yoon, and Wonjung Min, eds. 2021. *Transnational Hallyu:*

The Globalization of Korean Digital and Popular Culture. Lanham, MD: Rowman and Littlefield.

Lamont, Michèle, and Virág Molnár. 2002. "The Study of Boundaries in the Social Sciences." *Annual Review of Sociology* 28: 167–95. https://doi.org/10.1146/annurev.soc.28.110601.141107.

Lee, Jeehyun Jenny, Rachel Kar Yee Lee, and Ji Hoon Park. 2020. "Unpacking K-pop in America: The Subversive Potential of Male K-pop Idols' Soft Masculinity." *International Journal of Communication* 14: 5900–5919.

Lee, Min Joo. 2020. "Touring the Land of Romance: Transnational Korean Television Drama Consumption from Online Desires to Offline Intimacy." *Journal of Tourism and Cultural Change* 18 (1): 67–80. https://doi.org/10.1080/14766825.2020.1707467.

Lo, Adrienne, and Jenna Chi Kim. 2012. "Linguistic Competency and Citizenship: Contrasting Portraits of Multilingualism in the South Korean Popular Media." *Journal of Sociolinguistics* 16 (2): 255–76. https://doi.org/10.1111/j.1467-9841.2012.00533.x.

London, Oli. 2021a. "Oli London - Koreaboo." OliLondonVEVO, May 1, 2021. YouTube video, 3:29. https://youtu.be/uaJKTJlcuYY.

London, Oli (@OliLondonTV). 2021b. "Transracial is a thing! . . ." Twitter, June 29, 2021. Reposted by lagoslately, Instagram, July 1, 2021, https://www.instagram.com/p/CQzSQ1VgQoM/.

Lyan, Irina. 2019. "Welcome to Korea Day: From Diasporic to *Hallyu* 'Fan-Nationalism.'" *International Journal of Communication* 13: 3764–80.

———. 2021. "'Koreans Are the Israelis of the East': A Postcolonial Reading of Cultural Similarities in Cross-Cultural Management." *Culture and Organization* 27 (6): 507–25. https://doi.org/10.1080/14759551.2021.1955254.

———. 2023. "Shock and Surprise: Theorizing the Korean Wave through Mediatized Emotions." *International Journal of Communication* 17: 29–51.

Lyan, Irina, and Alon Levkowitz. 2015a. "Consuming the Other: Israeli Hallyu Case Study." In *Hallyu 2.0: The Korean Wave in the Age of Social Media*, edited by Sangjoon Lee and Abé Mark Nornes, 212–28. Ann Arbor: University of Michigan Press.

———. 2015b. "From Holy Land to 'Hallyu Land': The Symbolic Journey Following the Korean Wave in Israel." *Journal of Fandom Studies* 3 (1): 7–21. https://doi.org/10.1386/jfs.3.1.7_1.

McCloud, Sean. 2003. "Popular Culture Fandoms, the Boundaries of Religious Studies, and the Project of the Self." *Culture and Religion* 4 (2): 187–206. https://doi.org/10.1080/0143883003200135674.

Oh, David C. 2017. "Black K-pop Fan Videos and Polyculturalism." *Popular Communication* 15 (4): 269–82. https://doi.org/10.1080/15405702.2017.1371309.

"I Was Probably Korean in a Previous Life"

Oh, David C., and Chuyun Oh. 2017. "Vlogging White Privilege Abroad: *Eat Your Kimchi*'s Eating and Spitting Out of the Korean Other on YouTube." *Communication, Culture and Critique* 10 (4): 696–711. https://doi.org/10.1111/cccr.12180.

Otmazgin, Nissim, and Irina Lyan. 2014. "Hallyu across the Desert: K-pop Fandom in Israel and Palestine." *Cross-Currents: East Asian History and Culture Review* 3 (1): 32–55. https://doi.org/10.1353/ach.2014.0008.

———. 2018. "Fan Entrepreneurship: Fandom, Agency, and the Marketing of Hallyu in Israel." *Kritika Kultura* 32: 288–307. https://doi.org/10.13185/2987.

Park, Michael K. 2015. "Psy-zing up the Mainstreaming of 'Gangnam Style': Embracing Asian Masculinity as Neo-minstrelsy?" *Journal of Communication Inquiry* 39 (3): 195–212. https://doi.org/10.1177/0196859915575068.

Rosa, Jonathan, and Nelson Flores. 2017. "Unsettling Race and Language: Toward a Raciolinguistic Perspective." *Language in Society* 46 (5): 621–47. https://doi.org/10.1017/S0047404517000562.

Rosenau, Sara Haskin. 2022. "Mock Koreaboo: Appropriating Appropriation." MA thesis, University of Colorado.

Saeji, CedarBough T. 2018. "No Frame to Fit It All: An Autoethnography on Teaching Undergraduate Korean Studies, on and off the Peninsula." *Acta Koreana* 21 (2): 443–59.

Said, Edward. 1978. *Orientalism*. London: Routledge.

Shifman, Limor, and Elihu Katz. 2005. "'Just Call Me Adonai': A Case Study of Ethnic Humor and Immigrant Assimilation." *American Sociological Review* 70 (5): 843–59. https://doi.org/10.1177/000312240507000506.

Sue, Christina A., and Tanya Golash-Boza. 2013. "'It Was Only a Joke': How Racial Humour Fuels Colour-Blind Ideologies in Mexico and Peru." *Ethnic and Racial Studies* 36 (10): 1582–98. https://doi.org/10.1080/01419870.2013.783929.

Tuvel, Rebecca. 2017. "In Defense of Transracialism." *Hypatia* 32 (2): 263–78. https://doi.org/10.1111/hypa.12327.

Watson, Cate. 2014. "A Sociologist Walks into a Bar (and Other Academic Challenges): Towards a Methodology of Humour." *Sociology* 49 (3): 407–21. https://doi.org/10.1177/0038038513516694.

Wolfers, Solvejg, Kieran File, and Stephanie Schnurr. 2017. "'Just Because He's Black': Identity Construction and Racial Humour in a German U-19 Football Team." *Journal of Pragmatics* 112: 83–96. https://doi.org/10.1016/j.pragma.2017.02.003.

Won, Yong-Jin, Huikyong Pang, Jun-hyung Lee, and Marisa Luckie. 2020. "'코리아부(Koreaboo)': BTS Universe가 미운 퍼즐 한 조각" ["Koreaboo, a Missing Piece of the BTS Universe Puzzle"]. *Korean Journal of Journalism and Communication Studies* 64 (4): 471–99. https://doi.org/10.20879/kjjcs.2020.64.4.013.

Yoon, Kyong. 2018. "Global Imagination of K-pop: Pop Music Fans' Lived Experiences of Cultural Hybridity." *Popular Music and Society* 41 (4): 373–89. https://doi.org/10.1080/03007766.2017.1292819.

———. 2019. "Transnational Fandom in the Making: K-pop Fans in Vancouver." *International Communication Gazette* 81 (2): 176–92. https://doi.org/10.1177/1748048518802964.

———. 2022. *Diasporic Hallyu: The Korean Wave in Korean Canadian Youth Culture.* Cham, Switzerland: Palgrave Macmillan.

8

······

Hallyu Dreaming

*Making Sense of Race and Gender
in K-dramas in the US Midwest and Ireland*

······

REBECCA CHIYOKO KING-O'RIAIN

When *Squid Game* burst onto Netflix in 2021, few had predicted that it would become Netflix's biggest hit ever with 111 million viewers and US$891 million in "impact value" (Lachapelle 2021). Fans of Korean dramas who live outside of Korea, however, were not surprised, having long been viewers of Korean content on streaming platforms such as Netflix, Rakuten Viki, and Amazon Prime. Prior Korean dramas on streaming platforms laid the groundwork for interest in Korean content outside of Korea, often referred to as the Korean Wave or Hallyu, that help lead to the unprecedented success of *Squid Game*. Why has Hallyu taken hold recently in non-Asian countries, and how does a fan's race, class, or gender background come to shape how they interpret the Korean dramas they are watching in local terms in the Midwest of the United States and on the island of Ireland?

This chapter explores these research questions through comparative survey, interview, and ethnographic research with fans of Korean dramas, focusing on Latina, Black, and White fans in the US Midwest and White fans on the island of Ireland (north and south). It investigates how Korean dramas are used as emotional resources through local cultural strategies to support non-hegemonic identities and practices in racialized translocal contexts. In particular, it extends racial translocalism through an analysis of ethnographic data on some of the ways that the process of racial translocal understanding is constructed. It argues that understandings of Korean masculinity, gleaned through watching K-dramas, motivates American midwestern fans, within their local contexts as Latinx or Black women, to take action (join fan groups, learn Korean, travel to Korea) as an alternative to what they deem in their local contexts as undesirable "toxic masculinity" and as an attempt to deal with forms of exclusion in their local lived experiences. For Irish fans, Korean dramas are a much needed break from their everyday lives, often from working-class positions, and provide a vehicle for dreaming of global mobility and getting off the island of Ireland.

Why Are Korean Dramas Popular?

Theories of cultural proximity predicted that Korean dramas would be popular in other Asian countries (inter-Asian cultural exchange), extending South Korea's "soft power" in the region, because of similar experiences of rapid modernization and cultural or geographic "closeness" to Korea (Kim and Bae 2016). For example, Ik-ki Kim and Sang Joon Bae (2016) argue that Confucian and other Asian cultural values (filial piety, etc.), which deeply permeate K-drama, would resonate with socially conservative values of receiving Asian countries. One of these values is sexual modesty, and relative to US content available in the region, there are fewer graphically sexual scenes in traditional terrestrial Korean television, which is tightly controlled by the Korean Communications Standards Commission (KCSC). The KCSC claims that "it enforces strict regulations on depictions of sexuality because such scenes would 'destroy Korean moral sensibility and ethics'" (M. J. Lee 2020a, 108), and this may be one reason that K-dramas are appealing to non-Korean, Muslim, Latinx, and Black fans.

Other authors posit that K-dramas contain broader themes with wider appeal that gain new audiences as platforms such as Netflix and Rakuten Viki rapidly expand across the world. As Hyejung Ju explains, this is because of a "high degree of emotional involvement" with the dramas and feelings of pleasure through "affective consumption" of Korean dramas (2020, 32). Lisa Longenecker and Jooyoun Lee found that "K-dramas can develop storylines that can appeal to a wider range of audiences ... and presents the possibility that Korean popular culture has the capability to win minds of non-Asian audiences" (2018, 121), which could reverse the tide of popular culture from West to East, introducing a "contra-flow" (Thussu

Hallyu Dreaming

2006). This generates an increasing interest in Asian popular culture flowing from East to West. However, not all dramas become popular or successful in the global market, and these studies do not explain why K-dramas, in particular, might have taken hold among specific social groups or in particular translocal contexts, such as with fans of color in Chicago or in Ireland.

Prior studies have focused on the contents and flow of the Korean Wave (Y. Kim 2021; Yoon and Jin 2017; Kuwahara 2014; Jin 2016), but this chapter shifts the focus to the "shore" (the transnational digital audience) upon which the Korean Wave falls. This chapter explores an alternative explanation—that the appeal of K-drama to non-Asian viewers is due to how these Korean drama narratives help these viewers interpret, and re-interpret, their own local racial, gender, and class context (see Yoon 2019). In this sense, the study works from data collected from the bottom up to center fan voices, experiences, and emotions in digital Korean drama encounters that often go unheard—specifically those of non-White US fans, male fans, older fans, fans with fewer resources, and non-US fans.

Focusing less on the content of the Korean Wave and more on the transnational reception of Korean media, Ingyu Oh (2017), writing about Korean popular culture fans, argues that the cultural proximity explanation essentializes Confucian cultural values and that the appeal of K-dramas has more to do with these emotional outcomes (melancholia) or parasocial relationships (one-way mass emotional relationships from fans to actors) that the dramas incur for viewers in their local contexts. In particular, he argues that this appeal is related to how it allows the audience to devise strategies for addressing the experience of marginalization and exclusion. Borrowing from Judith Butler, David Eng and Shinhee Han (2019a, 2019b) refine this idea as "racial melancholia," which are the "histories of racial loss that are condensed into a forfeited object whose significance must be deciphered for its social meaning." Hua Hsu explains that "[o]ur inability to comprehend the reason for our melancholia pushes us further into our subconscious depths, and manifests as a kind of permanent mourning" (2019). The object in this case study is the Korean dramas that create social meaning tied to a sense of racial and gendered melancholia for non-Asian viewers.

This sense of loss and mourning, in facing gender and racial inequality, has driven some to seek solace in Korean drama. Min Joo Lee found that images of Korean men in dramas drove non-Asian women not only to avidly watch Korean dramas but led some to travel to Korea—seeking what Lee calls "transnational intimacy" (2020b)—a possible racialized form of gendered melancholia to quell a feeling of lack and fill a gap in their lives. These types of social actions are difficult to explain with melancholia alone but might be seen as "cultural resources or orientations" (M. J. Lee 2020b) that help explain the popularity of K-drama with non-Asian fans as a way to cope with gender and racial exclusion in the American and Irish contexts.

Building on these insights, this chapter illustrates how fans of Korean dramas in the US Midwest and Ireland also interpret these dramas through gendered, racialized, and classed lenses from within their own lived experiences and use them to "dream" of a globally mobile life. Hyunji Lee explains, "Although many Western fans are drawn to K-dramas because they provide a fantasy escape into a different world that holds the promise of a predictable yet enticing romance with beautiful, caring men, K-dramas and K-drama fandom also provide opportunities to develop and expand cultural knowledge, perspectives and worldviews" (2017, 376).

The fans in this study yearned to learn the Korean language and travel to Korea, in part to fulfill this fantasy, which developed through strong emotional connections to what they thought Koreans and Korea were. In a study of K-drama fans in Spain, Kyong Yoon, Wonjung Min, and Dal Yong Jin found that "the fans ... (are) engaging with Korean dramas as a new cultural resource by which they fantasize about alternative and possible lives. ... they engaged with K-pop as a way of rethinking their local contexts, imagining an alternative future, seeking personal growth and exploring intercultural understanding" (Yoon, Min, and Jin 2020, 140, 143), but they do so from their own locally gendered and racialized standpoints.

This chapter shows that K-drama motivates interest among its fans because they find a new (often digital) social world in which they can participate—the fandom itself. They experience the community of fans as a welcoming "affinity space." "Affinity spaces within digitally mediated networks function as 'contact zones' where K-pop is introduced to other cultures" (Min, Jin, and Han 2019, 613). This is most obvious in the case of racialization; for example, Wonseok Lee and Grace Kao discuss how Black fans of BTS or #BlackARMYs "not only reminded other fans of racism within the fandom, but also asked BTS and their fellow ARMYs to support

Hallyu Dreaming

BLM" (2021, 70). In another example, Crystal Anderson in her chapter in this volume illustrates how Black YouTube reactors to K-pop videos use "Black joy" to position their experiences and themselves in relation to Korean popular cultural material.

This chapter illustrates two main ways that fans interpret K-dramas through their own local lenses and lived experiences. First, in terms of gender, Korean dramas offer alternative notions of masculinity, which are racialized and essentialized as Korean (or Asian more generally) "soft masculinity." This is a counter to hegemonic toxic masculinity in the United States and Ireland. Second, fans use the above understanding of Korean men to reimagine their lives by learning Korean (or as Min Joo Lee's chapter in this volume examines, how they dream of actually becoming Korean) and traveling or relocating to Korea to feed their dreams of global mobility and cosmopolitanism.

Methods

From 2018 to 2022 (in person until the pandemic in 2020), I conducted participant-observation (at K-pop concerts, disco nights, film screenings, fan club gatherings, and conventions), conducted surveys (110 in Chicago in July 2018 and 100 in June 2019 in London—including some European respondents), and conducted qualitative in-depth interviews (30 in Europe and United States) with various types of Korean popular culture fans (both drama and music). This chapter draws on data from the United States and Ireland (north and south). The project received institutional ethical approval, and all the interviewee identities have been given pseudonyms to protect their privacy.

Interviewees were sampled through purposive sampling seeking general self-identified fans of Korean popular culture; that is, they were selected from fan forums, from fan clubs, at in-person fan events, at concerts, and elsewhere, and I did not seek any particular type of fan (opinion leaders, people of color, etc.). Therefore, findings are not generalizable to the larger fan population but do give a broad view into the lives of fans of Hallyu outside of Asia. The ethnography was more focused and conducted in person in Chicago and London. Many studies of Korean popular culture describe the typical international fan as female and White (M. J. Lee 2020b). However,

King-O'Riain

this chapter focuses more particularly on non-traditional fans (non-White fans, male fans, older fans, fans with fewer resources, and fans outside of the United States), a growing and important group, to examine how racialized, gendered, and classed narratives in their own lives constitute an affinity space within the Korean drama fandom. The fanbase in Chicago (drawing fans from all over the Midwest) and in Ireland (drawing fans from both north and south) demonstrates a striking diversity in fans' ages, ethnicities/races, class backgrounds, and geographic locations—defying the stereotype of K-drama and K-pop fans as teenage girls.

From my own surveys at K-pop concerts in Chicago and London, the responses show that there is a strong gendered element in the fandom with 85 percent indicating female and 15 percent male identity. To date, there is little reliable data on the racial/ethnic breakdown of Korean popular culture fans, so my survey results from Chicago are particularly telling. Table 8.1 illustrates the racial/ethnic breakdown of fans surveyed in Chicago (n = 110), reflecting an American racial context.

In 2018, 55 percent of all Chicago-based fans described themselves as non-White, but only 15 percent identified as Asian or Asian Pacific Islanders (API). Michelle Cho explains that early on in the Korean Wave (Hallyu) in North America, the majority of fans were women of color as K-wave (K-pop, K-drama, *manhwa*—comic books, etc.) and the fandom was a safe "space for people not interested in mainstream popular culture" (Cho 2021), so in one sense, it is not surprising to see many Latina and Black fans in the Midwest.

TABLE 8.1. Racial/Ethnic Self-Identification of Survey Participants in Chicago

	n	*Percentage*
WHITE/CAUCASIAN	49	45%
HISPANIC/LATINO	24	22%
BLACK	13	12%
ASIAN/API	17	15%
MIXED	7	6%

Hallyu Dreaming

Findings

US FANS IN THE MIDWEST MAKING SENSE OF KOREAN DRAMA MASCULINITY

Fans in the US Midwest say they watch K-dramas because they are interesting and better written, but they also strive to watch because the "cultural difference" is appealing to them. Carina, a twenty-four-year-old Latina from Iowa, explains that Korean dramas are not "cringey" like the telenovelas her mother watches with bad acting, poor production quality, and ridiculous storylines. She likes learning about Korean cultural practices (informal/formal language, religious ceremonies, cultural practices in drinking, health and house cleanliness) as well as Korean products (phones, cars, food, beauty, fashion). However, it still remains the case that she is making sense of these new cultural symbols through her own Mexican American interpretive lens. For Carina, her familiarity with telenovelas and the fact that they are not realistic or are overacted means that she judges them to be cringey and lack authenticity, but her lack of familiarity with Korean culture means she is more likely to take what she sees in K-dramas at face value. In particular, Carina is enchanted with the Korean men in the dramas she watches, and that, she explains, is how she chooses which dramas she will watch—that is, if they star her favorite Korean male actor rather than by genre. Next, I turn to analyze how these gendered meanings from K-dramas interact with racialization processes in order to contribute to their popularity.

ASIAN MASCULINITY RE-IMAGINED?

First, I examine understandings of Korean masculinity for fans in the US Midwest (interviews, ethnography, and surveys sampled in Chicago). In the survey that I conducted in Chicago in 2018, I asked fans to name three words to describe Korean men. As Vanessa, an eighteen-year-old Latina from Chicago, was filling out the survey, I held her water bottle in line at a K-pop concert, and she stopped halfway through the survey to ask me for clarification on what I meant by a question. She said, "I only know about Korean idols. I don't know any 'normal' Korean men."

King-O'Riain

However, most of those surveyed were happy to list adjectives to describe "Korean men," and many openly gushed about Korean men and used language to describe Korean men that I found radically different from long-held stereotypes of Asian men as emasculated and asexual (Espiritu 1997, 91). When asked, the most often used adjectives to describe Korean men (when they listed them) were tall, handsome, talented, hardworking, old school, traditional, polite, stylish, cute, amazing, manly, and masculine. This description of Korean men is the polar opposite to the past images of Korean men (and Asian men more generally). Past visions of Asian masculinity in US popular culture portrayed Asian men as sexless Asian sidekicks (who never get the girl), such as Charlie Chan, the Chinese laundryman, or feminized as "servants" and domestic laborers doing women's work such as laundry and cooking (Espiritu 1997, 91). Grace Kao, Kelly Stamper Balistreri, and Kara Joyner found that Asian men in the United States suffered in the dating market from these images that portrayed Asian men as "geeky and undesirable men, unable to attract women" and that "more than 90% of non-Asian women said they would not date an Asian man" (2018, 52).

The new image of Korean men, portrayed in dramas, shifts notions of masculinity as a site of remasculinization and a reinscription of bodily work (worked-out body, weight lifting, fit, six pack/choco abs, etc.) onto Asian male bodies. "The new look is urban and cosmopolitan: a slim face with large eyes, high cheekbones and a straight nose with a tall, trim body and long legs. And viewers actually get to see the abs and the legs" (Lie 2015, 106). This was a theme mentioned repeatedly in my interviews with K-drama fans, and many eagerly looked forward to "shower scenes" in K-dramas in which they might catch a glimpse of the worked-out Korean male body. Other authors such as Crystal Anderson argue that masculinity with Korean popular music stars "manifest overlapping masculinities, a range of masculinities that occur simultaneously, which reflect both Korean and American, especially African American, cultural elements" (2014, 118). These overlapping masculinities "disrupt emasculating stereotypes and challenge Western-based modes of masculinity" (128), and this might contribute to how multiple masculinities are understood by fans coming from many cultures.

These overlapping masculinities are grounded in Korean dramas' images

Hallyu Dreaming

of Korean men as having an athletic ability/body work alongside gentlemanly attitudes. Male leads often come across as "new men" who do not portray traditional notions of sexism but appear to have genuine respect for women. This should not come as a surprise as most K-dramas are written by Korean women. Masculinity in mainstream K-dramas, for the most part, is also unquestionably heterosexual, although there is a growing catalog of Boys' Love dramas featuring homoerotic love, which is enjoyed by female fans and which has inspired a growing number of titles of homoerotic fanfiction on creative platforms such as Wattpad.[1] Fans perceived and enjoyed K-dramas because they provided a temporary escape into an attractive and romantic racialized and gendered fantasy where they can experience innocence and respect; expect happy endings; and watch beautiful, caring, and feminized guys as a contrast to their own everyday lives in which they may not feel respected by toxic masculinity in their own (for Carina, Latinx) communities. They are creating a comparison between the soft masculinity they see in the drama and the toxic masculinity that they experience locally. K-dramas help provide an archetype of an alternative masculinity, which can be engaged every day through viewing K-dramas. While we will discuss that many of these images may not be that realistic, for these fans, who may never go to Korea or meet a real Korean man, the dramas provide a fantasy that allows them to envision a different man than the one they have in front of them in the West. Julia Trzcińska and David C. Oh argue in this volume that this emotion comes from female fans feeling empowered to have new gendered experiences and through imagining both feminine and masculine characteristics, such as through K-pop idols on TikTok.

MANLY, BUT FEMININE . . .
FLOWER BOYS AND SOFT MASCULINITY

The shift in masculinity as seen in K-dramas can, in part, be explained through the notion of the transformation and reconstruction of South Koreanness that is driven by the "transcultural hybridization" processes between Korean traditional masculinities and global masculinities (Jung 2010) but also by fans' racialized understandings. Sun Jung explains, "Western desire for the Other is expressed, transformed, and redefined by consuming hybrid South Korean masculinity. . . . it is different from earlier Orientalist desires towards the primitive Other. This desire is ambivalent because it seeks the strangeness of Otherness and, at the same time, the familiarity of modern 'coolness'" (2010, 31–32). The linking of modern coolness to Korea is racialized when laid upon the bodies of Korean male actors.

One of the predominant initial reactions to the masculinity of the Korean actors in this study was that although they are masculine and no longer nerdy, asexual undesirables, they were still locally decoded as more feminine than men in the West or having soft masculinity (Lee, Lee, and Park 2020). Korean men could appear feminine (wearing makeup) and good at domestic labor (cooking) in the dramas, typically feminine attributes, but still be considered masculine and heterosexual men. However, female fans did not dislike femininity in men nor read it as a sign of homosexuality the way that it might have been in an earlier era. I met Mary in Chicago standing in line waiting for entry to a K-pop concert. We were a similar age (forties to fifties), and she asked me why I was at the concert as it is still unusual to see middle-aged women at K-pop venues. She explained to me that she and a friend had traveled by car (over eight hours) from Minnesota for the concert. Mary described herself as a "forty-something, White American woman." She explained what she likes about "flower boys": "Also, the concept of *flower boys* is almost completely unknown, at least in America. For men to wear so much makeup and care for their skin is seen as feminine and sometimes considered homosexual. It frustrates me to no end how narrow minded some people can be in regard to standards of beauty in other cultures." US midwestern fans were often struck by the fact that one of the main criticisms they hear about K-dramas is that the men are too beautiful or that they "all look gay." The tight connection between gender (masculinity) and assumed sexual orientation (homosexuality) was racialized and read onto Korean male bodies who are gendered as "feminine men," but this is now imbued with desirable attributes.

PJ, a White dad in his fifties from the Chicago suburbs, his sixteen-year-old daughter, and I were chatting in line to get drinks at a K-pop concert in Chicago. Being the same age as myself, he leaned in and said in a whisper, "Can you explain something to me? I don't get the androgyny. These Korean guys wear makeup regularly, color their hair, pierce their ears. They look like girls!" The gender ambiguity unsettled many men from the Midwest,

Hallyu Dreaming

203

like PJ, who described himself to me as a "traditional working-class guy," and they "couldn't get used to" boys who "look like girls." Fans, including his daughter, however, reported that it was precisely this gender ambiguity and softer form of masculinity that was the primary appeal.

RESISTING TOXIC MASCULINITY: "KOREAN MEN JUST RUIN IT FOR YOU"

In addition to physical appearance, the personalities and values of Korean male actors were gendered and racialized. In 2018, at a K-pop concert in Chicago, as the summer heat and humidity took hold and the line of thousands of fans snaked around the concert venue, I struck up a conversation with Lucia, a thirty-something Mexican American mother, and her teenage daughter in line in front of me. After we established which songs we like best and who our biases are, the conversation turned to K-dramas we have recently watched and are recommending to each other. We talked about Lucia's favorite actors (she is a Ji Chang-wook fan who had just finished watching the *K2* drama). When we began to talk about the main character, she swung around and sighed and said to me, "Korean men just ruin it for you!" Taken aback by her comment, I asked her to clarify what she meant. She continued, "All other men come up short compared to them. They are natural, funny; they are gentlemanly. There are things about Korean culture that are similar to my Mexican culture: family-oriented, men are men and protect women, they are kind to women, respect women; it is not all sexualized and graphic the way it is with American dramas."

Drawing parallels and critiques between portrayed Korean and Mexican masculinity revealed the desire for "men who are men and protect women" but are also respectful men. For Lucia, this is clearly opposed to US dramas, which she claims are predominantly "whiter than white," and perhaps White men who are not respectful family-oriented men, but who, in her view, are overly sexually aggressive. Lucia, has not had a chance to travel to Korea and knows no Korean men in real life, but the image of Korean masculinity has made her hold local Mexican American men she meets up to a higher standard. This may impose impossible (and unrealistic) standards upon other men, but it allows Lucia to hold her standards high even if these standards are "ruined" by K-drama masculinity.

King-O'Riain

In Chicago, female-identified viewers, primarily Muslim, Latina, and Black American women, mentioned the absence of graphic sex scenes, fewer portrayals of graphic violence, and less aggressive forms of masculinity in K-dramas. This is despite having little exposure to, nor holding, Confucian or Asian cultural values. For example, Gabrielle, a twenty-two-year-old Black American woman from Chicago, explained to me that she is "sick of seeing all those light-skinned girls in bikinis grinding in [Black American] rap videos" and considers the portrayal of women in K-pop music videos and dramas to be much more respectful to women. Just from watching K-dramas, Gabrielle developed strong feelings about Korean men as more respectful. She was not alone. With only 5 out of 210 K-drama surveyed fans having been to Korea, most K-drama fans stated that they know very little about Korean culture and have not met a real Korean person. Yet, like Gabrielle, they voraciously consume K-dramas. The fans' understandings, developed or imagined, are in resistance to or reaction to toxic masculinity. Importantly, their desire for soft or new masculinity is highly racialized as Koreanness (racially) signifies difference, otherness, exoticization, and the possibility of a differently desirable masculinity—ironically, in direct opposition (attraction rather than repulsion) to prior images of Asian men. As Jeehyun Jenny Lee, Rachel Kar Yee Lee, and Ji Hoon Park argue, "Masculinity as stemming from an Asian culture further accentuates its difference from White, hegemonic masculinity, inadvertently contributing to the maintenance of the binary opposition of Asian and White masculinity" (2020, 5914).

Many of those I interviewed in Chicago were fed up with what they labeled toxic masculinity prevalent in the United States and particularly present in some rap and hip hop music and videos (broadly racialized as Black music), and they argued that it was more prevalent in recent years and more cavalierly expressed on digital media.[2] Min Joo Lee explains that this is because "they characterized Korean men as the racial and sexual *other* who served as the antitheses of the purportedly hypersexual men and sexually oriented cultures from which they came" (2020a, 117). The "otherness" of Korean soft masculinity for Desiree, a Black American fan in her twenties from the South Side of Chicago, is an alternative to the "booty call" and disrespect by some Black men present in local Black culture. However, her understanding of Korean men is arguably an iteration of Orientalism and

Hallyu Dreaming

racialized objectification, which perpetuates the binary opposition between Korean and Black American masculinity.

The fans in Chicago clearly did not mock Asian masculinity (such as in the Psy "Gangnam Style" phase in 2012), but valorizing the Korean man as the perfect man flattens difference in racially exoticizing ways. This comparison reinscribes the link between Korean men, and Asian men more generally, with femininity in contrast to US and Irish toxic masculinity. While such a contrast is interesting in thinking about global masculinities, it could also just be a new form of objectifying Asian men with feminine qualities adhering to Asian male bodies without realizing that patriarchy and toxic masculinities exist in Korean society as well. So while Korean masculinity may make them question toxic hegemonic masculinity in their own Latinx and Black local cultures, it may also reinscribe feminine, and in some cases, unrealistic forms of masculinity upon Korean men, which obscure fairly persistent forms of patriarchy present in contemporary Korea. Nonetheless, this is now posed as a desirable alternative to toxic hegemonic masculinity. The fans' interpretations are less of an expression of understanding of lived reality of masculinity in Korea and more of a reflection of where they are within their own local contexts and relationships with men in their own racialized and gendered communities.

IRISH DREAMS OF GLOBAL MOBILITY

Even so, K-dramas and the Korean masculinity portrayed within them continue to transport viewers, if only temporarily, into dreams of cultural and global mobility, quelling the feeling that their life lacks certain satisfaction and feeding the melancholia that Eng and Han (2019) write about. For most fans, their interest in Korea comes from watching K-dramas, and they dream of learning Korean and visiting or moving to Korea. In this sense, they wish for new cultural experiences and to meet new people who are not like themselves. Ultimately, fans' exposure and negotiations with new racialized forms of gender in K-dramas are underpinned by dreams of global and cultural mobility. Ironically, they invert the image that Korean and Korean American woman have of White men from the United States. As Nadia Kim explains, "Korean women's gender strategies, i.e., the ways they addressed Korean patriarchy . . . used the ideal of the gender progres-

King-O'Riain

sive white American man as the bar against which they challenged Korean men as patriarchal, hence backwards in the 'third world' sense" (2006, 532).

Irish fans, who see Korea as being "worlds away" both geographically and culturally, mentioned the "exotic" or unfamiliar parts of K-dramas as attractive and as a motivating force for why they watch them. They often used their perception of Korean culture's uniqueness and difference to demarcate it from their everyday lives in Ireland. Underneath this appreciation for Korean culture, food, and customs was a deep longing to travel to Korea, to meet a Korean man, and to imagine their lives there as an escape from the grind of their everyday lives at home. As Hyunji Lee writes:

> Western fans enjoy K-drama for the escape it provides and the desire to develop a better understanding of different cultures. Their experience, thus, exhibits hybridity; it is a complex mixture of fantasy and realism—a desire to participate in a romantic fantasy world and to embrace pop cosmopolitanism. I believe that the information, ideas, and cultural values depicted in K-drama that Western fans recognize, learn, and embrace as "Korean" paradoxically add authenticity to K-drama's content, creating a "real" cultural, yet fantasy, experience for those who crave something different. . . . And I argue that K-drama functions as a tool for fans to gain knowledge, expand their cultural views, and differentiate themselves from their local culture. (2017, 377)

Often this desire to learn more about Korea, including language, food, and culture, was a manifestation of dreams of mobility out of their present jobs, life, locations, and relationships and into an "exotic" place where a Korean man will make their lives better. In reality, while many K-drama fans are trying to learn Korean, most still need subtitles in English, which frustrates them. They view Korea as a place where there are polite and respectful people and particularly men who respect women, contributing to a changing understanding of Asian masculinity more generally in the United States. As Kelly Chong and Nadia Kim argue, new forms of Asian American masculinity, which they call "the model man," are emerging in terms of interracial relationships with White women. They write, "'The Model Man,' a hybrid masculinity construction that combines the elements of White hegemonic masculinity and model minority-based 'Asian' masculinity, is co-opted and deployed by men assexual/romantic capital—especially in re-

Hallyu Dreaming

lation to White women—because it enables the men to present themselves as desirable romantic partners" (2022, 674). They argue that the increasing desirability of Asian American men to White women is supported in part by media images of Asian American men, and this is true even outside of the United States and Ireland.

There was a strong local dimension to these global dreams, which after all were unlikely to "come true" for any but a tiny minority as many would have to consider emigration. Irish people have often had to emigrate due to the high cost of living in Ireland and the lack of housing and employment opportunities. Key to the credibility of the global dream was to differentiate themselves in their local setting and to explain why and how watching K-dramas made them "different" from their peers. Many of the Irish fans I spoke with said that they feel if they traveled to Korea, they would be familiar with Korean culture. Jean, an eighteen-year-old male fan from Northern Ireland, explained to me, "It (Korean culture) doesn't really surprise me as much anymore, the landscape and surroundings, it looks like a very peaceful country. Oh how I'd love to go there!" I found the reference to peace particularly interesting as on the day that the interview took place in May of 2019, North Korea had launched ballistic missiles tests, reminding South Korea that peace on the Korean peninsula is fragile. Jean was keenly aware of the concept of peace living in Northern Ireland where the peace agreement between Catholics and Protestants remains under challenge in the current era by the pressures of Brexit and the fact that the Assembly still struggles to cooperate.

Rachel, a twenty-two-year-old White Irish woman who works at a local café in the midlands in the Republic of Ireland, watches K-dramas every chance she can. She does not particularly like the repetitive and demanding parts of her job, but she likes the people she meets at work. She tells me how she is working hard each day, striving, keeping going, to think of a life beyond her daily routine. She dreams of escaping and going on a trip to Korea, but her friend who would accompany her does not have a passport. We exchange some of our favorite dramas, and then she explains why she wants to go to Korea.

> RACHEL: I would love to go to just travel and go "oh my God that is
> where they filmed this" or "that is the premise of this one," because

King-O'Riain

they do that all the time where they are based in Seoul, and it would be really cool to walk around there and see the big blue buses and the little markets that they have. I would love to try it and at the same time, would I like it?

INTERVIEWER: Before you started watching Korean dramas, did you know anything about Korea?

RACHEL: No, and it is weird, I do know a bit now, but at the same time if you asked me who the president was or who a big important leader is, I would still be a bit like, no.

INTERVIEWER: But culturally?

RACHEL: Culturally, I would know a bit now. Watching K-dramas, you learn they are really polite, always have to bow and sort of . . . If you are drinking, you sort of cover yourself when you drink on your own, and it wouldn't be like here where someone would just say cheers and you'd all down it and stuff. You take your shoes off in the house. I love that idea. We should totally do it!

Detailed knowledge of and interest in a "distant" culture further separated her from her peers. She said it stigmatized her and that her friends would not watch the K-dramas with her; it was a differentiating factor in her local social contexts, but it did draw her into close affinity with other fans of K-dramas whom she chatted with via X, formerly called Twitter. Ultimately, her understanding echoes Cordula Weisskôpple's definition of translocal as "securing one's own existence . . . in a new space" (2013, 288). Of the few fans in the sample who had visited Korea, Kay, age twenty-two, who hails from Northern Ireland, explained to me that she was surprised by many things in Korea as they were different from the dramas she watched at home. Her biggest surprise was that Korean people in Seoul do not really speak with strangers (herself) at all, and she found it really difficult to speak with, much less befriend, Korean men. She did go to one club in Hongdae where she was approached by Korean men asking her if she was "open minded" or if she "lived alone." She said she avoided this type of Korean man as they were not sincere, but she found it almost impossible to meet what she termed a "real Korean" man.

Fans described Korean food and culture as wonderful and interesting, and they had very positive images of Korea. Georgia, a self-described

Hallyu Dreaming

Koreaboo living in Dublin, said that she has a good idea of what Korea is like from the dramas and that there would not be too much culture shock since she "sees" and "hears" Korean culture through TV dramas every day. However, reality may be very different for her when she visits. The reality of youth unemployment in Korea, low marriage and fertility rates, gender inequality, and an increasingly competitive education system seem to pass her by in her imagination of a better life in Korea (see KOSTAT 2022; OECD 2021). In some ways, it may not matter, because what is working for her as the cure for melancholia is the imagined fantasy and feel-good factor or affinity of watching K-dramas, much like romance novels have functioned for housewives (Radway 1984) to provide an escape from the everyday grind as well as a romantic lead (or second lead) to represent the kindness and attention that they may not receive in their own lives.

For Irish fans in particular, K-dramas also led to thoughts of emigration, a historical and now recurring trend of young Irish people leaving Ireland due to lack of affordable housing, jobs, and career prospects. Given the Irish context, both economic and, in the north, political instability shape Hallyu dreams as a way of coping with marginalization in Irish society. This dream of global mobility, however, was often underpinned by the perception that fans had specifically of Korean men. Rachel, from above, explained to me she found the display of affection between men in Korean dramas interesting, and she mentions that Korean male friends tend to put their arms around each other more than men in Ireland (skinship). She adds, "I think guys here [in Ireland] find it very hard over here to be like they are hugging and they are not gay, that is so weird." She liked the more fluid and affectionate masculinity she saw portrayed in K-dramas and that was part of the attraction of watching them for her. James, age twenty-three, from Ireland explained to me the differences between what he saw as Korean masculinity and Irish masculinity.

INTERVIEWER: Do you think there is a style of masculinity in some K-dramas?

JOHN: Oh God yes. . . . obviously they are a lot more "feminine" that is a whole other argument, but by Irish standards, they are feminine. . . . People will be bothered by it because that is how people are, people don't like change. I don't particularly care . . .

King-O'Riain

For both Rachel and James, the alternative, more feminine Korean masculinity is appealing and something that they see as positively different and a reason to want to travel to Korea to experience firsthand. Finally, K-dramas, and Hallyu or Korean cultural content more generally, are providing a vision of a wider world to many fans—a familiar difference in their lives. Even those who have very limited means can dream of social and global mobility by learning Korean and traveling to Korea.

Conclusion

This study has explored the K-drama fandom in the US Midwest and Ireland and fans' perceptions and thoughts about Korea and Korean culture/people from viewing K-dramas. The chapter finds that K-drama fans in the Midwest of the United States and in Ireland have different motivations for watching K-dramas. Although their responses are overwhelmingly positive about Korean language and culture and about how being a fan has motivated them to want to learn Korean and travel to Korea, much of their perceptions are formed in the context of their racial, gendered, and classed positions within their own cultures and societies.

Fans from the US Midwest talked more about the visions of Korean masculinity and how they desired the respect and attractiveness that soft masculinity provided them in combating their melancholia of what they termed toxic masculinity in their everyday experiences. For Irish fans, the vision of Korean masculinity and Korea more generally provided a vehicle for dreaming of mobility out of Ireland to try something new. This transcultural object then signals a dream of global cosmopolitan mobility for Irish fans and a way to imagine an alternative masculinity for American fans in the Midwest.

There are limits to these fan imaginaries. The engagement with K-drama does not transform their views of masculinity in ways that directly challenge White and Western hegemonic masculinity but rather produces an alternative, feminized masculinity that is also desirable. While male K-drama actors, in particular, provided an alternative to hegemonic toxic masculinity for midwestern fans, they did not actually provide a total break from past stereotypes of Asian men in the United States. Contrary to undoing past stereotypes of Asian men as gendered feminine, the new ideal of the Korean

Hallyu Dreaming

211

actor is heavily racialized, and while they are now considered sexually and socially desirable, they are still seen as having soft masculinity compared to White men. For midwestern female fans, their consumption of K-dramas may represent how they use their own particular "racial and economic capital to live their romantic/sexualized fan desires."[3]

In particular, racialized visions of Korean masculinity do seem to create a particular affinity with fans, which fills a gap in their lives and differentiates them from other fandoms and their peers. Affinity fan spaces on digital social media platforms created strong emotional (parasocial) relationships between fans and Korean actors, but not all fans are in the same positions within and outside of the affinity fan space, and these positionalities are uniquely raced, classed, and gendered, shaping reception and understanding of K-drama content. This chapter has provided two contrasting examples of how this happens in practice—for fans in the US Midwest around Korean masculinity and for Irish fans around global mobility.

Notes

1. For more on analyses of Boys' Love dramas in Asia, see Baudinette (2024).

2. For more on the relationship between Black Americans and Korean popular music, see Anderson (2020).

3. See David Oh and Benjamin Han's introduction to this volume.

References

Anderson, Crystal S. 2014. "That's My Man! Overlapping Masculinities in Korean Popular Music." In *The Korean Wave: Korean Popular Culture in Global Context*, edited by Yasue Kuwahara, 117–32. New York: Palgrave Macmillan.

———. 2020. *Soul in Seoul: African American Popular Music and K-pop*. Jackson: University Press of Mississippi.

Baudinette, Thomas. 2024. *Boys Love Media in Thailand: Celebrity, Fans, and Transnational Asian Queer Popular Culture*. London: Bloomsbury Academic.

Chin, Bertha, and Lori Hitchcock Morimoto. 2013. "Towards a Theory of Transcultural Fandom." *Participations: Journal of Audience and Reception Studies* 10 (1): 92–108.

Cho, Michelle. 2021. "BTS for BLM: K-pop, Race and Transcultural Fandom." Center for Asian Studies at UTD, January 30, 2021. YouTube video, 1:30:44. https://youtu.be/ToZ7Tvyuklo.

Chong, Kelly H., and Nadia Y. Kim. 2022. "'The Model Man': Shifting Perceptions of Asian American Masculinity and the Renegotiation of a Racial Hierarchy of Desire." *Men and Masculinities* 25 (5): 674–97. https://doi.org/10.1177/1097184X211043563.

Eng, David, and Shinhee Han. 2019a. "Asian American Melancholia and Disassociation." Asian American Writers' Workshop, May 15, 2019. YouTube video, 1:30:43. https://youtu.be/Z4DErB04V_A.

———. 2019b. *Racial Melancholia, Racial Dissociation: On the Social and Psychic Lives of Asian Americans.* Durham, NC: Duke University Press.

Espiritu, Yen Le. 1997. *Asian American Women and Men: Labor, Laws, and Love.* Thousand Oaks, CA: Sage Publications.

Hsu, Hua. 2019. "The Stories We Tell, and Don't Tell, about Asian-American Lives." *New Yorker*, July 17, 2019. https://www.newyorker.com/books/under-review/the-stories-we-tell-and-dont-tell-about-asian-american-lives.

Jin, Dal Yong. 2016. *New Korean Wave: Transnational Cultural Power in the Age of Social Media.* Urbana: University of Illinois Press.

Ju, Hyejung. 2020. "Korean TV Drama Viewership on Netflix: Transcultural Affection, Romance, and Identities." *Journal of International and Intercultural Communication* 13 (1): 32–48. https://doi.org/10.1080/17513057.2019.1606269.

Jung, Sun. 2010. *Korean Masculinities and Transcultural Consumption: Yonsama, Rain, Oldboy, K-Pop Idols.* Hong Kong: Hong Kong University Press.

Kao, Grace, Kelly Stamper Balistreri, and Kara Joyner. 2018. "Asian American Men in Romantic Dating Markets." *Contexts* 17 (4): 48–53. https://doi.org/10.1177/1536504218812869.

Kim, Nadia Y. 2006. "'Patriarchy Is So Third World': Korean Immigrant Women and 'Migrating' White Western Masculinity." *Social Problems* 53 (4): 519–36. https://doi.org/10.1525/sp.2006.53.4.519.

Kim, Youna. 2021. *The Soft Power of the Korean Wave: Parasite, BTS and Drama.* London: Routledge.

Kim, Ik-ki, and Sang Joon Bae. 2016. "The Korean Wave in Laos: The Case of Glocalized K-pop." *Korean Regional Sociology* 17 (2): 21–43.

KOSTAT (Statistics Korea). 2022. Marriage and Divorce Statistics in 2022. https://kostat.go.kr/board.es?mid=a20108110000&bid=11774&tag=&act=view&list_no=424779.

Kuwahara, Yasue. 2014. *The Korean Wave: Korean Popular Culture in Global Context.* New York: Palgrave Macmillan.

Lachapelle, Tara. 2021. "Netflix Is Winning Streaming's Own 'Squid Game.'" *Bloomberg Opinion*, October 19, 2021. https://www.bloomberg.com/opinion/articles/2021-10-19/netflix-earnings-squid-game-keeps-subscribers-in-the-fold.

Lee, Hyunji. 2017. "A 'Real' Fantasy: Hybridity, Korean Drama and Pop Cosmopolitans." *Media, Culture and Society* 40 (3): 365–80. https://doi.org/10.1177/0163443717718926.

Lee, Jeehyun Jenny, Rachel Kar Yee Lee, and Ji Hoon Park. 2020. "Unpacking K-pop in America: The Subversive Potential of Male K-pop Idols' Soft Masculinity." *International Journal of Communication* 14: 5900–5919.

Lee, Min Joo. 2020a. "Intimacy beyond Sex: Korean Television Dramas, Nonsexual Masculinities, and Transnational Erotic Desires." *Feminist Formations* 32 (3): 100–120. https://doi.org/10.1353/ff.2020.0042.

———. 2020b. "Touring the Land of Romance: Transnational Korean Television Drama Consumption from Online Desires to Offline Intimacy." *Journal of Tourism and Cultural Change* 18 (1): 67–80. https://doi.org/10.1080/14766825.2020.1707467.

Lee, Wonseok, and Grace Kao. 2021. "'Make It Right': Why #BlackLivesMatter(s) to K-pop, BTS, and BTS ARMYs." *Journal of the International Association for the Study of Popular Music* 11 (1): 70–87.

Lie, John. 2015. *K-pop: Popular Music, Cultural Amnesia, and Economic Innovation in South Korea*. Berkeley: University of California Press.

Longenecker, Lisa M., and Jooyoun Lee. 2018. "The Korean Wave in America: Assessing the Status of K-pop and K-drama between Global and Local." *Situations* 11 (2): 105–27.

Min, Wonjung, Dal Yong Jin, and Benjamin Han. 2019. "Transcultural Fandom of the Korean Wave in Latin America: Through the Lens of Cultural Intimacy and Affinity Space." *Media, Culture and Society* 41 (5): 604–19. https://doi.org/10.1177/0163443718799403.

Oh, Ingyu. 2017. "From Localization to Glocalization: Contriving Korean Pop Culture to Meet Glocal Demands." *Kritika Kultura* 29: 157–67. https://doi.org/10.13185/KK2017.02907.

Organisation for Economic Co-operation and Development (OECD). 2021. "Gender Wage Gap." https://data.oecd.org/earnwage/gender-wage-gap.htm.

Radway, Janice A. 1984. *Reading the Romance: Women, Patriarchy, and Popular Literature*. Chapel Hill: University of North Carolina Press.

Thussu, Daya Kishun. 2006. "Mapping Global Media Flow and Contra-flow." In *Media on the Move: Global Flow and Contra-flow*, edited by Daya Kishan Thussu, 10–29. London: Routledge.

Weissköppel, Cordula. 2013. "Translocality in Transnational Space: Sudanese Migrants in a Protestant Church in Germany." *Urban Anthropology and Studies of Cultural Systems and World Economic Development* 42 (3/4): 255–303. http://www.jstor.org/stable/24643191.

Yoon, Kyong. 2019. "Transnational Fandom in the Making: K-pop Fans in Vancouver." *International Communication Gazette* 81 (2): 176–92. https://doi.org/10.1177/1748048518802964.

Yoon, Kyong, Wonjung Min, and Dal Yong Jin. 2020. "Consuming the Contra-flow of K-pop in Spain." *Journal of Intercultural Studies* 41 (2): 132–47. https://doi.org/10.1080/07256868.2020.1724907.

Yoon, Tae-Jin, and Dal Yong Jin. 2017. *The Korean Wave: Evolution, Fandom, and Transnationality*. Lanham, MD: Rowman and Littlefield.

9

······

When K-pop Meets Islam

Cultural Appropriation and Fan Engagement

······

YOUNG JUNG

Although K-pop propagates global fandom, recent incidents of K-pop performances appropriating Muslim costumes or religious practices raise questions about cultural conflicts for both international K-pop fans and K-pop industries. When SM Entertainment was marketing its well-known group NCT U's "Make a Wish" (2020) using the mosque design, Muslim K-pop fans were so angry about this insensitive cultural appropriation that they mobilized online movements. When a girl group, 2NE1, released the album *Crush* (2014) and member CL's solo track "MTBD" (mental breakdown) released a music video featuring a verse from the Qur'an, Muslim K-pop fans could not tolerate its inappropriateness.

This study aims to understand how international Muslim K-pop fans' online engagement regarding K-pop performances' appropriating Muslim elements reflects situated fan identities and fan practices and how Muslim K-pop fans' religious identities intersect with racial and ethnic identities complicating K-pop fans' solidarity. Like other chapters in this volume that have concerns about "specific racial identities" in contextualized reception, this chapter shares a central interest in racially and locally specified fandom and how these specific fan identities encounter religious identities. The study tries to contextualize international fan communities' ways of communicating different ideas and perspectives about cultural appropriation and expressing cultural awareness. By centering divisions of fan communities, this study challenges a global fandom of Korean popular culture and complicates the understanding of pan-ethnic fan solidarity. I argue that international Muslim K-pop fans' engagement in fan practices illustrates fan division intersecting racial and religious identities, which does not always harmonize well with their fan identities. Fans who can deal with their Muslim identities and K-pop aesthetics tend to accept K-pop performances' appropriation of religious decorations. In contrast, fans who think their religious identities and enjoying K-pop aesthetics are incompatible tend to agonize over K-pop's use of mosque designs or phrases from the Qur'an. Fans' avowed identities as fans and religious identities are in constant tension to create a translocal identity embedded in their locally specific racial and religious identities. While some international Muslim fans tolerate K-pop's appropriation of religious content, other Muslim fans who think of their religious identities as irreconcilable leave their fandom or express deep frustration. Both cases tend to take actions such as requesting apologies or mobilizing online forums. This unique intersecting position shapes how international Muslim K-pop fans respond and negotiate cultural appropriation, which goes beyond just the simple notion of global hybrid fan identities.

This study also makes a meaningful addition to reception studies of the global fandom of Korean pop culture and media. This field of research has been fast growing recently, but there is not much literature about the Arab world's readings of Korean pop culture. Reflecting the widespread popularity of Korean popular culture in the Middle East, scholars in this region have started researching the reception of Korean popular cultural products (Lyan and Levkowitz 2015; Lyan, Zidani, and Shifman 2015; Otmazgin and Lyan 2014). Nissim Otmazgin and Irina Lyan's (2014) study examines how Israel and Palestine K-pop fans constitute mediated and localized fan communities, illustrating unique examples of the globalization of pop culture. Irina Lyan and Alon Levkowitz argue that TV series fandom is a "symbolic pilgrimage" (2015, 2) by analyzing Israeli Hallyu fans' Korean TV drama reception. The Middle East and Northern Africa (MENA) is a rarely studied region in the field of Korean pop culture's global fandom. While the Middle East welcomes Korean popular culture due to an absence of historical conflicts and Korea's "in-between status" between the West and the rest of the world (Lyan, Zidani, and Shifman 2015), the images of the Middle East in South Korean media are still focused on "threatening"

When K-pop Meets Islam

terrorists or barren deserts.[1] Considering this unbalanced cultural exchange between Far Eastern and Middle Eastern countries, the research on Korean popular culture's MENA reception can become an important space to gauge the spectrums and trajectories of globalization of popular culture.

The chapter focuses on four case studies to examine how K-pop fans react to the appropriation of Muslim religious practices. In particular, I analyzed fan responses expressed in their comments to YouTube videos. The four cases are NCT U's merchandise and stage setting; Monsta X's I.M's teaser for the album *Duality* (2021); the dance competition show *Street Woman Fighter* (2021); and the rapper CL's "MTBD" video controversy. I also analyzed two Muslim fans' YouTube videos and their responses. A focus group interview was conducted to contextualize interracial dynamics regarding religion and Korean pop culture reception in January 2022. Five different racial participants were recruited for a two-hour conversation about the recent incidents regarding K-pop artists' appropriation of Muslim elements. One Iranian American female, one Pakistani American female, one White American female, one Black American female, and one Korean American male were invited to the focus group interview. All five interviewees were active K-pop fans who had been engaged in online and offline fan club activities for over two years. I showed them six videos—four original music videos related to issues and two YouTube videos, "Islamophobia in K-pop" (sparklyeon 2021) and "Let's Talk: Kpop and Islamophobia" (yoonist 2021), created by Muslim K-pop fans—and let them have a free conversation for about two hours. After identifying the six relevant YouTube videos, I read several times all selected online fan responses and transcribed focus group interviews to identify themes about the research question: How do K-pop fans engage with fan practices regarding Muslim appropriations? Notes were taken to identify recurring themes and patterns of fan responses and engagement with the incidents. The data set was selected from all responses of the six YouTube videos and transcribed interview texts between December 2021 and August 2022 and was coded using the software Taguette to thematize fan engagement regarding Muslim appropriations. As most social media responses are anonymous, the racial and regional identities of fans whose online responses are analyzed are unknown except for the focus group interviewees. However, the fans analyzed in this chapter can be characterized as active K-pop fans who have been involved in diverse

Jung

fan activities or consumption of K-pop products for a considerable time, international Muslim K-pop fans or Anglophone K-pop fans who can communicate in English, and avid social media users who express their K-pop fandom.

Global Fandom of Korean Popular Culture and the Arab World

Korean popular culture is not just visible in East Asian vicinities. Its global fandom and reception have now spread to all continents, including South America, Europe, and Africa.[2] The international fandom of Korean popular culture is mainly due to the global accessibility of social media. Teenagers and youth who feel comfortable using digital media and middle-aged folks who use social media for many reasons are exposed to globally circulated media products. YouTube is an essential site for international fans to easily access Korean popular cultural products. It produces fan responses and fandom activities such as response videos, cover dance videos, or commentary videos. Fans circulate preferred items and reproduce their comments by posting, tweeting, reposting, and retweeting among fan communities (Duffett 2013). Social media has become the central platform for the formation and evolution of the international fandom of Korean popular culture.

The Arab world's reception of Korean popular culture is one of the least studied in the field of global fandom studies. Contemporary studies of popular culture and Islamic studies take pop culture as a meaningful site of resistance against established canonical texts of literature and cultural products. Treating pop culture as "low culture" is prominent in Arab culture, which considers religious canons and classical literature more meaningful and necessary than commodified popular cultural products (Hamamsy and Soliman 2013). Intersecting fields of popular culture and Islamic studies pay attention to the everyday lives of the Muslim world by illuminating subjugated and alienated subjectivities and by challenging the binarism between the high and low cultures' conceptualizations and tradition and modernity (LeVine 2008; Nieuwkerk, LeVine, and Stokes 2016).

One of the main topics in the field of popular culture and Islamic studies is the (in)compatibility of Islamic values and the everyday lives and desires that popular cultural products represent (Mulya 2021). Sacred images of di-

When K-pop Meets Islam

vine representations are respected as traditional canons and cultural assets, while everyday lives' mundane temporality and human desires are treated as secular impurities (Weintraub 2011). However, both popular culture and Islamic values are disseminated and saturated in people's everyday lives in the Muslim world. Muslim K-pop fans encounter conflicting moments where visible sexualities and the liveness of corporeal representations conflict with their own religious beliefs and practices. Still, Muslim K-pop fans consume Korean popular cultural products more open-mindedly than Western products, as the former reveal less violent content than the latter.

APPROPRIATION OF ARAB CULTURE AND MUSLIM PRACTICES IN K-POP

The Arab world is one of the most foreign cultural heritages in South Korea. Although the contact between Korea and the Arab world can be traced to the Goryeo Dynasty (918–1392), contemporary Korean society has little knowledge about the Arab world and Muslims.[3] The only artistic representation of the Arab world known to Koreans is *A Thousand and One Nights*, which is circulated widely with various Korean translations. Other than these Arabic folktales, Korean kids barely heard anything about Arab culture or civilization growing up until September 11, 2001, when the signifier of the Arab world became layered with Third World terrorist countries. When about five hundred Yemeni refugees sought asylum in Jeju Island, Korea, between 2016 and 2018, they encountered hostile Islamophobia and xenophobia.

Conversely, Korean popular cultural products are widely consumed in the Arab world and among Muslims (Lyan, Zidani, and Shifman 2015; Lyan and Levkowitz 2015; Noh 2011; Otmazgin and Lyan 2014). Some Arab K-pop fans create their own fan sites and engage in diverse fandom activities (Sun Jung 2011; Syed and Kwon 2019; Yoon 2019), and other Arab countries' broadcasting companies produce various versions of parodies of Korean TV dramas.[4] The presence of Muslim communities in Korea has had little influence on media images of the Islam world in Korea because, in population size, Muslims in Korea still belong to the minority.[5]

The Arab world in Korea is mystified mainly due to the lack of information about Arab civilization and history (Eum 2017; Grayson 2002;

Jung

220

Sun 1971; Koo 2018).[6] The world history textbooks of South Korea briefly deal with the ancient records of the Ottoman Empire and the formation of Muslim communities in the Middle East. The Arabic language is an optional foreign language taught in public schools. Most foreigners living in South Korea are from the United States, Europe, Russia, South Asia, and China. Korean people have few chances to interact with Arab people and learn about the Arab world unless they travel or study abroad in the Middle East.

Korean pop culture reveals this kind of popular unconsciousness of mystifying and fantasizing about an unknown object. K-pop's stateless atmosphere, which adds mystery with exotic landscapes and elements, seems to be a way to maximize the commercial interests of K-pop industry producers targeting the international market. While many musical characteristics of K-pop are known as appropriation of Black music (Gardner 2019; S.-Y. Kim 2020), the contextual appropriation using Korean lyrics and sociohistorical backgrounds of Korea makes K-pop more globally appealing and accessible. However, the recent incidents in K-pop music videos and performances using Arab cultural elements are far from contextual adaptation or creative appropriation. Unlike Korea's acceptance of Americanization during and after the Korean War that shaped modern Korean cultural identity somewhere between "off-white and blackish" (K. H. Kim 2021, 13), K-pop's adoption of Arab and Muslim elements is an ahistorical appropriation. Most K-pop artists do not understand the sociohistorical meanings of the adopted elements of their performance; hence, the backlash related to Arab cultural appropriation tends to be settled upon the agencies' official apologies.

Appropriation and *adaptation* are sometimes treated as sibling words (Nicklas and Lindner 2012; Sanders 2016) in literary and artistic fields. However, cultural appropriation is often defined broadly as any taking of something in one culture by an individual or group of another (Young 2008, 1–5), and the objects of cultural appropriation are various, including intellectual property, cultural expression or artifacts, history, and ways of knowledge (Scafidi 2005, 9). As globalization influences the everyday lives of modern lifestyles, cross-cultural encounters in the form of cultural appropriations happen frequently. I define *cultural appropriation* in this study as "any use of established cultural, historical, and religious components of

When K-pop Meets Islam

another culture without crediting or respecting the contexts often expressed in the forms of commodified artifacts or practices."[7] Despite categorizing different types of cultural appropriation as object appropriation, content appropriation, style appropriation, and subject appropriation (Young 2008), the targets and spectrum of appropriation are so broad that it is sometimes hard to trace the effects of the original cultural product. K-pop's adoption of Arab and Muslim elements is not a vague example that can allow the perspective of intertextuality or hybridity. It is closer to the appropriation that can have "corrosive effects" (Ziff and Rao 1997, 9) on the heritage of Arab culture and Muslim religious practices.

The current cultural appropriation of Arab elements in K-pop can be categorized as visual, aural, and textual. Visual appropriation is expressed through costumes, makeup, stage settings, and merchandise. NCT U's merchandise shaped like a Muslim mosque, Taeyoung's Arab-style costume, and the stage setting of NCT U's "Make a Wish" are typical examples of visual appropriation. Aural appropriation in K-pop usually inserts the sound of praying or reciting verses from the Qur'an in the middle of the song. The dance competition show *Street Woman Fighter*'s teaser music video and the solo title of CL's "MTBD" include the sound of reciting verses from the Qur'an. Textual appropriation is revealing the verses from the Qur'an on the costumes, stage settings, or tattoos. I.M's concept photo for his debut solo album *Duality* shows the singer's T-shirt, including the verses from the Qur'an.

These recent K-pop music videos and performances appropriate Arab and Muslim elements to maximize uniqueness and foreignness, not necessarily adopting foreign elements contextually or thematically to the given music performances. A mystified atmosphere aided by Arab decorations and Muslim sounds strengthens K-pop performance of non-national and futuristic characteristics. While non-Muslim international K-pop fans can be captivated by the charm of exotic and mysterious K-pop performances, many Muslim K-pop fans feel conflicted by irrelevant misuses of their cultural and religious elements. In this sense, K-pop's cultural appropriation of Arab elements results in an unexpected cultural clash between the K-pop industry and the Muslim world and in cultural othering in which newly emerging hegemonic K-pop products and performances exploit other cultural components. This is different from a non-Western

Jung

nation appropriating Western culture in that K-pop's appropriation of Arab elements targets maximizing its commercial benefits. While K-pop's musical hybridity is largely influenced by Western pop, particularly African American music (Anderson 2020, 17–24), the recent K-pop employment of Arab elements complicates the notion of "Koreanness" in an expanding petti-imperialistic way. A new soft power, Korean pop contents suggest an alternative global culture within rising social media environments and accompany transnational fan culture, but they sometimes raise conflicting issues among the heritage culture of another world.

International Muslim Fan Engagement

In the following section, I argue that international Muslim K-pop fans' engagement in fan practices illustrates fan division intersecting racial and religious identities, which does not always harmonize with their fan identities. In the shadow of the so-called global fandom of Korean popular culture, international Muslim K-pop fans struggle with stereotypical racial and religious images while grappling with multifaceted fan identities. Few of them leave K-pop fandom, and most try to figure out how to make sense of the conflicts between religious beliefs and aesthetic pleasure. Except for a few fans who leave K-pop fandom, the following evidence illustrates how K-pop audiences' transcultural fan identity takes precedence over their religious identity as Muslims in their negotiation of cultural appropriation.

WHOSE FAULT? EMOTIONAL EXPRESSION OF DISAPPOINTMENT

One of the most common responses among international Muslim K-pop fans regarding Muslim appropriation is an emotional one, often expressed as anger, disappointment, and distrust. Muslim fans' emotional reactions reveal a variety of expressions, ranging from immediate anger to resentment and protesting the object that caused outrage through incremental disappointment and cold treatment. Reactions toward cultural appropriation are vividly emotional, using direct vocabulary about fans' first feelings of how much they were hurt and disappointed by the irresponsible use of their religious symbols and practices. Most of these emotional responses

When K-pop Meets Islam

are accompanied by Muslim identifications. It seems that clarifying the identity of Muslims is a prerequisite for Muslim K-pop fans to be angry. Emotions of anger, disappointment, sadness, and despair are rationalized only by the identity of Muslims. This creates an atmosphere in which non-Muslim international fans must reveal their religious identity when conversing.

> I feel very overwhelmed, and my tears almost come down; how can they do this? You should know that they are very malicious and despicable because they touch the most precious of *what we Muslims have*. Thank God for the grace of Islam.

> *I am a Muslim*, and this is so heartbreaking for me.

> Personally, *as a Muslim K-pop fan* who loves K-pop and also TEDDY [Park] as a producer, seeing the Qur'an being used like this makes me so sad. I really hope nothing like this happens again.

> This made my heart sink. I couldn't hear it before this video, but now I can hear it very clearly. I'm pretty disappointed. Not in CL; she did nothing wrong but in Teddy. I still enjoy this song, however. I don't think it will ever feel the same, though. (*I am a Christian*, by the way.)[8]

These YouTube responses illustrate how international Muslim K-pop fans feel about the stage setting and costumes upon watching NCT U's "Make a Wish" and CL's "MTBD." Right after the perfect group choreography with an enticing whistle sound, Taeyoung's Arab-style costume foregrounds the scene in the original music video SM released on October 12, 2020. The colorful and flashy mosque-style stage background then moves in three dimensions, mystifying the NCT U group members' dance. In the middle of CL's hip hop song "MTBD," the sound of a call to prayer (*adhan*) is embedded as a background sound to the playful rap (Otterbeck and Ackfeldt 2012).

Focus group conversation revealed uncomfortable tension among participants when they discussed the Arab-style stage and fashion of NCT U. Because all the participants in the focus group conversation were college students, they seemed to know how to express their opinions politely and

Jung

224

politically correctly. Still, the debate heated up over how far cultural appropriation could be allowed and who should take responsibility for cultural appropriation. The Black American participant's statements raised questions about mutual cultural respect and cultural understanding that the current K-pop industry does not consider seriously.

> As a non-Muslim and a very secular Christian, I think the setting is so cool. NCT U makes a perfect song this time with a beautiful stage. I understand Muslim fans are intimidated by the Arab-style stage decoration, but pop music can express anything. Isn't it the freedom of art? (Korean American participant)

> There is a certain limit to the expression of art. Imagine a K-pop song that includes a verse insulting Jesus or a nation or a race. Can you still enjoy the song? I still stan NCT, but I think they should apologize for misusing mosque design. (Pakistani American participant)

> We don't need to be a Muslim to understand that this is wrong. K-pop agencies like SM do not respect different cultures or different religions. Given that K-pop itself has appropriated Black music, how come they don't respect other cultures? (Black American participant)

Some Muslim fans tried to understand the background sound of "MTBD" by prioritizing CL's musicality and her hip hop spirit. Many comments under the music videos include Muslim fans' ambivalent feelings about the inserted sound. One of the Muslim fans commented on his/her inner conflict: "I really love her, but I love being a Muslim, too. This is the last thing I could do for Islam." This international Muslim K-pop fan revealed a chasm between a loyal fandom and a Muslim identity. Particularly, when they encounter music videos or concerts, including praying sounds or reciting of the Qu'ran, Muslim fans' inner conflicts between their religious identity and fan identity worsen. In comparison, religious identities are closer to existential ways of being, and fan identities are closer to ways of belonging. Both religious and fan identities constitute the core qualifications of young Muslim K-pop fans. If they feel that their sacred religious customs and practices have been insulted, an arrow of criticism will inevitably go to the subject of insult and destruction. However, many Muslim K-pop listeners

When K-pop Meets Islam

do not desert their loyal fandom even if they see the conflict between the two different identities. Instead of criticizing K-pop artists who committed offensive cultural appropriations, most Muslim fans, particularly loyal K-pop fans, tried to understand their idols' mistakes by acknowledging that many K-pop artists and producers do not know enough about Islam culture and the Muslim religion.

WHOSE RESPONSIBILITY? FAN DIVISION

The second typical response among international Muslim K-pop fans regarding Muslim appropriation is an argument about who is responsible. As online conversations get heated, international fans' involvement creates an argumentative forum about who is at fault regarding inappropriate cultural appropriations. Many international K-pop fans who participate in this kind of conversation are aware of the environment and production systems of the K-pop industry, so they do not criticize K-pop artists directly.

> I feel bad for NCT, like they didn't design the background images or pick the concept. Cultural appropriation is a big deal, yeah, but like, don't go hating or something on the boys, this might just be me, but I feel like everyone expects idols to know everything and anything about all the cultures and religions in the world. You can't expect them to know what's right or wrong about religions or cultures they have little to no knowledge of. I saw an article and stuff on Twitter saying that fans are using the fan sign video calls to "educate" the member by "educating" the English-speaking members so they can rely on the information to the rest of the members [l]ike . . . they're not the problem! It's sBs and SM (though it's more likely sBs because they made the background screen images, right?).

As this YouTube response illustrates, many international fans do not criticize K-pop artists' performances for appropriating Arab cultural elements or religious practices. It seems to be the logic of these generous fans that they cannot blame K-pop artists just because they danced and sang on a stage decorated by the agency or stage design director. In addition, international fans are already very much inclined toward their beloved K-pop artists, so they are ready to forgive and accept even if the artists

Jung

have committed some religious and cultural disrespect for their attractive musicality. The generosity of these K-pop fans toward their favorite stars on stages and in performances that seem to blaspheme Muslim religions shows that it may be ambiguous to divide the boundaries between creative labor and responsibility, given that the K-pop production environment is a space of collaboration by various artists, including art directors, stage directors, and makeup artists. Moreover, these loyal fans tend to negotiate their expectations toward their beloved idols. They acknowledge K-pop as a byproduct of capitalist systems to maintain their fantasy of K-pop stars even when the products clash with their religion.

A White college student also mentioned that if there were someone to blame in the situation, it would be the people and institutions that created it. She rationalized her opinion by explaining that in many problematic cases, producers, stage directors, costume directors, or makeup specialists are involved with a specific concept of a music video, so it is hard to pin down whose responsibility it is for the final product's aesthetic style and authenticity. This White college student tried to balance her perspective by adding that these producers do not educate their performers enough. This is a similar logic to that of Muslim K-pop fans who excuse recent incidents of K-pop's cultural appropriation of Arab cultural elements.

Still, some international fans question the idols' social responsibility as public figures whose voices and performances are expressions of personal tastes and sociocultural representations.

> I don't think it's fair not to include the idol in the responsibility. A lot of times, people will, when it's like good stuff, they will give credit to the idol, but when it's bad stuff, they'll say, oh, it's the company. (Iranian American)
>
> It is very interesting that fans expect their idols to participate in social movements like BLM but excuse Arab appropriations. I don't understand why K-pop idols can be excused for certain cases. We love our idols because they make voices for us. (Black American)

Iranian and Black American college students tried to show a balanced perspective about the cases. Even if the Iranian college student is a loyal K-pop fan of a couple of girl groups, including CL, she tried not to lose her critical mind regarding issues such as Arab cultural appropriations.

When K-pop Meets Islam

The Black American college student's statement resonates with the recent K-pop artists' involvement with social movements. Whether K-pop artists need to have political voices or not is a complicated issue. Still, some international K-pop fans expect their idol groups to show social responsibility as public influencers.

One of the most heated discussions regarding Arab cultural appropriations is whether religious expressions and aesthetic concepts represented in K-pop performances can coexist without cultural conflicts. Some secular Muslim fans show tolerance toward the cases in which Arab cultural appropriations are visible. Still, many Muslim fans feel disrespected and argue that religious expressions should not be used for the concepts or aesthetics of K-pop performances.

> We are offended because Al-Quran is not supposed to be used for entertainment purposes. We are not saying that CL is totally at fault; CL probably didn't know about it when she was recording it. Nevertheless, the person who put the Quran verse in there should apologize. We are just asking the person who is responsible for this to apologize. If you are a Muslim, you should actually feel something. Even people who are not Muslim are on our side. We are trying to defend Islam so that no one will use Al-Quran for entertainment purposes again. The sound of the call to prayer is not for a remix. Please respect our religion.

Here, international Muslim fans argue that divine sound, particularly the call to prayer or verses from the Qur'an, cannot be used for pop music or "entertainment purposes." Such arguments correspond to the theoretical idea that strict customs dominate the sacred and secular dichotomy. According to this dichotomy, even in Muslim and Islamic traditions, the music sound used in sacred religious rituals should be considered separate from sensual music composed for public pleasure.

As fans' comments illustrate, borrowing Islamic symbols and sound to make K-pop concepts diverse and hybrid is most likely due to K-pop agencies' ignorance. Even if some agencies consider global market strategies to draw international fandom, such as constituting idol groups by inserting a few foreigners, singing in foreign languages, and promoting sales by preparing fan meetings in local areas, unexpected cultural clashes can happen, particularly when K-pop artists' acts, attires, or performances'

Jung

decorations or sounds desecrate religious identities. Fan division regarding Muslim appropriations shows that fans' perspectives on whether they can reconcile with appropriated religion depend on individual fans' tolerance and the levels of understanding of the complexities of cultural encounters.

AGGRESSIVE ACTIONS

The third common way of responding to Muslim appropriation in K-pop is with aggressive actions such as requesting apologies, submitting petitions, or suggesting undoing fandom. These responses can be expanded versions of emotional reactions in that international Muslim fans request actual results to solve the emotional distress and frustration. At the same time, these responses are closer to fans' activism and fan practices in realizing fan identities.

> As a Muslim, I'm very disappointed. I'm just disappointed in their new song in general. I'm not Shea but that use of that line was very disrespectful; I actually started losing my interest in them even though I know it was SBS's doing, but SBS is still going to do their videos and decorations, so I just don't want to get disappointed or feel like this again.

> The worst part is NCT's company just ignored the accusations. Am I the only one who thinks that fans should stop streaming NCT for a while so that their company takes action? Like the intention for this is not the loss of NCT but their company.

> I think the best thing would be if YG, Teddy, or CL released a statement addressing this issue. But I don't think CL made this part of the song. She just wrote some lyrics, so I think it was Teddy who made this part.

> RESPECT OUR RELIGION! APOLOGIZE TO ALL MUSLIMS!

All these YouTube responses request taking action based on their different religious identities and different levels of engagement with K-pop fandom. The first and second responses are to NCT U's "Make a Wish," the third response is to CL's "MTBD," and the fourth response is to the dance competition show *Street Woman Fighter*'s teaser music video. Both the first and second responses urge international fans to undo their NCT fandom to give the company a warning sign. Even if the first response's author clarifies their intention not to follow the song "Make a Wish," we can still tell that this fan used to love NCT's music very much in the phrase "I just don't want to get disappointed."

Unlike NCT U's official music video, which still uses mosque-style decorations and Arab fashion, CL released a statement apologizing for the engineer's misuse of a call to prayer and changed the background sound soon after the incident. Similarly, when the Mnet channel released a teaser music video that inserted the sound of a call to prayer for its show, offended Muslim fans requested an immediate apology. Most loyal fans who experienced anger and frustration at the insult to their religion seem to be able to defuse their rage if given a sincere apology and responsible action. This reflects the view of many Muslim K-pop fans that K-pop fandom and religious beliefs can coexist. Just as youth culture can be found in the Islamic world resisting religious authority and dogma through popular culture, international Muslim fans seem to see room for compromise regarding K-pop's exotic body image and futuristic musicality, even if it undermines the sanctity of their daily religious beliefs. Of course, individual fans' loyalty to K-pop groups and fidelity to their religious practices will play a role in this receptivity.

Fandom is often expressed as a participatory culture (Jenkins 1992), a resistant network community that can form alternative opinions and perspectives on leading issues (Jenkins, Ito, and boyd 2016). International Muslim fans participating in an online discussion on the above matters constitute alternative fan communities that can draw many more followers, discussants, researchers, and even activists. When we had a class discussion about I.M's teaser music video that includes a verse from the Qur'an on a T-shirt, my original intention was to let students know examples of indiscernible cultural appropriation and to ask questions about what efforts the K-pop industry and the actors in charge of K-pop production can make to enhance mutual cultural understanding. Interestingly, three Muslim K-pop fan students suggested writing a group petition to send to the South Korean government requesting a nationwide correction of Arab cultural appropriation in K-pop performances. Even if I offered to translate into Korean a completed draft of the petition letter, and about 80 percent of my students were avid K-pop fans, the three Muslim students could not proceed with the petition due to other students' indifference or different opinions. Muslim students' aborted efforts and other racial group students' different responses make me think of fan division regarding their racial and religious identities.

INTELLECTUAL REACTIONS

Although not a typical response pattern, intellectual reactions to Muslim appropriation in K-pop are visible among social media user fans. These fans research the issues and then create educational videos for public awareness or upload lengthy responses to explain their perspectives. For instance, the educational video "Islamophobia in K-pop" drew 84,733 views as of August 15, 2022, and described representative cases of Muslim appropriation of K-pop and Muslim fans' Twitter movements such as #SMStopDisrespectingIslam (sparklyeon 2021). More than six hundred comments under this video show diverse international fans' different opinions regarding K-pop's appropriation of Islam culture. As YouTube is now a mainstream medium (Burgess and Green 2018), fan users' uploading of educational videos has global effects that can ignite international movements, raise global awareness among users, and produce different versions of educational videos.

Okay as a Muslim, let me give my opinion. 1. Well I'm not a Shia, but I know for a fact that this is very disrespectful. disrespect. Like seriously, SM or SBS, before you use something, get yourself educated about it. This is so rude, and as a person who has over 10 Shia friends, I know this pain. 2. Dancing with a holy thing around is NOT okay. Well, what if we Muslims did the same to you people? I know for a fact you won't shut up and charge at us. 3. Imam Hussein is a very important person to the Shia and Sunni. You think it's funny to let put those words be written there and y'all dancing to it. Ya Allah! No. And if you don't know, Imam Hussein was murdered in Karbala. Yes, murdered and Shia always cry on that day. 4. Please do not send hate comments to NCT. They are not in control of their backgrounds. So plz don't send hate. Maybe educate them. That's all I have to say and SM if you are reading this then educate yourself on things before you use them.

When K-pop Meets Islam

Educational videos usually lead to lengthy comments like the above example and create an online forum on YouTube where many international K-pop fans are engaged in virtual discussions about the cases. This kind of lengthy comment is usually accompanied by sub-followers who form related conversations expressing followers' agreement or disagreement. Some response writers request following and responding; others use catchwords and persuasive phrases to draw more followers.

Notably, international Muslim K-pop fans who identify their Muslim identities express such broad opinions toward K-pop's cultural appropriation that myriad forums are open for endless discussions. If popular educational videos draw appreciative responses first, lengthy comments induce another debate on the related topics. Fan-created educational videos and accompanied online forums contribute to the widening cultural understanding of international K-pop fans and audiences.

Conclusion

This study analyzed international Muslim K-pop fans' responses to the cultural appropriation and commodification of Arab culture and Muslim costumes and religious practices. Focusing on critical fan activism and fan engagement questions, the current study argues that international Muslim fan practices illustrate the complexity of global fandom and fan division among different religious and racial identities. Muslim K-pop fans' response to the recent K-pop performances appropriating religious symbols for decorative purposes shows a diverse range of fan engagement: from the emotional expression of disappointment and distrust, to logical arguments debating who owns responsibility, to aggressive actions requesting apologies, to intellectual reactions educating international K-pop fans. A focus group conversation of two MENA, one Black, one White, and one Korean American K-pop fan reveals fan divisions in cultural understanding, illustrating how race and religion play crucial roles in shaping and negotiating fan identities.

Probably no other intercultural encounter better reflects the resurgent scenes of cultural clash and conflicts in global Korean pop culture fandom than K-pop's appropriations of Islamic culture and Muslim practices. K-pop's repetitive appropriations of Arab culture and Muslim practices

Jung

followed by superficial apologies reveals the dangerous dynamics of K-pop expansionism, which relates to unilateral and imperial diffusion logic without considering other cultures' characteristics and historical development. This study exemplifies how fans' perspectives and involvement with fan activities complicate theories of cultural appropriation. Not just agents who create and perform artistic works but also audiences and fans who consume and appreciate manufactured pieces contribute to deciding the acceptability of appropriated culture. This study also illustrates that international fans' engagement with fan activism can critically correct K-pop's negligence and irresponsible appropriations by creating an "alternative economy" (de Kloet and van Zoonen 2007, 328) against mainstream media productions. If global awareness of mutual cultural understanding rises, the production agencies will pay more attention to K-pop's application and adaptation of other cultural factors.

While international K-pop fans exemplify the possibility of cosmopolitan fan communities (Jenkins 2004), situated fan identities that sometimes conflict with fans' racial and religious identities raise questions about the global fandom of Korean pop culture. As K-pop increasingly draws diverse racial and ethnic fans across the globe, it is more important to analyze international fans' roles and responsibilities than to celebrate the global fandom of K-pop as a counterflow of mainstream pop culture. Future studies may explore various fields where different racial and religious fan groups encounter Korean pop culture.

Notes

1. For instance, one of the globally circulated Korean TV drama series, *Descendants of the Sun* (2016), starring Song Joong-ki and Song Hye-kyo, set the primary setting, Urk, as an imaginative place where the main characters meet and fall in love, borrowing typical images of the Middle East, bioweapons, terrorist attacks, kidnapping, gang violence, sexual trafficking, and the desert. The fictional name of Urk must be coined from the nation name of Iraq.

2. The Ministry of Foreign Affairs and the Korea Foundation of the South Korean government have published the annual *Jiguchon Hallyu Hyeonhwang* (Global Hallyu status) since 2014 to document each continent's and country's reception of Korean pop culture. This annual report includes specific information such as cultural characteristics, Hallyu status, the reason why local people like Korean pop

culture, things to consider for cultural communication, the status of Hallyu fan clubs, cultural events, and local culture of four continent groups—Asia/Oceania, America, Europe, Africa/Middle East—and over one hundred countries.

3. Korea has actually had trade and cultural exchanges with the Arab world for a thousand years. See Suil Jung (2002, 2005) for the cultural exchanges and shared histories between ancient Korea and the Arab world. One of the Goryeo Songs, *Ssanghwajyeom* (The Turkish bakery), talks about the contact between Koreans and "hoehoe," referring to the Inner and Central Asian Muslims (Lee 2017, 29–30).

4. Visible K-pop fandom in the Arab world contrasts with the non-existence of Muslim K-pop fandom in Korea.

5. Recent journalistic coverage says the population of Muslims in South Korea rose to 60,000 in 2020 due to diverse cultural contacts (okjebo 2020). However, the official statistics of the South Korean government still do not include the number of Muslims in its religious population. According to Statistics Korea (https://kosis.kr), the Muslim population is just one of the "other religions."

6. A nonprofit and incorporated foundation, Korea-Arab Society, was established in 2008 to promote mutual understanding of the culture and traditions of both South Korea and the Arab world. The main events of this foundation are the Arab Cultural Festival and the Korea-Middle East Cooperation Forum, among others. This foundation is funded by the Ministry of Foreign Affairs of the South Korean government (http://eng.korea-arab.org).

7. *Cultural theft* refers to any culturally appropriating acts causing legal conflicts and harm to the appropriated objects and heritage. Cultural appropriation is so widely practiced in fashion, movies, music, and art that some cases result in cultural theft. Still, in many cases the legal definitions of *cultural property* are vague.

8. All commentators' identifications cited in this chapter were deleted to protect their privacy, even if online users usually use unique IDs instead of real names. Emphases have been added.

References

Anderson, Crystal S. 2020. *Soul in Seoul: African American Popular Music and K-pop*. Jackson: University Press of Mississippi.

Burgess, Jean, and Joshua Green. 2018. *YouTube: Online Video and Participatory Culture*. 2nd ed. Cambridge: Polity Press.

CL. "CL (2NE1) - '멘붕 (MTBD)' MV." MADE MANAGEMENT, April 4, 2014. YouTube video, 3:15. https://youtu.be/9LvdPuDhewY.

De Kloet, Jeroen, and Liesbet van Zoonen. 2007. "Fan Culture—Performing Dif-

Jung

ference." In *Media Studies: Key Issues and Debates*, edited by Eoin Devereux, 322–41. London: Sage Publications.

Duffett, Mark. 2013. *Understanding Fandom: An Introduction to the Study of Media Fan Culture*. New York: Bloomsbury.

Eum, IkRan. 2017. "Korea's Response to Islam and Islamophobia: Focusing on Veiled Muslim Women's Experiences." *Korea Observer* 48 (4): 825–49. https://doi.org/10.29152/KOIKS.2017.48.4.825.

Gardner, Hyniea. 2019. "The Impact of African-American Musicianship on South Korean Popular Music: Adoption, Appropriation, Hybridization, Integration, or Other?" MA thesis, Harvard University.

Grayson, James Huntley. 2002. "Islam in Korea: A New World Religion." In *Korea—a Religious History*, rev. ed., 195–97. London: Routledge.

Hamamsy, Walid El, and Mounira Soliman, eds. 2013. *Popular Culture in the Middle East and North Africa: A Postcolonial Outlook*. New York: Routledge.

Jenkins, Henry. 1992. *Textual Poachers: Television Fans and Participatory Culture*. New York: Routledge.

———. 2004. "Pop Cosmopolitanism: Mapping Cultural Flows in an Age of Media Convergence." In *Globalization: Culture and Education in the New Millennium*, edited by Marcelo M. Suárez-Orozco and Desirée Baolian Qin-Hilliard, 114–40. Berkeley: University of California Press.

Jenkins, Henry, Mizuko Ito, and danah boyd. 2016. *Participatory Culture in a Networked Era: A Conversation on Youth, Learning, Commerce, and Politics*. Cambridge: Polity Press.

Jung, Suil. 2002. 이슬람 문명 [Islam Munmyeong; Islam civilization]. Seoul: Changbi Publishers.

———. 2005. "Goryeowa Islame Yeokdongjeogin Mannam" [Dynamic encounter between Goryeo and Islam]. In 한국 속의 세계 [Hanguksogye Seygye; World in Korea]. Seoul: Changbi Publishers.

Jung, Sun. 2011. "K-pop, Indonesian Fandom, and Social Media." In "Race and Ethnicity in Fandom," edited by Robin Anne Reid and Sarah N. Gatson, special issue, *Transformative Works and Culture*, 8. https://doi.org/10.3983/twc.2011.0289.

Kim, Kyung Hyun. 2021. *Hegemonic Mimicry: Korean Popular Culture of the Twenty-First Century*. Durham, NC: Duke University Press.

Kim, Suk-Young. 2020. "Black K-Pop: Racial Surplus and Global Consumption." *TDR/The Drama Review* 64 (2 (246)): 88–100. https://doi.org/10.1162/dram_a_00921.

Koo, Gi Yeon. 2018. "Islamophobia and the Politics of Representation of Islam in Korea." *Journal of Korean Religions* 9 (1): 159–92. https://doi.org/10.1353/jkr.2018.0006.

Korea Foundation. 2014. *Jigucheon Hallyu Hyeonhwang* [Global Hallyu status]. Seoul: Korea Foundation.

"Korea-Arab Society." 2022. Ministry of Foreign Affairs of the Republic of Korea and Korea Foundation. Accessed August 15, 2022. http://eng.korea-arab.org/.

Lee, Peter H., ed. 2017. *An Anthology of Traditional Korean Literature*. Honolulu: University of Hawai'i Press.

LeVine, Mark. 2008. "Heavy Metal Muslims: The Rise of a Post-Islamist Public Sphere." *Contemporary Islam* 2 (3): 229–49. https://doi.org/10.1007/s11562-008-0063-x.

Lyan, Irina, and Alon Levkowitz. 2015. "From Holy Land to 'Hallyu Land': The Symbolic Journey following the Korean Wave in Israel." *Journal of Fandom Studies* 3 (1): 7–21. https://doi.org/10.1386/jfs.3.1.7_1.

Lyan, Irina, Sulafa Zidani, and Limor Shifman. 2015. "When Gangnam Hits the Middle East: Re-makes as Identity Practice." *Asian Communication Research* 12 (2): 10–31. https://doi.org/10.20879/acr.2015.12.2.10.

Mulya, Teguh Wijaya. 2021. "Faith and Fandom: Young Indonesian Muslims Negotiating K-pop and Islam." *Contemporary Islam* 15: 337–55. https://doi.org/10.1007/s11562-021-00475-1.

Nicklas, Pascal, and Oliver Lindner. 2012. "Adaptation and Cultural Appropriation." In *Adaptation and Cultural Appropriation: Literature, Film, and the Arts*, edited by Pascal Nicklas and Oliver Lindner, 1–13. Berlin: De Gruyter.

Nieuwkerk, Karin van, Mark LeVine, and Martin Stokes. 2016. "Introduction: Islam and Popular Culture." In Islam and Popular Culture, edited by Karin van Nieuwkerk, Mark LeVine, and Martin Stokes, 1–20. Austin: University of Texas Press.

Noh, Sueen. 2011. "Unveiling the Korean Wave in the Middle East." In *Hallyu: Influence of Korean Popular Culture in Asia and Beyond*, edited by Do kyun Kim and Min-Sun Kim, 331–67. Seoul: Seoul National University Press.

okjebo. 2020. "한국의 이슬람교:'토종 무슬림'6만 시대 맞았다" [*Hangugui Iseulllamgyo: "Tojong Museullim" 6man Sidae Majatda*; Islam in South Korea: Entering the 60,000 "native Muslim" era]. *Yonhap News*, October 20, 2020. https://yna.co.kr/view/AKR20201019082900501.

Otmazgin, Nissim, and Irina Lyan. 2014. "Hallyu across the Desert: K-pop Fandom in Israel and Palestine." *Cross-Currents: East Asian History and Culture Review* 3 (1): 32–55. https://doi.org/10.1353/ach.2014.0008.

Otterbeck, Jonas, and Anders Ackfeldt. 2012. "Music and Islam." *Contemporary Islam* 6: 227–33. https://doi.org/10.1007/s11562-012-0220-0.

Sanders, Julie. 2016. *Adaptation and Appropriation*. 2nd ed. London: Routledge.

Scafidi, Susan. 2005. *Who Owns Culture? Appropriation and Authenticity in American Law*. New Brunswick, NJ: Rutgers University Press.

SMTOWN. "NCT U 엔시티 유 'Make A Wish (Birthday Song)' MV." October 12, 2020. YouTube video, 4:08. https://youtu.be/tyrVtwE8Gvo.

sparklyeon. 2021. "Islamophobia in K-pop." February 23, 2021. YouTube, 5:00. https://youtu.be/8nH2uNvv8_Q.

Sun, Yoon Kyung. 1971. "Islam in Korea." PhD diss., Hartford Seminary Foundation.

Syed, Md Azalanshah Md, and Seung-Ho Kwon. 2019. "*Hallyu* and Strategic Interpretation of Malaysian Modernity among Young Malay Women." *Asian Women* 35 (3): 1–24. https://doi.org/10.14431/aw.2019.09.35.3.1.

"2021지구촌 한류현황" [*Jiguchon Hallyu Hyeonhwang*; Global Hallyu status]. Ministry of Foreign Affairs of the Republic of Korea. Accessed August 15, 2022. https://www.mofa.go.kr/www/brd/m_4099/view.do?seq=367660.

Weintraub, Andrew N. 2011. "Introduction: The Study of Islam and Popular Culture in Indonesia and Malaysia." In *Islam and Popular Culture in Indonesia and Malaysia*, edited by Andrew N. Weintraub, 1–17. London: Routledge.

Yoon, Sunny. 2019. "K-Pop Fandom in Veil: Religious Reception and Adaptation to Popular Culture." *Journal of Indonesian Islam* 13 (1): 1–20.

yoonist. 2021. "Let's Talk: Kpop and Islamophobia." March 29, 2021. YouTube, 7:09. https://youtu.be/NyasUU6BT6s.

Young, James O. 2008. *Cultural Appropriation and the Arts*. Malden, MA: Blackwell.

Ziff, Bruce, and Pratima V. Rao. 1997. "Introduction to Cultural Appropriation: A Framework for Analysis." In *Borrowed Power: Essays on Cultural Appropriation*, edited by Bruce Ziff and Pratima V. Rao, 1–27. New Brunswick, NJ: Rutgers University Press.

10

······

"I Can Do Both"

Queering K-pop Idols through the
White Discursive Standpoint of TikTok Users

······

JULIA TRZCIŃSKA AND DAVID C. OH

In late 2021, TikTok users engaged in a new trend, using Todrick Hall's "Both" in their short, edited videos. Hall, often referred to as an LGBTQ+ community role model, sings about the complexity of his gender identity and how he can switch between different actions and often contradictory roles—those typically assigned to either men or women. Shortly after the song appeared on TikTok, it was embraced not only by non-binary and gender-fluid users but also by K-pop fans. The K-pop fans, who predominantly consisted of non-Asian international fans, enthusiastically edited and posted videos of their favorite idols, regardless of how the idols gender identify. The purpose of this chapter is to answer why K-pop fans joined this trend—playfully imagining their favorite *Korean* idols' gender identities as fluid. How does their ostensibly progressive queer objectification of K-pop idols produce problematic conservative, Orientalist meanings about Korean sexuality and masculinity?

Here, we are interested in analyzing and contextualizing the popularity of this trend among K-pop fans as an ambivalent example of empowering female "prosumption" but also of problematic racial fetishization by international fans (I-fans).[1] Taking fan pleasure in Korean idol boy bands' "soft" or "liminal masculinity" is one of the key reasons behind the popularity of K-pop (Jung 2011; C. Oh 2015, 2017). Because of hegemonic masculine norms in the United States and other parts of the West that draw binary gender distinctions and emphasize physical size and power as masculine (Kimmel 2006), many Western I-fans read soft masculinity as queer identities (Kuo et al. 2020). Some fans claim that K-pop idols and their performances provide a "safe space" to explore gender (Bell 2022), but preliminary research of this trend has shown little trace of fans' own gender exploration or performance; rather, they play with K-pop idols' gender, thereby violating a principal norm to allow people to define their own genders, such as through their choice of pronouns. In most cases, women fans play with men K-pop idols' gender identities to express heterosexual sexual attraction toward them.

While we see this trend as a chance to strengthen representations of gender fluidity in the media as well as an opportunity for gender-non-conforming play, we also argue that it is predicated on I-fans' perceived right to comment on and control *Korean* idols. This advances I-fans' self-empowerment at the expense of idols' agency over their own genders. This intersectional analysis, then, provides the means through which to understand the primacy of race in White fans' pleasures and practices. As Myria Georgiou (2020) notes, it is necessary to systematically study media (old and new) in the context of ethnic and racial studies, and it is important to remember that White supremacy is not ahistorical; rather, ideologies that had sustained it in the past travel, mutate, and adapt in the present. Racial ideologies are stubbornly persistent and guide Western interaction with the East. Mari Yoshihara (2002), for instance, notes that since the early twentieth century, White women have exerted power over East Asians—Chinese and Japanese—as a way of expressing authority and control, which was otherwise denied to them in the patriarchal societies in which they lived. Even among progressives, feminists of color have criticized White feminists for maintaining their proximity to White supremacy through their exclusion and marginalization of women of color (Moon and Holling 2020; Moreton-Robinson 2006). The point, then, is that people in historically marginalized groups sometimes resolve their own devalued condition by marginalizing others. Self-empowerment can come at the cost of another's oppression.

To understand the fans' edits and their motivations as well as the reactions of other fans, the first author analyzed forty-three short videos and 361 of the most popular comments to find the relationship between the texts

"I Can Do Both"

and audience feedback. To select a sample among the nearly twenty-five thousand TikToks available at the time of data collection, a purposive sample was collected that included the most popular videos, an indication of their reach.[2] Using MAXQDA software, the chapter features a mixed method study, combining content analysis and comparative analysis of fan discourse. The analysis uncovered representational and discursive patterns that affirmed gender fluidity and identity exploration, positioned a White female gaze on K-pop male idols, and reinforced racial stereotypes.[3] We argue that I-fans exoticized and fetishized Korean idols, treating them as objects of queer fascination and amusement. This chapter begins with a context for both the reception of Korean media among I-fans and their perception of K-pop idols' "soft masculinity." It then includes the two major themes of the chapter: I-fans project their desires of gender binarism onto K-pop idols by creating TikTok videos, and they also exhibit Orientalist desires by queering male K-pop idols.

"I Could Be Forever or I Could Be Just a Fling": Hybridization, Orientalism, and Othering

Many scholars of Korean popular culture argue that hybridity is a force that drives its global popularity (Shim 2006; Jin and Ryoo 2014), and some scholars have claimed that its popularity is a demonstration of a contra-flow that challenges Western cultural hegemony (J. O. Kim 2021). K-pop is especially notable for its hybrid integration of multiple music genres and the English language into locally meaningful performances (Jin 2016). Another reason for Korean media's popularity, especially among its predominantly female fan base outside Asia, is the reversal of the gaze. Women can change their position from being an object of male gaze–oriented media to becoming spectators themselves. There is also evidence that women viewers can redefine womanhood by drawing upon Korean dramas as a symbolic resource. In Vietnam, women constructed new identities and found alternative paths outside the one that traditional society imposed on them (Jang, Nguyen, and Kwon 2021).

Nevertheless, scholars, such as Marwan Kraidy (2005) point to the limitations of hybridization within existing regimes of global power. The mere presence of a contra-flow does not necessarily produce a mutual exchange of culture and values, but it can also reify the dominant or seemingly more attractive one—for example, dominant racial logics that privilege Whiteness (D. C. Oh 2017; Thussu 2007). As Oh and Han argue in the introduction to this volume, when Korean media are interpreted outside of Asia, it should be understood as cross-racial interpretation because of the changing local context where this interpretation takes place.

There is much evidence demonstrating that Western audiences, including fans, interpret Korean media as a form produced by a "cultural Other" (Mazaná 2014; D. C. Oh 2017; Yoon 2019). As Kyong Yoon, Wonjung Min, and Dal Yong Jin point out in the context of K-pop, transnational reception "involves the ongoing negotiation of otherness" (2020, 144). One often-discussed issue is the fetishization of idols, a consequence of media representations of Asians and Asian Americans that are intertwined with both gender and sexuality stereotypes (Fong-Torres 1995; Zhang 2010; Kuo et al. 2022). This is especially true for White fans who have relatively more discursive power to do so (D. C. Oh 2017). They often see their actions as appreciation of Korean culture, although it may, instead, be appropriation or distortion.[4]

This has more consequential implications when it comes to content creators and influencers on social media. Although content creators can play the role of cultural intermediaries or translators, they are simultaneously motivated to increase the reach of their social media posts.[5] This, in turn, can lead to a tendency among content creators to show Korean culture as exotic or strange, thereby extending postcolonial discourses (D. C. Oh and C. Oh 2017). I-fans sometimes fetishize K-pop idols or trivialize Korean pop culture or rely on distorted explanations of Korean culture. As an example of racist, sexist humor by I-fan content creators, Jeehyun Jenny Lee, Rachel Kar Yee Lee, and Ji Hoon Park (2020) share a case of an I-fan who created videos in which the audience is supposed to guess whether a presented idol is a man or a woman. This leads us to the second reason for K-pop's popularity—"soft masculinity." In the following section, we trace changes in I-fans' understanding of masculinity in Korean media in order to contextualize the videos.

"I Can Do Both"

"I Can Throw a Pitch, I Can Play Receiver":
Masculinity and I-fans

In Sun Jung's explanation of soft masculinity, she invokes the traditional Confucian ideology of the ideal man who possesses "a tender exterior and a strong inner will" (2011, 48). Her work shows that the transnational desire for Korean representations of soft masculinity is appealing to global audiences. Seok-Kyeong Hong (2021) further explains how masculinity, which had been understood as a traditional patriarch, was questioned for being unable to protect both the state and its women—first during the colonial era and then after the IMF crisis in 1997. This led to the desire for a different model of masculinity, which was addressed through Korean dramas. Exported to Japan at the turn of the century, the dramas appeared "culturally odorless" (Iwabuchi 2002). According to Ingyu Oh, "Hallyu is not really about Koreanness or Asianness but is about global cultural values of a female universalism" (2017, 164).

With the growing popularity of Korean media and K-pop taking the lead in the so-called Korean Wave, the concept of "liminal masculinity" (C. Oh 2015) was introduced a few years after Jung's widely acknowledged analysis. In her work, Chuyun Oh argues that "K-pop performers embody male femininity through their hybridized nuanced gender expressions" (2015, 70). Liminal masculinity in this approach is believed to be able to challenge rigid gender binaries that prevail in Western culture (Zaslow 2018). Although media representations of a different kind of masculinity—one that could contest the norm of hegemonic masculinity—could certainly be a source of empowerment for all genders, it is worth stressing that the reception of this new model is always grounded in the audience's own local gendered meanings and their ideas about Korean culture. Although liminal masculinity provides new models of masculinity, it does not overturn existing hegemonic masculine beliefs (Lee, Lee, and Park 2020). Instead, Hong (2021) argues that this gender reversal enables the female audience the power to gaze into the male world—to observe it, understand it, and form an intimate connection to it. K-pop fans use social media to maintain intimate relationships with idols and are let into their world; this virtual intimacy is created not only with idols but also with other fans, especially via fan-made content that maximizes female scopophilia (Hong

Trzcińska and Oh

2021). Furthermore, Chuyun Oh (2015) shows that by changing women's position in relation to media, Western viewers perform new gender roles and discursively empower themselves in hierarchical relations to their idols (e.g., "my boys," "babies"). Thus, it is important to understand how fan practices that empower (White) women can be based in the simultaneous elevation and marginalization of their favorite idols.

"Do Whatever Cheeky Freaky Deaky Thing That You Desire": TikTok and International K-pop Fandom

Social media are undeniably interconnected to K-pop fandom's growth, reaching audiences outside of Asia and leading to what Dal Yong Jin (2016) refers to as Hallyu 2.0. In addition to "soft power" benefits, Hallyu's social media reception has been mobilized for social activism, most notably K-pop fandom's participation in the Black Lives Matter movement. However, social media users also, at times, reinforce ethnic, racial, and gendered Othering (Jung 2012; Roy and Das 2002). In particular, TikTok has arguably become the leading site for Gen Z users, who constitute the largest part of K-pop fandom. What makes the platform popular is its focus on virality and its innovative features (Abidin 2021). This includes the "For You Page," which has been described as "one of the most addictive scrolling experiences on the Internet" (Zeng, Abidin, and Schäfer 2021, 3163), and the ability to creatively reuse memetic content. Recreating content, editing, and sharing it strengthen its value in participatory culture as spreadable media (Burgess 2008; Jenkins, Ford, and Green 2013; Washington 2016). Through these features, TikTok fosters the growth of transcultural fandoms, which prioritize cross-cultural communication and identification (Han 2017).

Its international engagement, however, makes it difficult for researchers to discern a TikTok user's country of origin, especially when they do not create content featuring themselves or their spoken language. For instance, the vast majority of the most popular K-pop content is created by and for fans who identify merely as I-fans, a form of distinction that builds solidarity among all non-Korean fans, who use English as their primary mode of communication. The "I" in I-fans implies that they differentiate themselves from Korean fans' (K-fans) interpretation of K-pop and engagement with idols. The "I" often assumes a globally cosmopolitan identity

"I Can Do Both"

that is constructed as more progressive and informed than the oft-derided Korean netizen, or "K-netz." Thus, the I-fan distinction constructs self-other boundaries between the in-group, I-fan, and the out-group, K-fan. Us-them boundaries are, of course, a common form of boundary marking and hierarchical formation in critical discourse analysis (Goodman and Rowe 2014), and it points to the ways that fan adoration of a cultural object does not necessarily lead to respect or admiration for people from that culture. In this mobilization of us versus them discourse, I-fans often (sub) consciously reinforce global White hegemony through the construction of the I/K-fan distinction.[6]

As K-pop artists attain immense global popularity, they must navigate the English language and Western societies to reach broader international audiences. Finding like-minded peers within their respective countries can prove challenging, so I-fans search online, and because of the global hegemony of English, they largely turn to Anglophone communities. Although I-fans are found around the globe, their online communities are not meritocratic spaces; rather, they are unequal spaces that are heavily structured by Western cultural values and discourses, including its White racial logics. I-fans often juxtapose K-pop culture with Western pop culture (Chan 2014). This comparison creates a self-perception of being "critical" of the perceived flaws within K-pop culture. The Western-centric view of being "right" is articulated through a disavowal of race and a claim to an "international identity."

This tendency toward "post-racialism" is a common feature of White racial discourse (Bhopal 2018), and the right to judge the Other is a common feature of Orientalism (Said 1978). A relevant illustration of this clash of values and perspectives is the recent controversy surrounding the boy group Enhypen's performance with women dancers onstage, which was heavily framed through the lens of I/K-fan dichotomy. Some portrayed K-fans as overly conservative due to their "Asian background," while I-fans were depicted as liberal and supportive, therefore "correct." Thus, studying racial *discourse* is crucial because it recognizes that discourse is not determined by actual identities but can emerge from a particular racial standpoint. While we cannot definitively know the racial demographics of online content creators and commenters due to the platform's anonymity and pseudonyms, analyzing racial discourse provides insights into the ideologies, narratives, and representations that perpetuate racial inequalities and discrimination (Sulé, Winkle-Wagner, and Maramba 2017). By doing so, scholars can uncover underlying mechanisms that sustain racial hierarchies and privilege, such as color-blind ideologies (Everson 2022) and soft racial framing (Ukpabi 2016). Moreover, studying online racial discourse enables critical analysis of concepts such as post-racialism, which denies the significance of race while upholding White racial dominance and the marginalization of people of color as the Other.

Studying online racial discourse is critical as it offers insights into the multifaceted expressions and experiences of racial topics in digital spaces (Stewart, Schuschke, and Tynes 2019). By exploring the quotidian aspects of life, like social media usage, researchers gain a more comprehensive understanding of how racial issues are perpetuated, challenged, and negotiated in the digital realm (Adams 2022). This approach sheds light on the complexities of racial conversations and how online platforms shape racial narratives and identities. Furthermore, it facilitates an exploration of race's intersectionality with other social identities (Willoughby-Herard 2014), providing a holistic perspective on the construction and reception of racial discourses. In this study, it is important to clarify that we do not make definitive claims about I-fans' ascribed or avowed racial identities. This is unknowable because commenters and creators of fan-edited TikTok videos cannot be reliably identified; rather, we, like other scholars of online racial discourse, argue that new media can articulate a White discursive position. In this study, White discursive positions are marked by superiority and objectification of the fan object as well as discourses of post-racialism masked by claims of universal "internationalism." Though there is no physical local space as described in this volume's introduction's explanation of racial translocalism, we argue that there are imagined digital cartographies of space in which the I-fans imagine themselves to occupy different territory than K-fans.

I-fans on social media act as opinion leaders, culturally translating and promoting Korean media, but they can also capitalize on idols' texts (Leung 2017). Moreover, while analyzing fan videos on YouTube, Chuyun Oh observed that K-pop fans can "openly, actively and playfully express desire and engage in their own ways of finding sexual pleasure in a public space" (2015, 72). This also seems to be true, at least to a point, for TikTok users

"I Can Do Both"

245

who use the song "Both" to create fan content about K-pop idols for other fans to enjoy. This is similar to the fan fiction and production of media that is constitutive of fan communities (Jenkins 1992), and it is emblematic of the participatory culture of online fandoms (Jenkins, Ito, and boyd 2016).

"Do You Want the Masculine or Feminine Side?": TikTok Trends and K-pop Idols

The trend utilizing Todrick Hall's "Both" gained popularity in December 2021. Most of the videos feature a segment of the song where the singer states, "I can be your boy toy, I can be your bride / I can shut my mouth, or I can open wide / Do you want the masculine or feminine side? / I can do both, I can do both." Typically, each verse is illustrated by different scenes or images, highlighting stark differences between feminine and masculine "sides." Notably, the lyrics are sexualized, thus queering both gender and sexual identities. As such, the objectification of K-pop idols in fan TikToks expresses sexual pleasure or humor in seeing idols perform masculinity and femininity.

Among the collected videos, the three that garnered the highest numbers of views, likes, comments, and saves featured Stray Kids' Hyunjin (2.9 million views, 705,300 likes, 7,177 comments, 100,800 saves), Stray Kids' Felix (1.1 million views, 276,600 likes, 1,485 comments, 30,200 saves), and BTS's Jimin (943,900 views, 278,900 likes, 1,619 comments, 43,200 saves). The data reveal two important findings. First, fan-made TikTok videos can achieve comparable popularity to official content from K-pop idols, as evident from Stray Kids' TikTok account. Second, I-fans are more inclined to save videos for future enjoyment than to leave comments. Of the featured artists, Jimin was the most favored idol with seven edits among the collected data. The frequency of idol appearances in the analyzed videos appears to align with the popularity of the groups outside of Asia, mainly consisting of third and fourth generation K-pop boy groups, such as BTS, NCT, Stray Kids, Enhypen, ATEEZ, and TXT.[7] Notably, only three videos feature women performers (Mamamoo's Moonbyul, TWICE's Chaeyoung, and IVE's Leeseo), and one is a video that gender-switches two artists— Itzy's Ryujin, a female idol, as masculine, and TXT's Beomgyu, a male idol, as feminine.

Trzcińska and Oh

The content used by fans to create their edits is mainly official stage performances (83.7 percent) and behind-the-scenes stills from photo shoots (also 83.7 percent). Fans also incorporate content from social media (67.4 percent), such as parts of idols' V Live streams or Instagram posts, but not to the extent one might expect, given social media's role as a channel for virtual intimacy between fans and idols.

Through the creation of TikTok videos, I-fans project their desires for gender binarism onto K-pop idols. They reference common gender discourses in many countries and cultures: "erectness, rigidness or stubbornness for masculinity and flexibility, softness, and curviness" for femininity (C. Oh 2015). The edits predominantly present either the male or the female side with little blending of the two aspects. Most of the edits follow a similar structure with clips presented interchangeably—one showcasing the male side ("boy toy"/ "masculine side") and the other displaying the female side ("bride"/ "feminine side"). For the verse "I can shut my mouth, or I can open wide," edits either adhere to the same order or use images of a literally closed/open mouth (e.g., laughter, yawning).

The aforementioned binary representation is clearly evident in the analyzed edits. Segments aimed at portraying the masculine side of idols depict them in dark clothes, often in suits or with ties, and sometimes show them with scars or bruises or covered in sweat. Although the idols are occasionally portrayed performing seductive movements, they are more commonly portrayed as still, composed, and emotionless, often using behind-the-scenes stills from photo shoots. The masculine portrayals reinforce characteristics associated with hegemonic masculinity in the West, including toughness, violence, and dominance (Zaslow 2018). The feminine side, however, is associated with bright colors, flowers, lace, and a sense of softness and purity. Femininity is also linked to longer hair, jewelry, and glittery makeup. Furthermore, the feminine side is often portrayed as youthful, silly, goofy, and cute, contrasting with the masculine side's rigidity and composure.

It is noteworthy that I-fans' edits solely utilize the idols' image and visual signifiers rather than gendered actions or perceived character. There are minimal instances of edits that use specific situations, even in a stereotypical manner, to portray either side. For instance, descriptions such as "a mother of the group," which fans commonly use for idols who show exceptional care toward other members, are not evident in the "Both" trend edits. This

"I Can Do Both"

emphasis on the visual aspect may partly be due to fans who do not understand Korean and rely instead on images when engaging with Korean media (Ono and Kwon 2013; D. C. Oh, 2017). Consequently, it represents a form of objectification that features the heterosexual female and gay male gaze, reducing idols to their physical appearance. The only behavior-oriented aspects present in the analyzed data are sexual innuendos.

The trend can be categorized as so-called thirst traps, which are posts intended to sexually entice viewers, a theme emphasized by the lyrics of the song itself. Nearly 63 percent of the edits include lip movements such as licking, biting, or seductive touching of one's lips. Chuyun Oh (2015) observes that such movements are typically associated with female sexuality, but in the edits, fans connect them to masculinity three times more frequently than to femininity. Other categories connected to sexuality, which are used in 44 percent of the edits, include pelvic thrusting and eyes that are closing while tilting one's head back. The presence of numerous sexual references in the analyzed TikTok videos indicates that their purpose is to provide pleasure for fans. This observation becomes particularly significant when considering the research that highlights the frequent sexualization of not only K-pop idols but also of trans, non-binary, and gender-fluid people (Anzani et al. 2021). Adopting the definition of sexualization as reducing people to their body parts or sexual functioning (Flores et al. 2018; Fredrickson and Roberts 1997), the "Both" trend exemplifies sexualization.

Both the content of the videos and the accompanying comments demonstrate that the primary focus of this trend is fans' sexual pleasure, not fans' gender identity expressions or support for idols' gender fluidity. Indeed, only two edits display gender ambiguity. These edits, dedicated to BTS's members Jungkook and Jimin, use a longer version of the song and do not adhere to the structure of one verse–one image/scene. Thus, the edits portray gender fluidity with many boundary-blurring elements. However, the comments under these two edits do not differ significantly from others, indicating that even though the edits could potentially open a discussion on non-binary gender portrayals, I-fans primarily seek personal enjoyment with this gender play.

Another element analyzed in the edits is the portrayal of dance. As Chuyun Oh notes, "the dancing body in western culture is doubly marginalized: for women, it is a sign of promiscuity; for men, it is a symbol of emasculation or homosexuality" (2015, 65). Scenes with idols dancing are more often associated with the masculine side (eighteen cases) than the feminine side (ten cases). Further strengthening masculine and sexual associations, dances are frequently performed in dark settings and with sexualized movements, such as lip or hip/pelvic movements, emphasizing sensuality.

Remarkably, neither the edits nor the comments explicitly mention Korea or Korean culture, which may reflect a form of racial color blindness. The only exception is a single image of modernized 한복 (hanbok), Korean traditional clothing. It is likely that this is shaped by tendencies to avoid explicit "racetalk" in White discourse (Bonilla-Silva and Forman 2000; Pérez 2013). K-pop fans, often serving as opinion leaders on Korea-related topics among their friends and relatives, may feel that clearly stating that idols are Koreans could be seen as fetishization. Alternatively, fans might have been socialized to avoid discussions about race in "international" spaces. As Alice Marwick and danah boyd (2010) argue, users in online spaces tend to revert to the ideologically safest posts because of "context collapse," the merging of different audiences in social media. Because of the nature of dominant discourse, in this case, White liberal racial logics of post-racialism are the least risky for I-fans.

Among the 361 comments, 86.5 percent are written in English, 9.9 percent in Thai, and the rest in either Indonesian, Polish, Spanish, or Portuguese (there were also cases of mixing English with other languages).[8] Approximately 70 percent of the comments express attraction toward the idol (e.g., "So I want both," "I love men who can do both," "Sir we want all of you"), and 59.2 percent show support for the idol (e.g., "stan leeknow for clear skin," "IT BOY OF KPOP. NO ONE CAN CHANGE MY MIND").[9] When fans express attraction, it is mostly romantic or sexual attraction to both "sides"—the masculine and the feminine. Attraction to only femininity or masculinity is much less frequent. Other comments include requests for edits featuring a different idol or praise for the creator's editing skills. Only seven comments are coded as self-identification, mainly in the form of "gender envy," typically associated with trans individuals at the beginning of their transitioning process. This suggests that I-fans are familiar with queer TikTok vernacular.

In general, K-pop fans treat queerness as a default identity. For example,

"I Can Do Both"

in the series "Your sexual orientation based on your bias," different creators determine viewers' sexual orientation based on their favorite member of a particular group. This indicates that heterosexuality is no longer seen as the dominant or obvious option within K-pop fandom, at least on TikTok. However, I-fans are also susceptible to ethnocentric misinterpretation of everyday culture in Korea, such as "skinship" or general closeness between people of the same gender as an example of homosexuality (Kuo et al. 2022).

Interestingly, there is minimal discussion about gender identity or the definition of femininity or masculinity in the "Both" trend videos. I-fans in the comments section frequently emphasize that the idols depicted are men, using phrases such as "my man can do both" or "the man you are . . ." Yet fans particularly admire the idols' "duality," a notion deeply ingrained in K-pop fandom and often the subject of memes and discussions. Duality refers to idols' ability to switch between sexy and cute personas, leading some I-fans to question whether it should be perceived merely as the ability to fit any given concept. Some I-fans view it as the idols' onstage and offstage persona and one person being "able to give you different forms of entertainment," whereas others discuss it in the context of cultural differences ("I think Western I-fans care so much because it isn't typical with our own celebs") or are even angry at other fans for obsessing over this notion ("Duality? More like they are normals [*sic*] humans who have a complex range of emotions and understand societal cues and can adjust their public persona to a situation!").[10] Based on the analysis of TikTok videos, comments, and other K-pop-related content, the different personas most associated with duality are romantic tropes such as the "bad boy," the "guy next door," or the "high school sweetheart," and K-pop idols who embody these various tropes are considered the most desirable. This echoes the desire expressed by Bae Yong-joon's fans that a man who is both tender and feisty is considered ideal (Jung 2011). Thus, the creation of edited videos in the "Both" trend once again highlights the primary purpose of such fan practices—expressing the fans' own desires.

Interestingly, the reaction of other users to the "Both" trend videos differs from previous analyses of similar fan-made texts. There is no apparent sense of guilt observed in the comments section for watching sexually loaded videos. I-fans embrace their enjoyment of the videos without feeling conflicted. In contrast, previous analyses focused on how fans question

Trzcińska and Oh

White hegemonic masculinity by reversing the roles of the spectator and the object, often leading to feelings of guilt or being labeled as "pervert" or "deviant" (C. Oh 2015).

"Cause Baby I Can Do the Dishes, I Can Wear the Pants": I-fans as a Double-Edged Sword

In the West and in societies strongly influenced by Western culture, there is an intense struggle for hegemonic White masculinity. Anything perceived as a challenge to heterosexual masculinity and traditional values, such as boys with pink toenails or using colorful crayons in school, is often strongly policed as a threat.[11] Although I-fans do not simply duplicate prevailing dominant discourses about the normative desirability of hegemonic masculinity in these societies, the analysis of the TikTok videos finds that they project Orientalist desires by queering male K-pop idols in contrast to male pop stars in the West.

Cosimo Marco Scarcelli, Tonny Krijnen, and Paul Nixon observe that "it is not the singular image, but the repetitive occurrence of representations in various media that articulate discourses on what gender and sexuality mean" (2021, 1066). This is particularly relevant in cases such as the "Both" trend, where overly simplistic and binary patterns and narratives are repeated due to the memetic quality of a trend. The irony of using a queer song to queer K-pop idols while reinforcing heteronormative and patriarchal gender binaries points to the complexities and poached nature of fan discourse as well as its tendency toward dominant culture meanings. In reaction to the most popular edits, which solely feature seductive images or emphasize the stark contrast between the masculine and feminine "sides," I-fans claim that a particular idol "owned the song" or that it was written for them. The desire for popularity and visibility within the fandom motivates creators' editing decisions. The edits spark discussions among I-fans about which idol fits the song's lyrics better, thus generating more engagement within the attention economy of TikTok.

In contrast, after analyzing TikTok videos that feature Western pop stars, interesting differences emerge that point to dissimilar treatment of Western stars and K-pop idols. Notably, the most popular videos mainly focus on White women. This suggests that it is less imaginable and less

"I Can Do Both"

desirable for fans to portray White men as possessing gender duality, thereby demonstrating the persistence of White hegemonic masculinity. Furthermore, in the edits of White celebrities, such as Billie Eilish, separate videos were created to display their masculine and feminine "sides." Their gender performance is also less sexualized—for example, presenting Billie Eilish either in revealing dresses or baggy hip hop–style hoodies. Interestingly, most of the videos were created by women. This further points to the White discursive position of the content creators. Korean men are objectified for heterosexual women fans' pleasure, whereas White women are represented in ways to encourage identification. Respect for the artists' self-image is more visible in fans' treatment of Western celebrities.

Although some differences in the creators' sexual orientation could be observed (with K-pop-related TikTok creators self-identifying as straight, bi-, or pan-sexual more often and Western celebrities' fans slightly more often identifying as gay), strong claims cannot be made because of insufficient clarity in creators' self-identification and their discursive standpoints. Videos created by gender-fluid or non-binary TikTok users, however, exhibit more artistic freedom, using a wider variety of angles and transitions. Non-binary and gender-fluid individuals engage the trend as a way to express personal gender expression, to contemplate their own body perceptions, and to encourage others to do the same, whereas for K-pop fans, it is mostly exploitative for their own entertainment. Additionally, comments on these videos differ somewhat with more instances of "gender envy," questioning of sexuality, and critical comments, which are absent in the K-pop part of the trend (e.g., "i can do both. i can be femine or femine [*sic*] but with different clothes"). It is worth noting that K-pop fans may have had less freedom in their edits, as they are only able to reframe existing images. However, there was still room to problematize gender binary logic, but non-queer identified I-fans generally chose not to do so.

I-fans generally lacked self-reflexivity regarding the potential consequences of the "Both" trend, making it relatively easy for them to fetishize K-pop idols by mainly reducing them to a means of satisfying their own desires, while overlooking the idols' potential needs for self-expression. That said, it is essential to stress that the content used by fans in their videos was all readily available online and, in most cases, officially released by the idols' agencies. While the fact that a sexy versus cute duality edit featured an underage idol (Leeseo from the group IVE, born in 2007) could be worrisome, it must be noted that the images used in the TikTok video were all official content. Although fans do indeed sexualize K-pop idols and engage in consuming exotic otherness (Yoon, Min, and Jin 2020), it seems that this is somewhat expected and enabled by entertainment companies. Official performances and images are designed for participatory culture that encourages the creation of viral, spreadable media.

Conclusion

The question of how soft or liminal masculinity can influence Western perceptions of Asian men and Western-influenced societies remains a topic of debate. On one hand, it portrays Korean men as attractive and handsome, challenging the desexualization of Asian men, but, on the other hand, the focus on their physicality can lead to the fetishization of Asian men. Although extremes on a binary of sexual desirability, they are ideologically joined by the Western gaze. The analysis of the "Both" trend on TikTok provides evidence that I-fans often exoticize and fetishize Korean idols, treating them as objects of queer play. Furthermore, dominant gender and racial norms continue to prevail in fan discourse, as viral videos with catchy songs and alluring images are much more widely viewed than those promoting meta discussions about fandom practices and racism. Nonetheless, it should not be solely attributed to I-fans' initiative, as K-pop idols and their agencies appear to capitalize on this type of reception.

Defining I-fans' role in this phenomenon is not straightforward. They face double stigmatization—as fans of popular cultural texts (seen as inferior) and fans of Korean media (still seen as exotic and Other). We also see many paradoxical situations. John Fiske (1992) writes that fans can take up subordinate positions to their idols, and K-pop idols are certainly seen quite often as otherworldly and unavailable, but at the same time we observe the reversal of the Cinderella complex and I-fans taking up the role of idols' protectors (C. Oh 2017). The "Both" trend on TikTok exemplifies how various themes and processes can overlap in international fans' reception and recreation of Korean media.

The analyzed trend emerged within an online space predominantly occupied by I-fans communicating in English and participating in a

"I Can Do Both"

sphere dominated by Western White culture, which serves as a shared experience for most of them. The utilization of common ground fosters mutual understanding among individuals from diverse backgrounds, but K-pop fans may not fully grasp the consequences of embedding their communication within such a hegemonic White cultural context. While the prevalence of Western White culture might facilitate the exploration of queer themes, which could prove challenging in the Korean-speaking internet sphere, it also leads to the replication of harmful discourses that advance Orientalism by projecting personal desires onto K-pop idols. It is crucial for fans to be mindful of these dynamics and their impact on the perception and representation of K-pop idols and culture. By comprehensively studying racial discourse, we are better able to comprehend and address the complexities of racial dynamics so that we may strive for more inclusive and just societies.

Notes

All the subheadings are lyrics from Todrick Hall's "Both."

1. Prosumption is a process in which a person takes over some of the activities performed by both producers and consumers.

2. The number of TikToks has increased to 36,200 as of July 18, 2022.

3. It must be stressed that all designations about race in the following text are made from the perspective of the first author, a Polish researcher.

4. Min Joo Lee's chapter in this volume discusses appreciation and appropriation.

5. The topic of content creators is explored by Crystal S. Anderson in her chapter in this volume, where she presents Black creators.

6. Interestingly, Korean fans also use such a differentiation, calling I-fans "overseas fans" (해외 팬), portraying them as an example of an out-group and proving that this division is seen by both parties. Nevertheless, Koreans fans' use of this term carries different connotations.

7. K-pop generations are typically classified based on the debut year of the groups. Not all of the fans agree on the same dates, but one of the most common classification groups K-pop generations as follows: first generation, 1990s–2003; second generation, 2003–2012; third generation, 2012–2017; and fourth generation, 2017 to the present.

8. Only comments in English, Polish, and Spanish were analyzed.

9. All the quoted comments have their original spelling.

Trzcińska and Oh

10. All the comments are from r/unpopularkpopopinions on Reddit.

11. This is a reference to Polish MP Janusz Kowalski's statement linking the use of colorful crayons in school to LGBTQ+ ideology.

References

Abidin, Crystal. 2021. "Mapping Internet Celebrity on TikTok: Exploring Attention Economies and Visibility Labours." *Cultural Science Journal* 12 (1): 77–103. https://doi.org/10.5334/csci.140.

Adams, Brienne A. 2022. "'Whole Self to the World': Creating Affective Worlds and Black Digital Intimacy in the Fandom of *The Misadventures of Awkward Black Girl* and *Insecure*." *Digital Humanities Quarterly* 16 (3).

Anzani, Annalisa, Louis Lindley, Giacomo Tognasso, M. Paz Galupo, and Antonio Prunas. 2021. "'Being Talked to Like I Was a Sex Toy, Like Being Transgender Was Simply for the Enjoyment of Someone Else': Fetishization and Sexualization of Transgender and Nonbinary Individuals." *Archives of Sexual Behavior* 50 (3): 897–911. https://doi.org/10.1007/s10508-021-01935-8.

Bell, Crystal. 2022. "How K-Pop Is Helping Fans Explore the Full Spectrum of Gender." *Nylon*, November 3, 2022. https://www.nylon.com/entertainment /gender-envy-in-k-pop-hyunjin-stray-kids.

Bhopal, Kalwant. 2018. *White Privilege: The Myth of a Post-Racial Society*. Bristol: Policy Press.

Bonilla-Silva, Eduardo, and Tyrone A. Forman. 2000. "'I Am Not a Racist but . . .': Mapping White College Students' Racial Ideology in the USA." *Discourse and Society* 11 (1): 50–85.

Burgess, Jean. 2008. "All Your Chocolate Rain Are Belong to Us"? Viral Video, YouTube and the Dynamics of Participatory Culture." In *Video Vortex Reader: Responses to YouTube*, edited by Geert Lovink and Sabine Niederer, 101–9. Amsterdam: Institute of Network Cultures.

Chan, Yvonne Yi Yan. 2014. "Looking at K-Pop as an I-fan: A Reflection of Mesmerizing yet Imperfect Identities." Honors thesis, Duke University. https://hdl .handle.net/10161/8615.

Dubino, Jeanne. 1993. "The Cinderella Complex: Romance Fiction, Patriarchy and Capitalism." *Journal of Popular Culture* 27 (3): 103–18. https://doi.org/ 10.1111/j.0022-3840.1993.00103.x.

Everson, David W. 2022. "Narrating the Territorial Foundations of Privilege: Racial Discourse and Indigenous Peoples." *Sociology of Race and Ethnicity* 8 (1): 213–28. https://doi.org/10.1177/23326492211043908.

Fiske, John. 1992. "The Cultural Economy of Fandom." In *The Adoring Audience:*

"I Can Do Both"

Fan Culture and Popular Media, edited by Lisa A. Lewis, 30–49. London: Routledge.

Flores, Mirella J., Laurel B. Watson, Luke R. Allen, Mudiwa Ford, Christine R. Serpe, Ping Ying Choo, and Michelle Farrell. 2018. "Transgender People of Color's Experiences of Sexual Objectification: Locating Sexual Objectification within a Matrix of Domination." *Journal of Counseling Psychology* 65 (3): 308–23. https://doi.org/10.1037/cou0000279.

Fong-Torres, Ben. 1995. "Why Are There No Male Asian Anchormen on TV?" In *Men's Lives*, 3rd ed., edited by Michael Kimmel and Michael A. Messner, 256–60. New York: Macmillan.

Fredrickson, Barbara L., and Tomi-Ann Roberts. 1997. "Objectification Theory: Toward Understanding Women's Lived Experiences and Mental Health Risks." *Psychology of Women Quarterly* 21 (2): 173–206. https://doi.org/10.1111 /j.1471-6402.1997.tb00108.x.

Georgiou, Myria. 2020. "Racism, Postracialism and Why Media Matter." *Ethnic and Racial Studies* 43 (13): 2379–85. https://doi.org/10.1080/01419870.2020.1784 450.

Goodman, Simon, and Lottie Rowe. 2014. "'Maybe It Is Prejudice . . . but It Is NOT Racism': Negotiating Racism in Discussion Forums about Gypsies." *Discourse and Society* 25 (1): 32–46.

Han, Benjamin. 2017. "K-Pop in Latin America: Transcultural Fandom and Digital Mediation." *International Journal of Communication* 11: 2250–69.

Hong, Seok-Kyeong. 2021. "Sharing Gender Imagination in East Asia: An Essay on Soft Masculinity and Female Digital Scopophilia in East Asian Mediaculture." In *Transnational Convergence of East Asian Pop Culture*, edited by Seok-Kyeong Hong and Dal Yong Jin, 113–26. London: Routledge.

Iwabuchi, Koichi. 2002. *Recentering Globalization: Popular Culture and Japanese Transnationalism*. Durham, NC: Duke University Press.

Jang, Haeyoung, Ngoc Tram Oanh Nguyen, and Seung-Ho Kwon. 2021. "Women's Empowerment and Transnational Consumption of *Hallyu* in Vietnam." *Asian Journal of Women's Studies* 27 (2): 184–207. https://doi.org/10.1080/12259276 .2021.1924482.

Jenkins, Henry. 1992. *Textual Poachers: Television Fans and Participatory Culture*. New York: Routledge.

Jenkins, Henry, Mizuko Ito, and danah boyd. 2016. *Participatory Culture in a Networked Era: A Conversation on Youth, Learning, Commerce, and Politics*. Cambridge: Polity.

Jenkins, Henry, Sam Ford, and Joshua Green. 2013. *Spreadable Media: Creating Value and Meaning in a Networked Culture*. New York: New York University Press.

Jin, Dal Yong. 2016. *New Korean Wave: Transnational Cultural Power in the Age of Social Media*. Urbana: University of Illinois Press.

Jin, Dal Yong, and Woongjae Ryoo. 2014. "Critical Interpretation of Hybrid K-Pop: The Global-Local Paradigm of English Mixing in Lyrics." *Popular Music and Society* 37 (2): 113–31. https://doi.org/10.1080/03007766.2012.731721.

Jung, Sun. 2011. *Korean Masculinities and Transcultural Consumption: Yonsama, Rain, Oldboy, K-Pop Idols*. Hong Kong: Hong Kong University Press.

———. 2012. "Fan Activism, Cybervigilantism, and Othering Mechanisms in K-pop Fandom." In "Transformative Works and Fan Activism," edited by Henry Jenkins and Sangita Shresthova, special issue, *Transformative Works and Cultures* 10. https://doi.org/10.3983/twc.2012.0300.

Kaye, D. Bondy Valdovinos, Aleesha Rodriguez, Katrin Langton, and Patrik Wikström. 2021. "You Made This? I Made This: Practices of Authorship and (Mis) Attribution on TikTok." *International Journal of Communication* 15: 3195–215.

Kim, Grace MyHyun. 2019. "'Do They Really Do That in Korea?': Multicultural Learning through Hallyu Media." *Learning, Media and Technology* 44 (4): 473–88. https://doi.org/10.1080/17439884.2019.1620768.

Kim, Ju Oak. 2021. "The Korean Wave and the New Global Media Economy." In *The Routledge Handbook of Digital Media and Globalization*, edited by Dal Yong Jin, 77–85. New York: Routledge.

Kimmel, Michael. 2006. *Manhood in America: A Cultural History*. 2nd ed. New York: Oxford University Press.

Kraidy, Marwan M. 2005. *Hybridity, or the Cultural Logic of Globalization*. Philadelphia: Temple University Press.

Kuo, Linda, Simone Perez-Garcia, Lindsey Burke, Vic Yamasaki, and Thomas Le. 2022. "Performance, Fantasy, or Narrative: LGBTQ+ Asian American Identity through Kpop Media and Fandom." *Journal of Homosexuality* 69 (1): 145–68. https://doi.org/10.1080/00918369.2020.1815428.

Lee, Jeehyun Jenny, Rachel Kar Yee Lee, and Ji Hoon Park. 2020. "Unpacking K-pop in America: The Subversive Potential of Male K-pop Idols' Soft Masculinity." *International Journal of Communication* 14: 5900–5919.

Leung, Lisa Yuk-ming. 2017. "#Unrequited Love in Cottage Industry? Managing K-pop (Transnational) Fandom in the Social Media Age." In *The Korean Wave: Evolution, Fandom, and Transnationality*, edited by Tae-Jin Yoon and Dal Yong Jin, 87–108. Lanham, MD: Lexington Books.

Marwick, Alice E., and danah boyd. 2010. "I Tweet Honestly, I Tweet Passionately: Twitter Users, Context Collapse, and the Imagined Audience." *New Media and Society* 13 (1): 114–33.

Mazaná, Vladislava. 2014. "Cultural Perception and Social Impact of the Korean Wave in the Czech Republic." In *The Global Impact of South Korean Popular*

Culture: Hallyu Unbound, edited by Valentina Marinescu, 47–63. Lanham, MD: Lexington Books.

Moon, Dreama G., and Michelle A. Holling. 2020. "'White Supremacy in Heels': (White) Feminism, White Supremacy, and Discursive Violence." *Communication and Critical/Cultural Studies* 17 (2): 253–60. https://doi.org/10.1080/14791420.2020.1770819.

Moreton-Robinson, Aileen. 2006. "Whiteness Matters: Implications of Talkin' Up to the White Woman." *Australian Feminist Studies* 21 (50): 245–56. https://doi.org/10.1080/08164640600731788.

Oh, Chuyun. 2015. "Queering Spectatorship in K-pop: The Androgynous Male Dancing Body and Western Female Fandom." *Journal of Fandom Studies* 3 (1): 59–78. https://doi.org/10.1386/jfs.3.1.59_1.

———. 2017. "'Cinderella' in Reverse: Eroticizing Bodily Labor of Sympathetic Men in K-Pop Dance Practice Video." In *East Asian Men: Masculinity, Sexuality and Desire*, edited by Xiaodong Lin, Chris Haywood, and Mairtin Mac an Ghaill, 123–42. London: Palgrave Macmillan.

Oh, David C. 2017. "K-Pop Fans React: Hybridity and the White Celebrity-Fan on YouTube." *International Journal of Communication* 11: 2270–87.

Oh, David C., and Chuyun Oh. 2017. "Vlogging White Privilege Abroad: *Eat Your Kimchi*'s Eating and Spitting Out of the Korean Other on YouTube." *Communication, Culture and Critique* 10 (4): 696–711. https://doi.org/10.1111/cccr.12180.

Oh, Ingyu. 2017. "From Localization to Glocalization: Contriving Korean Pop Culture to Meet Glocal Demands." *Kultura Kritika* 29: 157–67.

Ono, Kent A., and Jungmin Kwon. 2013. "Re-worlding Culture? YouTube as a K-pop Interlocutor." In *The Korean Wave: Korean Media Go Global*, edited by Youna Kim, 199–214. London: Routledge.

Pérez, Raúl. 2013. "Learning to Make Racism Funny in the 'Color-Blind' Era: Stand-Up Comedy Students, Performance Strategies, and the (Re)Production of Racist Jokes in Public." *Discourse and Society* 24 (4): 478–503. https://doi.org/10.1177/0957926513482066.

Roy, Ratan Kumar, and Biswajit Das. 2022. "Transcultural Flow in the Age of Globalization: Digital Platforms, Fandom and Mediated Culture in South Asia." In *Korean Wave in South Asia: Transcultural Flow, Fandom and Identity*, edited by Ratan Kumar Roy and Biswajit Das. Singapore: Palgrave Macmillan.

Said, Edward. 1978. *Orientalism*. New York: Vintage Books.

Scarcelli, Cosimo Marco, Tonny Krijnen, and Paul Nixon. 2021. "Sexuality, Gender, Media: Identity Articulations in the Contemporary Media Landscape." *Information, Communication and Society* 24 (8): 1063–72.

Shim, Doobo. 2006. "Hybridity and the Rise of Korean Popular Culture in Asia." *Media, Culture and Society* 28 (1): 25–44. https://doi.org/10.1177/0163443 706059278.

Stewart, Ashley, Joshua Schuschke, and Brendesha Tynes. 2019. "Online Racism: Adjustment and Protective Factors among Adolescents of Color." In *Handbook of Children and Prejudice: Integrating Research, Practice, and Policy*, edited by Hiram E. Fitzgerald, Deborah J. Johnson, Desiree Baolian Qin, Francisco A. Villarruel, and John Norder, 501–13. Cham, Switzerland: Springer.

Sulé, V. Thandi, Rachelle Winkle-Wagner, and Dina C. Maramba. 2017. "Who Deserves a Seat? Colorblind Public Opinion of College Admissions Policy." *Equity and Excellence in Education* 50 (2): 196–208. https://doi.org/10.1080 /10665684.2017.1301836.

Thussu, Daya Kishan. 2007. "Mapping Global Media Flow and Contra-flow." In *Media on the Move: Global Flow and Contra-flow*, edited by Daya Kishan Thussu, 11–32. London: Routledge.

Ukpabi, Ifeanyichukwu U. 2016. "Please, Read the Comments: Exploring the Racial Dialectic of Online Racial Discourse." Thesis, Georgia State University.

Washington, Myra. 2016. "Asian/American Masculinity: The Politics of Virility, Virality, and Visibility." In *The Intersectional Internet: Race, Sex, Class, and Culture Online*, edited by Safiya Umoja Noble and Brendesha M. Tynes, 61–79. New York: Peter Lang.

Willoughby-Herard, Tiffany. 2014. "'The Only One Who Was Thought to Know the Pulse of the People': Black Women's Politics in the Era of Post-racial Discourse." *Cultural Dynamics* 26 (1): 73–90. https://doi.org/10.1177/09213740 13510802.

Yoon, Kyong. 2019. "Transnational Fandom in the Making: K-pop Fans in Vancouver." *International Communication Gazette* 81 (2): 176–92. https://doi.org /10.1177/1748048518802964.

Yoon, Kyong, Wonjung Min, and Dal Yong Jin. 2020. "Consuming the Contra-flow of K-pop in Spain." *Journal of Intercultural Studies* 41 (2): 132–47. https://doi.org/10.1080/07256868.2020.1724907.

Yoshihara, Mari. 2002. *Embracing the East: White Women and American Orientalism*. New York: Oxford University Press.

Zaslow, Emilie. 2018. "Pink Toenails and Princess Boys: Contemporary Discourses of Boys' Gender-Fluidity in USA Television News." *Journal of Children and Media* 12 (3): 243–57. https://doi.org/10.1080/17482798.2018.1457552.

Zeng, Jing, Crystal Abidin, and Mike S. Schäfer. 2021. "Research Perspectives on TikTok and Its Legacy Apps: Introduction." *International Journal of Communication* 15: 3161–72.

Zhang, Qin. 2010. "Asian Americans beyond the Model Minority Stereotype: The Nerdy and the Left Out." *Journal of International and Intercultural Communication* 3 (1): 20–37. https://doi.org/10.1080/17513050903428109.

Zheng, Robin. 2016. "Why Yellow Fever Isn't Flattering: A Case against Racial Fetishes." *Journal of the American Philosophical Association* 2 (3): 400–419. https://doi.org/10.1017/apa.2016.25.

Contributors

CRYSTAL S. ANDERSON is an affiliate faculty member in African and African American Studies at George Mason University. She works in the fields of Transnational American Studies, Black Internationalism, and Global Asias. Her first book, *Beyond the Chinese Connection: Contemporary Afro-Asian Cultural Production* (2013), uses the films of Bruce Lee to interpret cross-cultural dynamics in post-1990 novels, films, and anime. Her 2020 book, *Soul in Seoul: African American Popular Music and K-pop*, explores the impact of African American popular music on contemporary Korean pop, R&B, and hip hop and the role of global fans as the music press. In addition to publishing articles and book chapters on K-pop, she also manages several digital humanities projects, including *KPK: Kpop Kollective*, the oldest and only public scholarship site for K-pop. A veteran blogger on Asian popular culture, she is also a former associate chief editor for *hellokpop*.

BENJAMIN M. HAN is an associate professor in the Department of Entertainment and Media Studies in the Grady College of Journalism and Mass Communication at the University of Georgia. His research focuses on global media, race and television, and the cultural intersections between East Asia and Latin America. He is the author of *Beyond the Black and White TV: Asian and Latin American Spectacle in Cold War America* (Rutgers University Press, 2020). His work has been published in the *International Journal of Communication*; *Critical Studies in Media Communication*; *Media, Culture and Society*; and *Television and New Media*. He is currently completing his second book, titled *Reckoning with the World: South Korean Television and the Latin American Imaginary*. He is also working on a new book project about Netflix Korea and global television.

WOORI HAN (she/her) is a lecturer in media and communications at the Department of Communications, Drama and Film at the University of Exeter, UK. Her research centers on media and cultural activisms, popular culture, and the body at the intersection of race, gender, sexuality, and class. In particular, she examines how digital media and cultural production have become a critical site where contested global and local sexual politics and networked affect can construct social movement, backlash, and new subjectivities. Han's research on cultural translation of transnational feminist movements, feminist media critiques, and queer cultural activism has been published in *Communication, Culture and Critique; Media, Culture and Society;* and *Korea Journal.* She holds a PhD from the Department of Communication at the University of Massachusetts Amherst and was a postdoctoral fellow at the Center for Advanced Research in Global Communication and the Center on Digital Culture and Society at the University of Pennsylvania.

LAURA-ZOË HUMPHREYS is an associate professor in the Department of Communication at Tulane University. She is working on two book projects: an ethnography of how gender shapes informal media economies and a study of a previously unidentified transnational film genre—the bureaucrat comedy—as it developed in state socialist and liberal capitalist contexts. Her first monograph, *Fidel between the Lines: Paranoia and Ambivalence in Late Socialist Cuban Cinema* (Duke University Press, 2019), combines ethnography, archival research, and film analysis to demonstrate how political paranoia and struggles over allegory in cinema shape the public sphere. Her current research is supported by the National Science Foundation, the Wenner-Gren Foundation, and the Louisiana Board of Regents (ATLAS program), and her work has also appeared in *boundary 2, Discourse,* and *Social Text,* among others.

YOUNG JUNG is an assistant professor of the Korean studies program, Department of Modern and Classical Languages at George Mason University. Her research is at the crossroads of migration studies, sense of place studies, media studies, and gender studies. She also has a thorough grounding in the history of modern Korean and Korean diasporic literature and popular culture. One of her recent essays, "Squid Games, Transcultural Fan Parodies: Black and Queer Adaptations," appeared in *The Hallyu Project*. Her current research project, "Division and Connections: Korean Popular Culture Fans' Racial Dynamics," examines the racial dynamics of Korean popular culture fan communities and explores the (im)possibilities of constructing pan-racial fan communities. She is currently completing the book titled *Korean Kirogi Families: Placemaking, Belonging, and Mothering*.

REBECCA CHIYOKO KING-O'RIAIN is an associate professor of sociology at Maynooth University, Republic of Ireland. She works in the fields of Asian/Asian American popular culture; people of mixed descent, critical mixed-race studies; race/ethnicity, beauty, and Japanese Americans; and emotions, technology, and globalization. She has published in *New Media and Society, Global Networks, Ethnicities, Journal of Ethnic and Migration Studies, Journal of Intercultural Studies, Sociology Compass*, and *Journal of Asian American Studies*, as well as in many edited books. She is the lead editor of *Global Mixed Race* (New York University Press). Her book *Pure Beauty: Judging Race in Japanese American Beauty Pageants* (University of Minnesota Press) examined the use of blood quantum rules in Japanese American beauty pageants. Her current research explores globalized interpersonal and interactive forms of bodily culture in Asian popular culture (Korean and Japanese popular music and dramas) and digital media.

DONNA LEE KWON is an associate professor of ethnomusicology at the University of Kentucky. She holds a PhD in ethnomusicology from the University of California, Berkeley. She is the author of *Music in Korea: Experiencing Music, Expressing Culture* (Oxford University Press, 2011). Her research interests include North and South Korean music, East Asian and Asian American music, gender and the body, and issues of space and place. Many of these interests are addressed in her second book, *Stepping in the Madang: Sustaining Expressive Ecologies of Korean Drumming and Dance* (Wesleyan University Press, forthcoming). She has also published in the journals *Ethnomusicology, Music and Politics*, and *Ecomusicology Review*. Donna has served in various roles in the Association for Korean Music Research, the Society for Ethnomusicology Council, the Board of the Society for Ethnomusicology, and the *Ethnomusicology* journal. As a new YouTuber, she also has a channel exploring Korean pop culture called *Hallyu Like That!*

Contributors

MIN JOO LEE is an assistant professor in the Department of Asian Studies at Occidental College. She received her PhD in gender studies from UCLA. Her first book project examines the transnational popularity of romantic Korean television dramas. More specifically, she examines the gendered and racial politics surrounding how some White heterosexual women fans of Korean television dramas develop racialized erotic fantasies about Korean men and subsequently travel to Korea to form intimate relations with Korean men in real life. Her research interests include Korean popular culture, race and gender politics in contemporary Korea, and the intersection of new technology and sex. She is working on launching a new research project on the racial and sexual politics surrounding the creation and transnational dissemination of Korean illicit pornography (molka).

IRINA LYAN is an assistant professor and the head of the Korean studies program at the Department of Asian Studies, the Hebrew University of Jerusalem. She is a sociologist who explores South Korea's national images, imagery, and imagination and their impact on its economic miracle, also known as the Miracle on the River Han, and its cultural miracle, also known as the Korean Wave or Hallyu. Irina is the recipient of prestigious scholarships and awards, including the Principles of Cultural Dynamics Fellowship at the Freie Universität Berlin, the World Association for Hallyu Studies article award, and a postdoctoral fellowship at the University of Oxford. Her academic papers have appeared both in leading critical management studies journals such as *Organization, Culture and Organization*, and *Critical Perspectives on International Business* and in cultural and media studies outlets such as *International Journal of Communication, Cross-Currents: East Asian History and Culture Review*, and *Kritika Kultura*.

DAVID C. OH is an associate professor at Syracuse University. He is the author of *Second-Generation Korean Americans and Transnational Media: Diasporic Identifications, Whitewashing the Movies: Asian Erasure and White Subjectivity in U.S. Film Culture*, and *Navigating White News: Asian American Journalists at Work*. He has written a few dozen articles on Asian/American representation vis-à-vis Whiteness, Asian American identity and media, intersectional representations of multiculturalism in South Korean popular media, and transnational audience reception of Korean

Contributors

264

media. Finally, he serves on several editorial boards, and he was a Fulbright Senior Scholar in South Korea in 2018–19.

MOISÉS PARK is an associate professor of Spanish and has taught literature, cinema, and culture in the Department of Modern Languages and Cultures at Baylor University (Waco, TX) since 2016. He holds a PhD from UC Davis. His research interests are literature, film, masculinity, Otherness, Orientalism, and popular culture. He is author of twenty articles and book chapters as well as *Figuraciones del deseo y coyunturas generacionales en literatura y cine postdictatorial* (2014). He co-edited *Here Comes the Flood: Perspectives of Gender, Sexuality, and Stereotype in the Korean Wave* (2022). He is currently working on a monograph examining representations of Korea(s) in the Americas. His first poetry book, *El verso cae al aula*, was published in 2017. His second poetry book, *Poemas marciales*, was published in Spanish and English in 2019.

JULIA TRZCIŃSKA is an assistant professor at the University of Wrocław, Poland. She holds a PhD in political science and administration and is the author of *The Presidential Campaign in the Republic of Korea in 2017: The Role of Social Media*. She is a member of the Bosch Alumni Network, and she graduated from the Confucius Institute at the University of Wrocław. She is a member of the World Association for Hallyu Studies, the Polish Communication Association, and the Polish Political Science Association. Her main research interests are political communication, soft power, public diplomacy, and fan studies. In her research, she primarily uses content and frame analysis. Since 2017, she has been writing about Polish K-pop fans, as well as South Korean soft power, and she has been teaching courses at the University of Wrocław and Jagiellonian University.

Contributors

265

Index

Abelmann, Nancy, 35
abjectness, 21, 99, 103
acculturation vs. cultural appropriation, 55
adaptation vs. cultural appropriation, 221
adoption and adoptees, 175
affinity, transcultural: cross-race, 6; and fandom as affinity space, 197; forms of, 19; and hope for future, 17–18, 19; and hybridity, 75–77, 92–93; intra-race, 14; and masculinity in K-drama, 197, 209, 212; and minority capital, 173–74, 182, 184–85, 187; and selective cultural appropriation, 77; as term, 9
age: and fan demographics, 156; and positions in K-pop groups, 42
agency: of audience, 8, 12; and consent, 85; of K-pop idols, 23, 62, 239; and tanning, 91
AleXa, 109
ambivalent mimicry, 119n4
American Song Contest, 109
Anderson, Benedict, 183
Anderson, Crystal, 201
Ang, Ien, 80
anime, 76, 126–27, 153, 172, 178
Ansari, Aziz, 86
"Arirang," 123, 184

ARMY fandom, 3, 8, 197–98
ARTCOR (Club Amistad de Arte Coreano), 126–30, 131–32, 140, 141, 142
Asian Americans: and pan–East Asian identity, 14; and queer identity, 14, 111; visibility of, musicians, 21, 98–118
assimilation: assimilated difference in K-pop, 101; defined, 55; role of humor in, 175
Athique, Adrian, 8
audibility of Asian American musicians, 21, 110–18
audience: agency of, 8, 12; and diasporic consumption, 13–14; vs. fans, 7–8; and interpretation of text through local culture, 13–14; reception studies, 7–8
authenticity: and Asian American artists, 101, 115; and Black identity, 79; and cultural appropriation, 55, 62; and K-drama, 200, 207; and Korean American language skills, 175; and performativity of race, 81; and reality dating shows, 75, 79, 85, 87, 88

The Bachelor, 74, 79–80
Bae, Sang Joon, 195
Bae Yong-joon, 85, 250
Balistreri, Kelly Stamper, 201

bards, 113

beauty industry and skin-whitening products, 61, 90–91, 92

beauty standards: and colorism, 21, 75, 81, 87–93, 107–8; and fantasies about becoming Korean, 183; and K-pop, 21, 42, 60–61, 107–9, 139–40; and pan-Asian ideal, 61; and reality TV, 75, 81, 87–93; weight and height, 42, 107, 108; White standards as norm, 107–8

Beomgyu (TXT), 246

Bhabha, Homi K., 76, 119n4, 176

Black culture: appropriation of, 34–35, 43–45, 150, 177–78, 221, 223; and Black identity, 16, 36–37, 40, 79, 177–78; and Black joy, 20, 33–48; and Korean-Black conflict narrative, 35, 38

blackface, 61

Black fans: and hybridity, 16; and K-drama, 22, 199, 205–6; and K-pop reaction videos, 16, 20, 33–48; scholarship on, 16–17

Black Lives Matter, 10, 16, 197–98, 227, 243

Black music: as category in US, 100–101; and Cuban fans, 141; influence on K-pop, 34–35, 43, 107, 164, 221, 223; influence on Seo Taiji, 158, 162

Blackpink, 4, 43, 57, 101, 135, 140, 166

Black Twitter, 81

body and embodiment: body type and beauty standards, 42, 107, 108–9; hybridity of body, 3; male body in K-drama, 201; and transracialism, 20, 52–69

Bollywood, 14

"Both" (Hall), 23, 238, 246–54

boyd, danah, 249

Boys' Love dramas, 202

Brock, André, 37

Brown, Chris, 43

BTS: ARMY fandom, 3, 8, 197–98; and Black Lives Matter, 197–98; and Cuban fans, 123, 132, 133, 134; English usage, 166; and gender fluidity in fan-made TikTok videos, 246, 248; masculinity and beauty, 139; and reaction videos, 43; and Seo Taiji, 156; success of, 3, 4, 99, 101

capitalism: alternatives to, 10, 16, 21, 127–32, 141; Black video reactions as subverting, 20, 34, 46–48; and cultural appropriation, 227; Korea's success in, 21, 46–47; and Latin American aspirations, 17

Casa Cuba Corea, 126, 137–38

celebrities in reality TV, 79, 82

censorship and Seo Taiji, 150, 155

Chaeyoung (TWICE), 246

Chariots of the Gods? (von Däniken), 163–64

Chile: civil unrest in, 10, 157; in Korean media, 157; and othering of Rapa Nui, 22, 149–67

Chin, Bertha, 9

China: appropriation of Chinese culture, 67; China-Cuba relations, 137; and K-pop artists, 41

Cho, Margaret, 98, 104

Cho, Michelle, 199

Choi, Andrew, 21, 100, 103–4, 106, 110–14, 118

Choi, David, 114

Chong, Kelly, 207

Chun, Elaine, 175

Chung, Hye Jean, 159

CL (2NE1), 216, 218, 222, 224, 225, 227, 229–30

class: and colorism, 88–89; and Cuban

Index

fans, 132, 140–41, 150–51; and reggaeton, 21, 151
classical musicians, 101
clothes and costumes: and Asian
American artists, 110, 116, 117; and
Cuban fans, 135, 137–38, 139; and cultural appropriation of Chinese culture, 67; and cultural appropriation
of Islam, 222; and fantasies about
becoming Korean, 60, 181, 183; and
gender fluidity in fan-made TikTok
videos, 249, 252; *hanbok*, 60, 137–38,
181, 183; and masculinity, 139; and Seo
Taiji, 158
Cloud, Dana, 79–80
Coachella, 102
code-switching, 119n7
collective identity of fandom, 8
colonialism: and colorism, 89–91,
92; and cultural appropriation of
Rapa Nui, 159–60, 164, 165, 167; and
hybridity as survival strategy, 75;
Japanese colonization of Korea, 68,
130, 242; legacy of racism, 12; and
masculinity, 20; and mimicry, 176;
and modernity, 123–24; and racial
translocalism concept, 11–12; Whiteness as colonial invention, 89
colorism, 21, 75, 81, 87–93, 107–8
Confucian values, 58, 195, 196, 242
consent, 84, 85, 86
consumers vs. fans, 47
coolness, 203
cosmetics: and masculinity, 139–40, 203;
and transracialism, 52, 61
cosmetic surgery: by K-pop idols, 60,
107; and transracialism, 20, 53, 58–62,
177, 183
cosmopolitanism: and Black identity,
16; and colorism, 75, 90; and fantasies

of global mobility, 198, 207, 211; and
mockery, 179; of transcultural fans,
12, 77, 178, 233, 243; and Whiteness,
15, 90
costumes. *See* clothes and costumes
country of origin, return to, 111–12, 113
Crush, 34
Cuban fans, 21–22, 122–42, 150–51
cultural appropriation: vs. adaptation,
221; vs. appreciation, 54–56; defined,
54–55, 221–22; and permission, 54,
67; transidentification as selective
appropriation, 77; White, of Black
music, 44
cultural appropriation by Koreans: of
Black culture, 34–35, 43–45, 150, 221,
223; of Islam, 22–23, 216–33; of Rapa
Nui, 22, 149–67
cultural appropriation of Koreans:
jokes and fantasies about becoming
Korean, 22, 77, 171–88; and Koreaboo,
176–77; Korean reactions to, 66–67;
and transracialism, 20, 52–69, 177
cultural proximity, 5, 9–10, 124, 130, 195,
196
cultural theft, 34–35, 234n6

dance: and cultural appropriation of
Islam, 218, 222, 229; and gender flu-
idity in fan-made TikTok videos,
248–49; and K-pop cover dancers,
18, 134–36; and Latin American fans,
17, 134–36
Dangun, 188n1
Dan tribe, 188n1
dating shows, 20–21, 74–93
Davichi, 161
De Luna, Elizabeth, 35
Desai, Jigna, 14
Descendants of the Sun, 233n1

Index

269

diasporas: and humor, 176; and media consumption, 13–14. *See also* Korean diaspora

diet, 60

digital piracy, 125–26

diplomacy and Korean-Cuban relations, 122–23, 126, 142

Docan-Morgan, Sara, 175

Dolezal, Rachel, 177–78

Dol hareubangs (stone grandpas), 164–65

Domínguez Santos, Magalys, 142

double consciousness, 37, 113

Dramaworld, 79–80

Du Bois, W. E. B., 5–6, 37

Dubrofsky, Rachel, 79, 81

Duffett, Mark, 37, 42, 47

Dumbfoundead, 116

Durham, Meenakshi Gigi, 14

Easter Island. *See* Rapa Nui

Eat Your Kimchi (YouTube channel), 176

Eilish, Billie, 252

Encounter, 133

Eng, David, 206

English: and Asian American artists, 105, 114–15; and code-switching, 119n7; and fans, 244; and mock-Asian accents, 175; use in K-pop, 101, 110, 165–67

Enhypen, 244

enunciation, third space of, 76

epicanthic folds and cosmetic surgery, 59, 61, 107

Eponymous. *See* Choi, Andrew

Epstein, Stephen, 107

e-sports, 2

EXO, 41

extraterrestrials and Rapa Nui, 153, 154, 158, 159–60, 163–64, 167

eyes, cosmetic surgery on, 59, 61, 107

Faker (Lee Sang-hyeok), 2

fanfiction, homoerotic, 202

fan labor: and cultural translation, 34, 41–42, 47; and curation, 42, 47; as legitimizing interests, 15

fans: age demographics, 156; vs. consumers, 47; cosmopolitanism of, 12, 77, 178, 233, 243; defined, 37; and expertise, 42; fan studies vs. audience reception studies, 7–8; fandom as affinity space, 197; fandom as participatory culture, 230; fan-nationalism, 178, 183; and gender demographics, 156; vs. other users, 7–8; and pilgrimages, 180, 217; as producers, 8; role of non-fans, 38–39, 46, 47–48; role of TikTok in fandoms, 243; White as default, 45–46, 166. *See also* Black fans; Cuban fans; identity; Muslim fans; videos by fans; White fans

fantasy: jokes and fantasies about becoming Korean, 22, 77, 171–88; K-drama and alternative masculinity, 22, 138–40, 194–212; K-drama and global mobility, 22, 194–95, 197, 198–206, 211–12. *See also* transracialism

Felix (Stray Kids), 238

femininity: and feminization of Asian men, 201; and gender fluidity in TikTok videos, 23, 238–54; Korean masculinity as feminine, 15, 139–40, 210–11, 241–42; strong femininity and K-pop, 140. *See also* masculinity; masculinity, Korean

Fernández, Macarena, 159

fetish tourism, 164–65

Fiske, John, 7–8, 253

Flavor of Love, 79

food and diet, 60

foreigners and foreignness: and abject-

Index

270

ness, 21, 99, 103; of Asian Americans, 99; Asians as perpetual foreigners, 11; and Korean citizenship, 57; and K-pop vs. Asian American music, 21, 101, 103–4, 106–7, 110; and openness of imagined communities, 183–84; of overseas Koreans, 56; and racial triangulation, 101, 106–8; and transracialism, 65. *See also* cultural appropriation; Orientalizing; othering

Foucault, Michel, 159

future and fantasies about becoming Korean, 185–87, 188

gaming, 2

"Gangnam Style" (Psy), 3, 101, 103

Garion, 36

gender: ambiguity in K-drama, 203–4; changes in gender ideals, 107; fan demographics, 156, 199; fluidity and fan-made TikTok videos, 23, 238–54; fluidity and queer identity, 14; and Seo Taiji fans, 158

Georgiou, Myria, 239

globalization: and colorism, 89; and Cuba, 130, 131, 141; and cultural appropriation, 221; scholarly focus on, 46–47

global mobility and K-drama, 22, 194–95, 197, 198–206, 211–12

Goa trance, 15

Gong Yoo, 2

Goryeo Songs, 234n3

"Gracias a la vida" (Davichi), 161

Grant-Smith, Michael, 39

Gray, Jonathan, 39

hair, 43–44, 139, 158

Hall, Todrick, 23, 238

Hallyu. *See* K-drama; Korean pop culture; K-pop

Han, Benjamin, 17, 76, 134

Han, Shinhee, 206

hanbok, 60, 137–38, 181, 183

Hardy, Antoine, 79

Harlow, Jack, 116, 117

Heart Signal, 78, 79, 82, 83, 84

hegemonic mimicry, 119n4, 162–63, 164

height and beauty standards, 107, 108

heterotopia, 159, 164, 167

hierarchies: and fandoms, 244; role of humor in, 175–76, 182

hip hop, 3, 34, 35–36, 107, 166–67, 205, 224–25

historically Black colleges and universities (HBCUs), 40–41

Hong, Seok-Kyeong, 242

Hsu, Hua, 196

humor: defined, 174; functions of, 174–76; indirectness in, 187; jokes and fantasies about becoming Korean, 22, 77, 171–88; about masculinity, 241; and mockery, 79–80, 176–79

Humphreys, Laura-Zoë, 17

Hwasa (Mamamoo), 42, 109

hybridity: and affinities with reality TV, 75–77, 92–93; and Black fans, 16; of body, 3; of Chileans, 162; and colonialism, 75; and counterflows, 12–13; and fantasies of traveling to Korea, 207, 208–10; of Korean masculinity, 3, 202–3; of Korean pop culture, 3, 58, 178, 240; pop culture as hybrid/third space, 76; of reality TV dating shows, 21, 75, 77–80, 92–93; as survival strategy, 75; as uneven, 12, 18, 76, 240–41; and White identification and desire, 15

Hyunjin (Stray Kids), 246

Index

271

identity: Black, 16, 36–37, 40, 79, 177–78; collective identity of fandom, 8; and diasporic consumption, 13–14; and hybridity, 75–77; and jokes and fantasies about becoming Korean, 22, 77, 171–88; Muslim identity and cultural appropriation of Islam, 22–23, 216–17, 223–33; pan–East Asian, 14, 57. *See also* Korean identity; queerness and queer identity

I.M., 218, 222, 230

imaginaries, transnational, 19–20. *See also* fantasy

imagined communities: and fantasies about becoming Korean, 174, 179; as open, 183–84

immigration: and colorism, 90; and Korean-Black conflict narrative, 35; role of humor in assimilation, 175

indentured labor in Cuba, 132, 136–37

Indian diasporic identity, 14

indigeneity, 10, 160, 162, 163–64

inferior/superior axis and racial triangulation, 101, 104, 107–8

in-groups: and fans, 244; and humor, 175–76

Irish fans and K-drama and global mobility, 22, 194–95, 197, 198–206, 211–12

irony bribe, 79–80

Isla de Pascua. *See* Rapa Nui

Islam: and cultural appropriation by Koreans, 22–23, 216–33; Korean Muslims, 220

Israel: fan labor as legitimizing interests, 15; Israelis as White, 173; jokes and fantasies about becoming Korean, 22, 77, 171–88

Itzy, 246

IVE, 246

Ives, Mike, 34

Jackson, Jason Baird, 55

Japan: colonization of Korea, 68, 130, 242; Japanese fans' interest in soft masculinity, 85; and study of Japanese language, 5

Jeju Island, 164–65, 220

Jenkins, Henry, 8, 178

Jeong, Ken, 98

Jimin (BTS), 62–68, 177, 246, 248

Jin, Dal Yong, 197, 241, 243

Johnson, E. Patrick, 81

jokes and fantasies about becoming Korean, 22, 77, 171–88

Joo, Rachael M., 107

joy, Black, 20, 33–48

Joyner, Kara, 201

JTBC, 74, 78. See also *Single's Inferno*

Ju, Hyejung, 195

Judaism: conversion to, 186; Korean connections to, 188n1

Jung, Hyeri, 12

Jung, Sun, 3, 85, 202–3, 242

Jungkook (BTS), 248

JYP Entertainment, 107

Kao, Grace, 16, 197–98, 201

KCON, 4

K-drama: and alternative masculinity, 22, 138–40, 194–212; Boys' Love dramas, 202; and Cuban fans, 21–22, 122–42, 150–51; and cultural appropriation of Islam, 233n1; as culturally "odorless," 242; and global mobility, 22, 194–95, 197, 198–206, 211–12; lack of violence in, 17; popularity of, 195–98; and sexual restraint, 138–39, 195, 205

Kellner, Douglas, 18–19

Keshi, 118

Kim, Claire Jean, 101, 104, 106

Index

272

Kim, Ik-ki, 195
Kim, Jenna Chi, 175
Kim, Ju Oak, 1–2
Kim, Kyung Hyun, 162–63
Kim, Min Suk, 140
Kim, Nadia Y., 108, 206–7
Kim, Yeran, 38
Kim Young-sam, 1
Kleisath, C. Michelle, 56
Kondo, Dorinne, 100
Korea: colonialism in, 68, 130; Cuban efforts to learn about, 125–29; and Cuban foreign relations, 122–23, 126, 142; and fan-nationalism, 183; government's role in Korean pop culture, 10; and national sound, 183–85, 188; and soft power, 11, 21, 122–23
Korea-Arab Society, 234n6
Koreaboo: mocking of, 176–79; term, 172. *See also* transracialism
"Koreaboo" (London), 177
Korean Americans: and Korean-Black conflict narrative, 35; Korean language skills, 175; racism toward, 45; visibility of Asian American musicians, 21, 98–118
Korean Communications Standards Commission, 195
Korean diaspora: and Cuba, 132, 136–37; and humor, 176; and Korean identity, 56; reactions to cultural appropriation, 66–67
Korean identity: defining, 56–58; fan concepts of, 57–58; and mixed-race Koreans, 56; and national sound, 183–85, 188; official concept of, 56–57; and overseas Koreans, 56; and Whiteness, 90
Korean language: and Asian American

artists, 114, 117; and fantasies about becoming Korean, 179, 183–84; and K-pop names, 166; and mockery, 175, 179; study of, 5, 179, 183–84, 197
Korean Nationality Act, 57
Korean pop culture: and exceptionalism, 6–7; government's role in, 10; hybridity of, 3, 58, 178, 240; Korean Wave term, 6; rise of, 1–3, 19; scholarship overview, 3–19; Third Korean Wave, 1–2. *See also* K-drama; K-pop
Korean War, 64
KOTRA, 126, 133
K-pop: agency of idols, 23, 62, 239; and Asian American musician visibility, 21, 98–118; and beauty standards, 21, 42, 60–61, 107–9, 139–40; and Black Lives Matter, 10, 16, 197–98, 227, 243; and civil unrest in Chile, 10, 157; cover dancers, 18, 134–36; duality of personas, 250; English use in, 101, 110, 165–67; and gender fluidity in TikTok videos, 23, 238–54; generations, 254n7; group vs. solo acts, 156; influence of Black music on, 34–35, 43, 107, 164, 221, 223; lack of racial "odor," 178; names in, 166; positions in, 42; reaction videos by Black Americans, 16, 20, 33–48; reaction videos by White fans, 45–46, 77; vs. rock, 152–53; Seo Taiji as pioneer of, 156, 158; success and global spread of, 2–3, 101
Kraidy, Marwan, 12, 18, 76, 240
Krijnen, Tonny, 251

labor, indentured, 132, 136–37
Larkin, Brian, 124

Index

273

Latin American fans: audience experiences, 17–18; Cuban fans, 21–22, 122–42, 150–51; fan labor in, 17; identity and affinities, 76–77; Latina fans and K-drama, 22, 194, 199, 200, 204, 205, 206; and telenovelas, 13–14. *See also* Chile; Mexico and Mexican fans

Lay, 43

Lee, Hyunji, 76–77, 207

Lee, Jeehyun Jenny, 177, 205, 241

Lee, Jooyoun, 195

Lee, Jun-hyung, 179

Lee, Min Joo, 77, 196–97, 205

Lee, Rachel Kar Yee, 177, 205, 241

Lee, Sangjoon, 46–47

Lee, Wonseok, 16, 197–98

Lee Sang-hyeok (Faker), 2

Leeseo (IVE), 246

Lee Soo-man, 107

Levina, Marina, 81

Levkowitz, Alon, 217

LGBTQ+ identity. *See* queerness and queer identity

Lie, John, 35, 47

Limitless, 134–36, 140

Linton, John, 68

Livingstone, Sonia, 7

Lo, Adrienne, 175

Lollapalooza, 102, 106, 116

London, Oli, 20, 53, 62–68, 177, 183

Longenecker, Lisa, 195

Love Island, 74, 82, 84

Lu, Jessica H., 38

Luckie, Marisa, 179

Lucumí, 131–32

Lyan, Irina, 15, 42, 52, 77, 217

Maira, Sunaina, 14–15

"Make a Wish" (NCT U), 216, 218, 222, 224, 225, 226, 229–30

male gaze, 166, 240, 242–43

Mamamoo, 42, 109, 246

manga, 126–27, 172, 178

manhwa (comic books) and webtoons, 2

Manigault-Bryant, LeRhonda, 54

Mapuche people, 161–62

Maragh, Raven, 81

Maria Isabel, 13–14

Marwick, Alice, 249

masculinity: as based in Whiteness, 10; and colonialism, 20; hypermasculinity of US soldiers, 64; liminal, 242; overlapping, 201; policing of, 251; and transracialism, 62–65, 185

masculinity, Korean: and asexuality trope, 2, 77, 138, 201; and beauty standards, 139–40; changes in, 201, 202–3; and coolness, 203; and dating shows, 75, 82–87; denial of, in Korean War, 64; in fan-made TikTok videos, 23, 238–54; as feminine, 15, 139–40, 210–11, 241–42; hybridity of, 3, 202–3; and K-drama, 22, 138–40, 194–212; and Latin American fans, 17, 138–40; and liminal masculinity, 242; and persistence, 85–86; and physical displays of affection between men, 210, 250; as queer or gay, 138, 139–40, 203–4, 239; and transracialism, 20, 53, 54, 185

The Masked Singer, 98

Mayer, Vicki, 13

McDaniel, Byrd, 41

media: and Black fans, 33–37; control of in Cuba, 125–26; diasporic consumption of, 13–14; Korean media as alternative to White, 6, 7; Korean media coverage of Chile, 157; Korean media coverage of Middle

Index

274

East, 217–18, 220; social media and accessibility of Korean pop culture, 219, 243

Meizel, Katherine, 109–10

melancholia and K-drama, 196–97, 206–12

#MeToo movement, 84

Mexico and Mexican fans: fan experience, 17, 18; and femininity, 140; indentured labor in, 137; and K-drama, 200, 204; and telenovelas, 13–14

Middle East and cultural appropriation by Koreans, 22–23, 216–33

Milli Vanilli, 162

mimicry, 119n4, 162–63, 164, 176

Min, Wonjung, 197, 241

Minaj, Nikki, 43

minbok, 117

minority capital, 173–74, 182, 184–85, 187

Miss A, 33

Mitski, 99, 103

mixed-race Koreans and Korean identity, 56

Mnet, 230

"Moai" (Seo Taiji), 22, 149–67

mockery, 79–80, 176–79

model minority: and fantasy of becoming Korean, 185; and K-pop vs. Asian American music, 101, 104–5; and masculinity, 207–8; and racial triangulation, 101, 106–8

modernity: alternatives to, and Cuban fans, 21–22, 122–25, 129–36; alternatives to, and hopes for, 9, 17–18, 19; and lightness, 108; as White, 123–24

Mongolian spot, 189n5

Moonbyul (Mamamoo), 246

Morimoto, Lori, 9

Morrison, Toni, 36–37

Morton, Brian, 54

"MTBD" (CL), 216, 218, 222, 224, 225, 227, 229–30

Mulenga, Natasha, 34

multivocality, 99, 100, 109–18

Mulvey, Laura, 166

Music Bank, 161

music festivals and representation of Asian vs. Asian American artists, 102–3, 106, 116, 117

Muslim fans: and cultural appropriation of Islam, 22–23, 216–33; Korean Muslims, 220

Naachal (Garion), 36

Nam, Eric, 21, 100, 104–5, 106, 110–11, 114–15, 117–18

nationalism: and colorism, 90; fan-nationalism, 178, 183; Korean national sound, 183–85, 188

Nazca Lines, 159, 163–64

NCT, 41, 229, 230

NCT Dream, 41

NCT 127, 41

NCT U: and cultural appropriation of Islam, 216, 218, 222, 224, 225, 226, 229–30, 231; membership changes, 41

Netflix: and colorism, 92; dominance of, 9; and sexually explicit content, 78; *Single's Inferno*, 20–21, 74–93; *Squid Game*, 1, 13, 194

new jack swing, 162, 163

Nishi, Xiahn, 20, 53, 58–62

Nishime, LeiLani, 80

Nixon, Paul, 251

North Korea and Cuban fans, 128

nostalgia: and dating shows, 82, 84–85, 86, 93; and fantasies of becoming Korean, 182, 187; and othering of Cuba, 133

Index

275

nu metal, 156, 158, 163

Nuna, Audrey, 21, 100, 105–6, 115–17, 118

"odor," lack of racial or ethnic, 178, 242

Oh, Chuyun, 18, 242, 243, 245, 248–49

Oh, David, 14, 16, 40, 45, 76, 80

Ono, Kent, 138

Orientalizing by Koreans: of Cubans, 124, 133–34, 142; and cultural appropriation of Islam, 221; of Rapa Nui, 22, 149–67

Orientalizing of Koreans: and asexual trope, 2, 77, 138; and desire, 15, 203, 205–6; and fantasies about becoming Korean, 174, 182; and oriental riff, 113; and queering of K-pop idols in TikTok videos, 238–54; reproduction of, in Korean pop culture, 11; and right to judge, 244

othering of Koreans: and Asian American musicians, 21, 99–100, 101, 103, 106–7; and dating shows, 77, 86–87; and desire, 15, 202–3, 205–6; and facial features, 59; and hybridity, 76–77; and K-drama, 204–7; and Korean masculinity, 77, 86–87, 204–7; and mockery, 176; and queering of K-pop idols in TikTok videos, 238–54; and right to judge, 244

othering of non-Koreans: of Cubans, 21, 124, 133–34, 142; and Goa trance, 15; of Rapa Nui, 22, 149–67

Otmazgin, Nissim, 15, 217

Pang, Hulkyong, 179

Panizza, Tiziana, 159

p'ansori (bards), 113

Parasite (2020), 1

Park, Han Woo, 17

Park, Ji Hoon, 177, 205, 241

Park, Teddy, 222, 224, 229

Park Jin-young, 107

past: Cubans as stuck in, 124, 133–34, 142; and jokes and fantasies about becoming Korean, 179–82

penis: phallic statues on Jeju Island, 164–65; reduction surgery, 63

performativity: of race, 81, 88; and sincerity, 79

permission and cultural appropriation, 54, 67

Pham, Vincent, 138

pilgrimages, 180, 217

piracy, digital, 125–26

plastic surgery. *See* cosmetic surgery

Polish fans, 16

Polynesians and othering of Rapa Nui, 22, 149–67

pop culture: as hybrid space, 76; as low culture, 219. *See also* Korean pop culture

postcolonialism: and alternative modernity in Cuba, 124, 131; and humor, 176, 241; and mimicry, 176; and racial ambiguity, 12; and Rapa Nui, 159, 160, 164, 165, 167; and transracialism, 20

post-racialism: and colorism, 91; and denial of racism, 6; gender fluidity in fan-made TikTok videos, 249; and humor, 175–76; and reaction videos by White fans, 77; and right to judge, 244

power: consumptive, 15; and cultural appropriation, 54–55, 58, 61–62, 64, 67–68, 155; and hybridity, 75–76, 240–41; and jokes and mockery, 175–76, 188; and reception, 11, 12–13, 18–19; White women's use of, 15, 239. *See also* soft power

Index

276

present and jokes and fantasies about
becoming Korean, 183–85
prosumption, 238
Psy, 3, 101, 103
punk, 156, 158, 163
purity and white skin tone, 87, 91–92
Pyongyang, 188n1

Qipao, 67
queerness and queer identity: and
androgyny, 14; Asian American,
14, 111; and Cuban fans, 139–40; as
default of K-pop fans, 249–50; and
K-drama, 202; Korean masculinity
reading as gay, 138, 139–40, 203–4,
239; and non-binary identification
of London, 62, 64–65; and physical
displays of affection between men,
210, 250; queering of K-pop idols in
TikTok videos, 238–54; sexualization
of trans and non-binary people, 248;
transracialism as similar to transgenderism, 64–65, 178
Qur'an and cultural appropriation, 216,
217, 222, 224, 225, 228, 229

race: Black fans and hypervisibilty of,
33–36; Black people as authority on,
34, 35; centering of, in scholarship,
4–6, 8–19; as central to US culture,
5; and colonialism, 12; Cuban fans
and anti-Blackness, 125, 140–41,
150–51; Korean media as alternative
to White media, 6, 7; mockery and
maintaining racial status quo, 174–
79; performativity of, 81, 88; racial
melancholia, 196; and racial "odor,"
178; racial triangulation, 101, 106–8;
and reality TV dating shows, 21; and
reggaeton, 21, 151; US ideologies of,

in Korea, 108. *See also* post-racialism;
transracialism
racial translocalism: defined, 6, 11;
scholarship overview, 11–19
racial triangulation, 101, 106–8
rap, 3, 35–36, 116, 156, 162, 205
Rapa Nui, cultural appropriation of, 22,
149–67
real and unreal in reality TV, 75, 79–80,
92–93
reality TV: and Cuba, 132–33, 134; and
dating shows, 20–21, 74–93
refugees, 220
reggaeton, 21, 141, 151
reincarnation and jokes and fantasies
about becoming Korean, 22, 171, 174,
179–82
religion: and Cuban fans, 131, 132; and
cultural appropriation of Islam, 22–
23, 216–33; spirituality and fantasies
about becoming Korean, 180–82, 188
rhinoplasty, 107
rock, 152–53, 154
Roggeveen, Jacob, 155
romance and non-Asian fans: Cuban
fans, 133, 136; and fantasies about
becoming Korean, 174, 185–87, 188;
and fantasies about Korean men, 2,
15, 75, 84–85, 185, 186, 197; and reality
TV dating shows, 20–21, 74–93;
and romantic tourism, 2, 5, 15; and
wholesomeness, 19, 21, 75, 83–85
Rondilla, Joanne, 89
Rosenau, Sara, 178–79
Ryujin (Itzy), 246

Said, Edward, 155, 174
savages cliché and Rapa Nui, 153, 159
SBS, 226, 229, 231
Scarcelli, Cosimo Marco, 251

Index

277

Schulze, Marion, 124, 127
Sealey, Kris, 66
Seo Taiji, 22, 149–67
Seotaiji Moai: The Film (2011), 157–58
Sesoko, Kay, 43–44
Seventeen, 135
sex and sexuality: and asexuality/emasculation of Korean men, 2, 77, 138, 201; consent and women's labor, 84, 85; cute vs. sexy presentation in K-pop, 252–53; and dating shows, 75, 77, 78, 82–84; and fantasies about becoming Korean, 174, 185–87, 188; hypersexuality of Afro-Caribbeans, 133–34, 135; and K-drama, 138–39, 195, 201–2, 204–6; lack of sexual explicitness in Korean TV, 17, 21, 75, 78, 83–85, 138–39, 195, 205; and Orientalizing and othering of Korean men, 2, 77, 86–87, 138; and queering of K-pop idols in TikTok videos, 239, 245–46, 248, 249, 250–51; sexualization of trans and non-binary people, 248. *See also* romance and non-Asian fans
sexism: and appeal of Korean masculinity, 139, 202; and reality TV dating shows, 21
sex workers, 64
Shimakawa, Karen, 103
SHINee, 33, 42
Sinawi, 156
sincerity, 79
Single's Inferno, 20–21, 74–93
skin color. *See* colorism
skinship, 210, 250
skin-whitening products, 61, 90–91, 92
SM Entertainment: and cultural appropriation of Islam, 216, 226, 231; groups and structure, 41; and influence of Black music, 107

#SMStopDisrespectingIslam, 231
Sneeze, Lauryn, 20, 39–48
socialism and Cuban fans, 122–36
soft power, 6, 7, 11, 21, 122–23, 155–56, 165, 195
Song, Myoung-Sun, 3
South by Southwest (SXSW), 102–3
spectators vs. fans, 8
Spickard, Paul, 89
spirituality and fantasies about becoming Korean, 180–82, 188
Squid Game, 1, 2, 13, 194
Ssanghwajyeom, 234n3
Stanfill, Mel, 45, 46, 165
Steele, Catherine Knight, 38
St. Lenox. *See* Choi, Andrew
Straubhaar, Joseph, 9
Stray Kids, 238
Street Woman Fighter, 218, 222, 229
Suga (BTS), 139
Swan, Anna Lee, 46
SXSW (South by Southwest), 102–3

tanning, 91
telenovelas, 13–14
television: global spread of, 1–2; Korean coverage of Chile, 157; Korean coverage of Middle East, 217–18; Korean engagement with Cuba, 132–33. *See also* K-drama; reality TV
temporality and jokes and fantasies about becoming Korean, 174, 179–88
terrorism and Korean concepts of Arab culture, 217–18, 220
Third Korean Wave, 1–2
third space, 76
thirst traps, 248
Tierra sola (*Solitary Land*, 2017), 159
TikTok videos and gender fluidity, 23, 238–54

Index

278

tokenization and representation of Asian vs. Asian American artists, 103–4, 105, 106
tokusatsu, 158
Too Hot to Handle, 74, 78, 82, 83
tourism. *See* travel and tourism
traditional music, Korean, 184
transcultural affinity. *See* affinity, transcultural
transgenderism and transracialism, 64–65, 178
transracialism: and Black cultural appropriation by Whites, 177–78; and cosmetic surgery, 20, 53, 58–62, 177, 183; and cultural appropriation by non-Koreans, 20, 52–69, 177; jokes and fantasies about becoming Korean, 22, 77, 171–88; and Koreaboo, 172; and transgenderism, 64–65, 178
travel and tourism: fantasies of traveling to Korea, 198, 207, 208–10; fetish tourism, 164–65; increase in tourism in Korea, 5; romantic tourism, 5, 15; and travel to country of origin, 111–12, 113
Traveler, 133, 134
triangulation, racial, 101, 106–8
Tuvel, Rebecca, 178
TWICE, 42, 101, 166, 246
2 Days & 1 Night, 133, 134
2NE1, 140, 216
TXT, 246

Ultraman, 158
United States and US fans: and alternative masculinity in K-drama, 22, 194–95, 197, 198, 199, 206–12; music categories in, 100–101; race as central to US culture, 5; reaction videos by Black Americans, 20, 33–48

Vargas Meza, Xanat, 17
videos by artists: by Asian American artists, 112–13, 116; and cultural appropriation of Islam, 22–23, 216–33; and cultural appropriation of Rapa Nui, 22, 149–67
videos by fans: on cultural appropriation of Islam, 218, 231–32; and gender fluidity in TikTok videos, 23, 238–54; reactions to transracialism and cultural appropriation, 53, 65–67; reaction videos as creative act, 41; reaction videos as cultural practice, 38–39; reaction videos by Black Americans, 16, 20, 33–48; reaction videos by White fans, 45–46, 77; role of non-fans in reaction videos, 38–39, 46, 47–48
Vietnam War, 64
violence: against Asians, 104; lack of, in K-drama, 17
Visigoths, 162
von Däniken, Erich, 163–64

Wanzo, Rebecca, 37, 46
WayV, 41
webtoons, 2
weeaboo, 172
weight and beauty standards, 107, 108–9
Weissköpple, Cordula, 209
White fans: and alternative masculinity, 15, 22, 194–212; consumption overview, 14–15; and cultural appropriation of Chinese culture, 67; default fan as White, 45–46, 166; and K-pop reaction videos, 45–46, 77; and queering of K-pop idols in TikTok videos, 238–54; transracialism by, 20, 52–69; use of power, 239. *See also* cultural appropriation; fantasy; romance and non-Asian fans

Index

279

whiteness: as colonial invention, 89; default fan as White, 45–46, 166; of Israelis, 173; of Koreans in Latin America, 134, 167; masculinity as based in, 10; and mockery, 178–79; modernity as White, 123–24; wanting to be White as default normal, 171–72; White beauty standards as norm, 107–8. *See also* colorism

White supremacy: and colonialism, 12, 91; and colorism, 87, 89, 91; and indigenous feats of engineering, 160

wholesomeness and reality TV dating shows, 21, 75, 83–85

women: and consent labor, 84, 85; in K-pop vs. rock, 152–53; and pressure of K-pop beauty standards, 60–61; and reversal of male gaze, 240, 242–43. *See also* Black fans; Cuban fans; Muslim fans; romance and non-Asian fans; videos by fans; White fans

Won, Yong-Jin, 179

yellowface, 52, 61
Yoon, John, 34
Yoon, Kyong, 176, 197, 241
Yoon Sang-hyun, 132
Yoshihara, Mari, 239
YouTube: as fan resource, 219; reaction videos as cultural practice, 38–39; reaction videos by Black Americans, 20, 33–48; reaction videos by White fans, 45–46, 77; role of non-fans in reaction videos, 38–39, 46, 47–48

Index